Hacking
Windows Vista™

Steve Sinchak

Wiley Publishing, Inc.

Hacking Windows Vista™

Published by
Wiley Publishing, Inc.
10475 Crosspoint Boulevard
Indianapolis, IN 46256
www.wiley.com

Library of Congress Cataloging-in-Publication Data

Sinchak, Steve.
  Hacking Windows Vista : / Steve Sinchak.
    p. cm.
  ISBN 978-0-470-04687-6 (pbk.)
  1. Microsoft Windows (Computer file) 2. Operating systems (Computers) I. Title.
  QA76.76.O63S5634 2007
  005.4'46—dc22
                                2007014921

To my fiancée, Stephanie, and to my family

Credits

Executive Editor
Chris Webb

Development Editor
John Sleeva

Technical Editor
Justin Korelc

Copy Editor
Nancy Rapoport

Editorial Manager
Mary Beth Wakefield

Production Manager
Tim Tate

**Vice President and
Executive Group Publisher**
Richard Swadley

Vice President and Executive Publisher
Joseph B. Wikert

Compositor
Kate Kaminski, Happenstance Type-O-Rama

Proofreader
Kathryn J. Duggan

Indexer
Melanie Belkin

Anniversary Logo Design
Richard Pacifico

Cover Design
Anthony Bunyan

About the Author

Steve Sinchak is an entrepreneur who has started several technology-related businesses. Steve is currently running a web development firm known as Advanced PC Media LLC, which owns and operates several Web sites geared toward computer enthusiasts. In addition to writing for his Web sites and running Advanced PC Media LLC, he works as a Systems Engineer for a Global 100 company in the financial services sector.

Steve has been working with computers for more than 15 years. Starting with a desktop that had a 286-based processor, 1MB of RAM, and Windows 3.1, he taught himself how to make Windows run faster on the slow hardware. Driven by a strong curiosity to understand how Windows works, he spent countless hours researching and experimenting with its inner workings and features. Over the years, he has worked closely with all versions of Windows. In 2005 and 2006, Microsoft honored him with the Most Valued Professional (MVP) award for his work with Windows and his contributions to the Windows community.

Contents at a Glance

Contents

Part III: Securing Your System

Chapter 14: Windows Security 251

Chapter 15: Internet Security 275

Acknowledgments

I want to thank my fiancée, Stephanie, for her support and understanding during all the time I had to take away from her in order to meet deadlines and get this book finished. Thank you for helping me with my other work and for taking care of me when I was short on time. I love you very much.

I also want to thank everyone who has helped me over the years succeed in the computer industry. I want to thank my Uncle Ron for his help in getting us our first 486 (with turbo button!) and many other computer upgrades over the years. I want to thank my Computer Science and Business professors at my alma mater, Marquette University, for teaching me exactly how a computer works, from high-level programming all the way down to the basic electric components.

I also want to thank everyone involved in this book at Wiley for their help and advice.

Introduction

The era of Windows Vista is finally here. The result of thousands of programmers and five years of work, Windows Vista is the most important and comprehensive release of Windows since 1995. Microsoft has never before paid so much attention to detail and invested so heavily in security. It has finally realized how important user experience truly is and has delivered a product that makes enormous strides in the right direction. Although Windows Vista makes previous versions of Windows antiquated, there are still many improvements to make. This book picks up where Microsoft stopped and helps you personalize and improve your Windows Vista experience.

Few products in the world have to cater to as many types of customers and satisfy as many needs as Windows Vista. Microsoft spent a lot of time gathering feedback to try to please all users with Windows Vista. Its effort is shown in the big improvements throughout the OS, but you can never make all users happy. Everyone has different preferences and likes different things. I am going to show you how to customize almost every aspect of Windows Vista. By the time you are finished with this book, your Windows Vista will look and feel as if Microsoft designed it just for you.

Performance is another major component of your Windows Vista experience. Windows Vista demands more out of your hardware than ever before. After all, when you add many new features, various types of automation, and a slick 3D user interface, you are going to need something more powerful than a computer that barely runs Windows XP. However, you also do not need to go out and buy a completely new computer. In this book, I show you how to fine-tune the settings and features in Windows Vista to make it run faster on hardware that is not exactly the cutting edge anymore.

Windows XP has had a horrible security track record since it was introduced many years ago. It seems like almost every month a handful of new critical vulnerabilities need to be patched. Above all, Microsoft has stressed security during the development of Windows Vista. Hundreds of new security features protect your computer from all types of threats. This book shows you how to take advantage of the new security features as well as how to tame some of the more annoying features such as User Account Control while still benefiting from the feature's protection.

Are you ready to customize, speed up, and secure your Windows Vista computer? Let's get started!

Whom This Book Is For

This book is intended for all Windows Vista users who are interested in customizing the operating system, improving the performance, and using the latest security features and tools to secure Windows Vista. Previous Windows experience is necessary for this book. Most of the topics in this book are geared toward a more advanced Windows user, but every section is written in a way that even beginner Windows users can understand.

How This Book Is Organized

In this book, you will find 16 chapters spread across three main parts. Each part covers a different theme and each chapter is broken down into sections supporting the chapter's topic. The first two parts are presented in logical operating system event order, such as boot, logon, and interface. The third part is laid out in order of steps.

Part I: Customizing Your Computer

Chapter 1 starts off by customizing the very first thing you see when you turn on your PC: the boot screen. Then I cover tweaking the settings of the logon screen and customizing its look. Chapter 2 shows you how to customize many aspects of the Start menu and the taskbar. Chapter 3 is all about customizing the desktop and the new Windows Sidebar. I even show you how you can make your own Windows Sidebar gadget. Chapter 4 covers customizing the look of the user interface by fine-tuning Aero Glass and completely changing the look of the interface with themes and visual styles. Chapter 5 shows you how you can customize all aspects of the Windows Explorer interface. Chapter 6 is all about customizing and tweaking Internet Explorer 7. Chapter 7 shows you how to customize Windows Media Player 11 as well as how to add a Media Center to your PC and customize it as well.

Part II: Increasing Your System's Performance

Chapter 8 introduces performance monitoring and benchmarking, using applications such as the Performance Diagnostic Console and Event Viewer to discover bottlenecks. Chapter 9 starts off with configuring your BIOS for maximum boot speed and various techniques to speed up the boot time, such as disabling unneeded services and features. Chapter 10 is all about speeding up your logon by removing unneeded startup programs as well as some other tips. Chapter 11 shows you how to speed up Windows Explorer and adjust the search indexer for maximum performance. Chapter 12 helps you optimize the core Windows components, such as using ReadyBoost, fine-tuning the paging file, and setting application priorities. Chapter 13 is all about speeding up your web browser and network.

Part III: Securing Your System

Chapter 14 helps you identify how vulnerable your system is as well as ways to better protect your computer, such as file and drive encryption. Chapter 15 is all about Internet security and protecting yourself with the latest tools, such as the new bidirectional firewall and Windows Defender. Chapter 16 guides you through techniques to protect your privacy by clearing stored personal history information from Internet Explorer and Windows Explorer.

Conventions Used in This Book

In this book, you'll find two notification icons — Tip and Caution — that point out important information. Here's what the two types of icons look like:

 Tips provide small, helpful hints to make hacks work better.

 A Caution alerts you to possible hazards that can result from the hacks.

Code, commands, filenames, and executables within the text appear in a monospace font, whereas content you type appears in **bold**.

What You Need to Use This Book

Windows Vista Ultimate is required to perform all tweaks and hacks mentioned in this book. You can use other versions of Windows Vista but you may find that certain sections do not work because that particular feature of Windows Vista is not in your version.

The Book's Companion Web Site

For links and updates, please visit this book's companion Web site at:

www.HackingWindowsVista.com

Hacking Precautions!

Although all the tweaks and hacks mentioned in this book have been tested, if a step is accidentally missed or a typo made, your computer may have severe problems. To make sure that you system is protected, I recommend that you utilize the Windows Vista System Restore feature as well as routinely back up your important documents.

To learn more about the backup utilities and System Restore features in Windows Vista, visit the help site located at http://windowshelp.microsoft.com/Windows/en-US/maintenance.mspx and look under the File backups and system recovery section.

Customizing
Your Computer

part

Customizing the Look of the Startup

Windows Vista has a great new look, but after a while, the new look can get old. With the help of some cool tools and tricks, you can customize many components of Windows Vista.

This chapter guides you through customizing two parts of your computer: the boot screen and the Welcome/Logon screen. I show you how to replace the boring boot screen and even how to activate a hidden boot screen.

Then this chapter moves on to a discussion of customizing the second part of your computer startup, the Welcome/Logon screen. This screen can be customized in several ways, such as customizing the user pictures and various settings that will allow you to increase your privacy and change the way the Logon screen behaves. I even show you how to change your Logon screen background.

Customizing the Boot Screen

Every time I turn on my computer, I am forced to stare at the boring Windows boot screen. I must admit that I found the moving bars amusing at first, but after a few months I became bored and wanted something different. Changing the boot screen is not something that Microsoft made easy; however, it is still possible with a few cool hacks.

Activating the hidden boot screen

Over the several years that Windows Vista was in the planning stages and in development, many promises were made about new features and enhancements. One of those promises had to do with high-resolution boot screens. This was going to be a great feature replacing the ancient 256-color boot screen that has been with Windows since Windows 95. Over time, as development of Vista was slipping behind schedule and developers were plagued with hardware compatibility problems with the high-resolution boot screen code, the feature was pulled from the final product.

Although this feature never made it into the released version of Windows Vista, there appears to be some parts of it left in the system. This section shows you a cool trick that will enable a hidden boot screen that looks like it was part of the high-resolution feature, as shown in Figure 1-1. It is nothing super fancy or elegant, but it sure is better than the boring boot screen that Vista shipped with, which looks like it is missing the Vista logo.

Figure 1-1: Hidden boot screen in Windows Vista

Before we proceed, note that some users have problems with using the hidden boot screen — possibly the reason why Microsoft hid it in the first place. If you are one of those users, simply boot into Safe mode and undo the steps for enabling the boot screen. Unfortunately, it is not currently known exactly what hardware has problems with the hidden boot screen. When you are ready, follow these steps to enable this boot screen on your PC:

1. Click the Start button, type **msconfig** in the Search box, and then press Enter.

2. When the System Configuration Utility loads, click the Boot tab.

3. Locate the No GUI boot box and select it, as shown in Figure 1-2.

4. Click OK and reboot your computer.

You should see the hidden boot screen after you reboot your PC. As I mentioned earlier, if you have problems with the hidden boot screen, just boot into Safe mode (hold down F8 when you boot up) and remove the check from the No GUI Boot box.

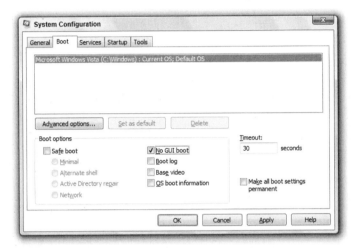

FIGURE 1-2: Using the System Configuration utility to enable the hidden boot screen

Customizing the boot screen image

The alternative boot screen that you just enabled in the preceding section is a great improvement compared to the boring moving progress bar that shows by default. However, this is still not good enough. With the help of a few cool tricks, you can create your own high-resolution, 24-bit boot screen without hacking any system files.

How is that possible? Thanks to the new language-independent operating system components in Windows Vista, some resources are stored in regional language files rather than the actual system components. This allows Microsoft to easily create a localized version of Windows Vista in any language by just creating new MUI (multilingual user interface) files that contain localized versions of bitmaps and text. Because MUI files are not digitally signed by Microsoft, you can make your own that has your own boot screen image in it, which allows you to customize the alternative boot screen to use any image you desire.

This new feature in Windows Vista provides a great enhancement and alternative to the traditional method of hacking system files as you had to do in previous versions of Windows to do things such as changing the boot screen. In addition, there is a great tool developed by Dan Smith called the Vista Boot Logo Generator that will automatically compile the boot images you select into an MUI file. This makes the overall process simple compared to trying to change boot screens, as you did in the past.

To get started, you need two images, one 800 × 600 and one 1024 × 768 image, both saved as 24-bit bitmap images. When you have those images picked out, resized, and saved, you are ready to follow these steps:

1. Visit www.computa.co.uk/staff/dan/?p=18 and download the latest copy of the Vista Boot Logo Generator and install it.

2. Click the Start button, type **vista boot logo**, and press Enter.

3. After the boot logo is downloaded, click the Browse for Images button in the 800 × 600 section and select your 800 × 600 24-bit bitmap image. Do the same for the 1024 × 768 section.

4. After you have both images selected, click File and select Save Boot Screen file as to save your MUI file. Save it to your desktop.

5. Next you need to replace the winload.exe.mui file located in c:\windows\system32\en-us with the file you just created. However, it is not as easy as a simple copy and paste because the Windows system files are protected. First, I recommend making a backup of the existing winload.exe.mui file so that you can copy it back if you have problems later. To get around the file protections, you need to take ownership of all the files in the en-us folder. Right-click the en-us folder and select Properties.

6. Select the Security tab and then click the Advanced button at the bottom of the window.

7. Select the Owner tab, and then click the Edit button.

8. Select your account from the Account list and check Replace owner on subcontainers and objects. Click OK to apply your changes.

9. Click OK to exit all the open Properties windows. You need to go back into the folder properties to change the file permissions. This time you will have more rights because you are now the folder owner. Right-click en-us and select Properties again.

10. Click the Security tab, and this time click Edit.

11. Click the Add button. Type in your username and click OK. Your account name should now appear on the Permissions list.

12. Select your account, and then select the Allow column for Full control, as shown in Figure 1-3.

13. Click OK to save your changes and OK once more to close the Properties screen. You will now be able to copy the winload.exe.mui file you made and saved to your desktop to c:\windows\system32\en-us. After you copy the file and reboot, you should see your new boot screen.

If you do not see your new boot screen and instead see the progress bar, make sure that you turned on the alternative boot screen as shown in the previous section. If you have any problems with your new boot screen MUI file, you can always boot using your Windows Vista install CD into a command prompt and can copy back the old winload.exe.mui file.

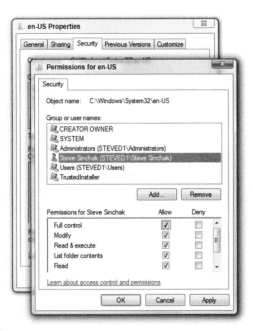

FIGURE 1-3: Giving your account full control over the
en-us MUI files to change the boot screen

Customizing the Logon Screen

Windows Vista included a slightly improved Logon screen similar to the one that was used
in Windows XP. Gone for good this time is the Windows NT–style classic Logon screen with
which many domain users are familiar (because it was included in the last several releases of
Windows). The new Welcome screen, as I called it in Windows XP, is here to stay, and is now
your only choice for logging on. Not much changed except for a few visual enhancements that
make the screen look more professional and make it fit in with the theme of the rest of the
operating system.

In Windows Vista, Microsoft has done a lot of work on securing the logon system by digitally
signing the logon components. This makes it next to impossible for anyone to modify the
Logon screen files, so it greatly increases the security of Vista. Unfortunately, it also makes it
next to impossible for people like us who want to customize the Logon screen; you can no
longer just hack a system file and replace some resources in it. Now, if you hack a system file
with a resource hacker and customize the images in it, the digital signature will be broken and
the file will no longer be used by Vista.

The days of customizing the Logon screen are over for now until someone writes an application that extends the Logon screen or someone releases a patch that disables the requirement for the Logon screen system files to be digitally signed.

So, is this the end of customizing the Logon screen? Not at all! You can still do a lot of useful tweaks to the Logon screen that will give the Logon screen a personal touch, such a changing user pictures, hiding users, customizing the Logon screen screensaver, and more.

Changing user pictures

Each user who is set up on your computer can associate an image that appears next to his or her name on the Logon screen, as shown in Figure 1-4. By default, you have the option to select a picture for your account when you install Windows. However, the screen that allows you to pick an image offers only a small selection of the pictures available to you. In addition, if you do not like the images that Windows has to offer, you can select any image file.

FIGURE 1-4: The Logon screen with an image next to the user's name

The process of changing a user's image is simple. Just perform the following steps and you will have it changed in no time:

1. Click the Start button, and then click your user picture, as shown in Figure 1-5.

FIGURE 1-5: Clicking your user picture to access your account settings

2. Select Change your picture from the middle of the list.

3. You will now be shown all the Windows user images that you can choose from. If you find one you like, click it, and then click the Change Picture button.

4. If you prefer a different photo, click Browse for more pictures to select and use any image file on your PC.

5. After you have selected your new image, your setting change is instantly applied. You can now close User Accounts and Control Panel.

Now you have changed your user image on the Logon screen; you have also updated the image used on the Start menu.

Hiding users on the Logon screen

One of the side effects of the new Logon screen is the list of all the user accounts on the computer. What if you created an account that you want only to run a service under? You do not want other users of your computer to even have the option to log on to that account because you designated it only to run a service. With the help of a simple Registry hack, it is possible to hide any account on the Logon screen so that it is no longer possible to log on to it (unless you turn on the Do not display last user name policy and manually type the username and password, as discussed later in this chapter).

Hidden away in the local system settings is the feature that Microsoft used in the past to hide system accounts from the Logon screen. In Windows Vista, the actual Logon screen hides system accounts, so the old method code was removed from the Registry. However, the functionality still exists. In the next few steps, I show you how to re-create the missing Registry code so that you can use this feature once again to hide your accounts:

1. Click the Start button, type **regedit** in the Search box, and then press Enter.

2. When Registry Editor loads, navigate through HKEY_LOCAL\MACHINE\ SOFTWARE\Microsoft\Windows NT\CurrentVersion\Winlogon.

3. You must now create a new key. Right-click the Winlogon folder, select New, and then select Key. Name this new key **SpecialAccounts**.

4. Right-click the new SpecialAccounts folder, select New, and then select Key. Call this new key **UserList**.

5. Now you are ready to add the name of the account that you want to hide. To add a name, right-click and select a new DWORD value, as shown in Figure 1-6.

6. When the new DWORD is created, enter the name of the user's account as the name of the DWORD. After you have done this, you can close the Registry Editor.

After you log off and back on or reboot, the user will not be displayed on the Logon screen. Keep in mind that no one will now be able to log on to this account interactively (as in having a graphical session). If you want to hide all accounts and just have a username and password box, the next section is for you. If you opt for that method, you can hide all accounts and still log on to them. You just need to remember the username and the password because no accounts will be listed any more.

If you ever change your mind and want the account to display on the Logon screen again, just delete the entry that you made in the list in the system registry, and everything will be back to the way it once was.

Clearing the last user logon

Every time you boot up your PC, all computer accounts and users who have logged on to it display on the Logon screen. This can be a big security risk because it shows the usernames of all accounts that someone can try to use to break into the computer. In addition, the Logon screen can become cluttered with user accounts. Therefore, it might be a good idea to enable the Do not display last user name policy. In previous versions of Windows that used the classic Logon screen, this policy would just clear the User name text box so that an attacker would have no clue about the last account used to log on. With the removal of the classic Logon screen in Vista, this policy behaves slightly differently by removing the Account list on the Logon screen and turning on basic User name and Password boxes, as shown in Figure 1-7.

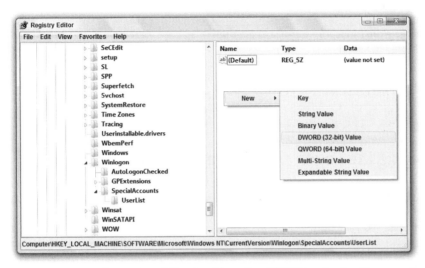

FIGURE 1-6: Using the Registry Editor to add another DWORD value for the name of a user who will be hidden on the Logon screen

FIGURE 1-7: Basic User name and Password boxes on the Logon screen

Using the policy is easy, if you choose to enable it. If so, just follow these steps:

1. Click the Start button, type **secpol.msc**, and press Enter.

2. When the Local Security Policy editor loads, navigate through Local Policies and then Security Options.

3. Locate the Interactive logon: Do not display last user name policy. Right-click it and select Properties.

4. On the Local Security Settings tab, select Enable, and then click OK.

5. Close the Local Security Policy editor and you are finished.

As soon as you log off or reboot, the new Logon screen settings will be present.

Changing the Logon screen screensaver

If you turn on your computer and let it sit at the Logon screen long enough, eventually the screensaver will appear. This setting can be tweaked so that you can set the screensaver that you want to see instead of the boring Windows default. Unlike changing your screensaver for your account when you are logged on, it is possible to change the Logon screen screensaver setting only by using the Registry. With the help of a few quick Registry hacks, you can fine-tune the screensaver that is displayed and other settings such as the screensaver Timeout value that determines how long before the screensaver is activated.

Follow these simple steps to customize your Logon screensaver:

1. Start the Registry Editor. Click the Start button, type **regedit** in the box, and press Enter.

2. When the Registry Editor starts up, navigate through HKEY_USERS\.DEFAULT\ Control Panel\Desktop.

3. Let's change the amount of time the system waits after the last activity was detected before starting the screensaver. To do this, right-click the ScreenSaveTimeOut entry and select Modify. The amount of time to wait is stored in seconds. By default, the system waits 600 seconds (10 minutes) before starting the screensaver. If you want to change this value to something shorter, such as 1 minute, just enter a new value, which for 1 minute would be 60. Then click OK to save your changes.

4. By default, the boring flat Windows Vista logo screensaver displays. Try something a little more exciting such as the Mystify screensaver. To do this, right-click and select Modify on the SCRNSAVE.EXE string value. Set the value to the full path of the screensaver you want to use. For example, I use C:\windows\system32\Mystify.scr for the Mystify screensaver. Refer to Table 1-1 for a list of Windows screensavers and the paths you can use. When you have finished making your change, click OK to save.

5. Close the Registry Editor. You are now finished. After a reboot, you will see your new screensaver.

Table 1-1   Windows Vista Screensavers

Screensaver Name	Full path
Aurora	C:\Windows\System32\Aurora.scr
Bubbles	C:\Windows\System32\Bubbles.scr
Logon (Windows default)	C:\Windows\System32\logon.scr
Mystify	C:\Windows\System32\Mystify.scr
Photos	C:\Windows\System32\PhotoScreensaver.scr
Ribbons	C:\Windows\System32\Ribbons.scr
Blank Screen	C:\Windows\System32\scrnsave.scr
Vista	C:\Windows\System32\ssBranded.scr
3D Text	C:\Windows\System32\ssText3d.scr

Displaying a security message

Would you like to display a message to your users before they can log on? Are any instructions necessary for users of your computers, such as "Do not shut down this computer!" or possibly a security warning informing unauthorized users that they are breaking the law if they try to log on to your laptop? All these are possible with the help of Group Policy. With just a few clicks, you can easily display a message to your visitors, as shown in Figure 1-8.

Using the Local Security Policy editor, you can turn this feature on. Follow these steps to activate it on your PC:

1. Click the Start button, type **secpol.msc**, and press Enter.

2. When the Local Security Policy editor loads, navigate through Local Policies and then Security Options.

3. Locate the Interactive logon: Message title for users attempting to log on policy. Right-click it and select Properties.

4. On the Local Security Settings tab, type a title that you would like to use for your message and click OK.

5. Locate the Interactive logon: Message text for users attempting to log on policy. Right-click it and select Properties.

6. On the Local Security Settings tab, type your message and click OK.

7. Close the Local Security Policy editor; you are finished.

As soon as you log off or reboot, the security message settings will be activated.

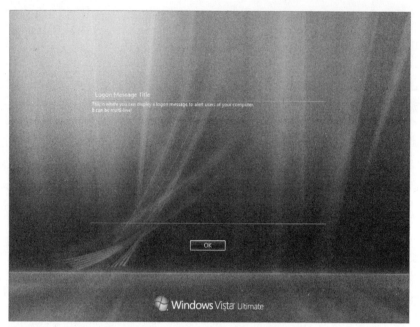

FIGURE **1-8**: Security message on a Windows Vista Logon screen

Enabling Num Lock by default

If you have a password that has both numbers and letters and you frequently use the number pad to enter part of your password, this hack is for you. I cannot count the number of times that I started to type my password and was then presented with a logon error telling me that my password was incorrect. I would sit there staring at the screen for a second before I realized that Num Lock on my keyboard was not on.

This is a great hack for every desktop computer with a full-size keyboard with a separate number pad. Turning on Num Lock by default on a laptop is not a good idea because usually most laptops do not have a separate number pad. Enabling this feature on a laptop will result in almost half of your keyboard functioning as the number pad, and you would be much better off using the numbers above the letters. To get started, follow these steps:

1. Click the Start menu, type **regedit**, and press Enter.

2. When the Registry Editor loads, navigate through HKEY_USERS\ .DEFAULT\Control Panel\Keyboard.

3. Locate the InitialKeyboardIndicators entry, right-click it, and select Modify. To enable Num Lock, enter **2** into the box. If you want to disable it, enter **0** into the box.

4. Then click OK to save the changes. That's it!

If you are on a laptop and you attempted to enable Num Lock even though I told you not to and need to fix your system, repeat the preceding directions but replace the value of InitialKeyboardIndicators with **0** to disable the feature.

Changing the Logon screen background

How would you like to be able to customize the background image used on the Logon screen just as easily as you change the background image of your desktop? With a cool and free utility from Stardock, this is now possible. The logon in Windows Vista is nice looking and much better compared to XP. However, if you are like me, and you probably are if you are reading this book, you want to customize the background your way. This section shows you exactly how to do that using Stardock LogonStudio for Windows Vista.

Let's get started. First, head over to www.stardock.com and download a copy of the latest version of LogonStudio for Windows Vista and install it. When you have finished, follow these steps to change your logon background:

1. Click the Start button, type **LogonStudio**, and press Enter.

2. When you install LogonStudio, a few logon backgrounds will come pre-installed. Just click a background and click Apply to change the logon background.

3. To use your own image, click Create a new Logon screen from the side menu.

4. Type in a name and then click the Browse button to locate your image, as shown in Figure 1-9.

5. After you have selected your image, click Save.

6. Select your new logon image and click Apply to see it in action.

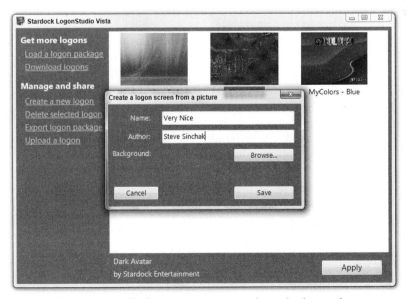

FIGURE 1-9: Using LogonStudio to create your own logon background

Summary

This first chapter can be thought of as the first step in the complete customization of every possible aspect of your Windows Vista. You started at the very beginning with enabling the hidden boot screen and you worked through to the Logon screen to customize it to meet your needs.

The next chapter helps you customize the user navigation components of Windows Vista. First, you learn all about customizing the updated Start menu in Vista. This chapter shows you how to get the most out of the new features. Then it shows you how you can customize the next most used component of Windows, the taskbar.

Customizing User Navigation

C ustomizing user navigation is the next stop on the Windows Vista
customizing road trip. In the preceding chapter, with the help of
some cool hacks, you were able to change and improve the boot
and logon screens. This chapter picks up where Chapter 1 left off and
shows you how to customize and improve the visual navigation elements
of Windows Vista.

This chapter starts with customizing the look and the contents of the cool
new Start panel. The improved Start panel in Windows Vista has many
useful new features, and I show how you can use them best. Then, I show
you how you can customize the new program list and customize almost
everything you see. If you don't like the new Start panel, you can then find
out how to get the old classic Start menu back. Then, I show you some cool
hacks to improve and customize the classic Start menu.

You also learn how to customize the taskbar on the bottom of your screen.
The taskbar is an essential part of navigating your computer. I show you
how to customize and improve its features and give you some new ideas on
how you can use it that may dramatically improve your experiences with
Windows Vista.

Customizing the Start Panel

The Start panel is what I consider the replacement for the traditional Start
menu that you may be familiar with if you were a pre-Windows XP user. I
call this the Start *panel* because it is not just a *menu* anymore. It is now a
collection of various shortcuts and features, all thrown onto one panel that
pops up. It offers many new features such as a dynamic list that includes
your most frequently run programs so that you can easily access them without having to navigate through All Programs. In addition, the Start panel
has replaced all the icons on the desktop except for the Recycle Bin so that
your desktop will look much cleaner and uncluttered. New in Windows Vista
is a Search box on the bottom of the Start panel. This new box enables you
to easily search through programs in the Start menu and search your computer for documents and launch commands like a traditional Run box.
Everything can be accessed from the Start panel now!

Today, tools and hacks allow you to customize the Start panel. Almost everything on it is customizable. You can add and remove icons and shortcuts, and you can even change the way it looks. You can even change the way the features on it, such as the Search box, work.

When you have finished reading these next few sections, you will have transformed your Start panel into something that works better for you and is much more useful for your everyday tasks.

Customizing navigation shortcuts

You will find many new navigation links on the Start panel that will help you navigate to various parts of Windows. All these shortcut buttons on the right side of the Start panel can be customized. Many can be removed completely, and others can be added. By default, you will see a button with your username followed by buttons for Documents, Pictures, Music, and Games. All these buttons are shortcuts to your personal folders. The next set — Search, Recent Items, Computer, Network, and Connect to — are more functional navigation shortcuts that allow you to jump to the most common system components. The last three shortcuts offer you a way to access system configuration components such as the Control Panel and Default Programs and a convenient shortcut to Help and Support for new users.

Some shortcuts are not displayed, such as the classic Run button, Printers, and Favorites. Other features, such as Display as Menu for buttons, that allow you to jump directly to a specific child item are also missing. This feature can be useful in some situations. For example, if you enable Display as Menu on the Computer button, you will see a list of drivers that you can jump directly to. This eliminates a few extra clicks that will help you get to where you want to go faster.

All these features and shortcuts are customizable on one screen. Follow these steps to access the Start Menu Customization screen:

1. Right-click the Start button and click Properties.

2. On the Start Menu tab, click the Customize button on the top right of the window. This loads the Customize Start Menu window, as shown in Figure 2-1.

3. Scroll through the list and make changes to the items as you see fit. Refer to the sections that follow for my recommendations.

4. When you're finished adjusting the options, click OK and OK once more to close Taskbar Properties. Your changes will be live instantly.

Now that you know how to change the settings, the next few sections guide you through my recommendations for creating a clean and powerful Start panel.

Hiding user folders

Having all the user folders on the Start panel can be useful for some but not for me. You are already given a button that has your username on it. Through that button, you can access your music, pictures, and documents. Having these extra folders visible is just cluttering the Start panel and taking up real estate that could be better spent.

FIGURE 2-1: Customizing the Start Menu window

To clean up the user folders, while on the Customize Start Menu window (shown in Figure 2-1), set these options:

- **Documents:** Select Don't display this item.
- **Music:** Select Don't display this item.
- **Pictures:** Select Don't display this item.
- **Games:** Select Don't display this item. You can reach the games through the normal Start menu.

Customizing system component and management shortcuts

The system component shortcut buttons and management buttons also take up a lot of space on your Start panel. I rarely find myself using any of these buttons with the exception of Search and Computer. The others I have in my Quick Launch bar, or you can find them in the system tray. Here are my recommendations for these two sections:

- **Connect To:** Clear the checkbox. You can access this in the system tray.
- **Computer:** Set to Display as menu.
- **Default Programs:** Clear the check box.
- **Help:** Clear the check box.

- **Network:** Clear the check box. You can access this in the system tray.

- **Printers:** Check. The only other place you can get this is in Control Panel, which is inconvenient if you print a lot.

- **Run:** Check if you like the old Run button. You can use the search box now as a Run box, too, but some may still like the old Run box. I do!

Tip While in the Taskbar and Start Menu Properties window (right-click the Start button and select Properties), I recommend removing the check next to Store and displaying a list of recently opened files. This removes the annoying Recent Items entry on your Start panel.

You are now finished customizing your Start panel. If you followed my recommendations, your Start panel will now look like Figure 2-2.

FIGURE 2-2: Slim Start panel

Customizing the Frequently Run Programs list

Every time you launch an application on your PC, Windows is watching. It keeps track of the applications you run to derive the list of frequently run programs. You can find the list of frequently run programs on the left side of the Start panel. This program list can be useful for quickly accessing your applications instead of navigating through the entire All Programs menu.

There are a few cool tweaks for the Frequently Run Programs list that will allow you to customize it to make it more useful for you. The next three sections show you how you can modify the icon size, change the number shown, hide applications from showing up, and pin applications to the list.

Customizing icon size

One way that I like to customize my Start panel is to decrease the size of the icons on the left so that I can fit more icons on the screen. Figure 2-3 shows the difference between a Start panel that has been switched to use small icons and the normal Start panel.

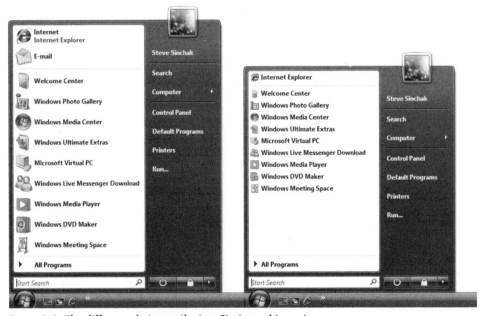

FIGURE 2-3: The difference between the two Start panel icon sizes

Changing the icons is easy. You just need to change one setting within the Start menu properties. To do so, follow these steps:

1. Move your mouse cursor over the Start button and right-click it, and then click Properties.

2. This brings up the Start Menu Properties menu that you used in the preceding section. Here you want to click the Customize button.

3. Scroll all the way to the bottom of the list and uncheck Use large icons.

4. Click OK to save your change and click OK once more to finish.

You have now made some more room so that you can display more frequently run programs on the Start panel. When you click the Start menu, you may notice that there are not any more programs showing up. That is because you also have to adjust the number of programs that will appear. The next section shows you how to adjust how many program shortcuts are displayed.

Tweaking the number displayed

By now you have changed the icon size of the Frequently Run Programs list so that you can fit more icons on the screen. Now you can increase the number of programs that will be displayed so that your list of programs will become even more useful. If you decide that you do not want to change the size of the icons, don't worry. You can still change the number of programs that display; you just can't display as many.

Changing the number of programs depends completely on personal preference. Do you like having a huge Start panel that stretches from the taskbar to the top of the screen? Do you like a Start panel with a small footprint? By design, the Start panel cannot contain more than 30 programs on the list. Very few users can display 30 items simultaneously because they must have their screen resolution set at a minimum 1280 × 1024, assuming that they are using the small icons. That high resolution is usually used only by owners of screens larger than 18 inches. The most common computer screen resolution is 1024 × 768. At that resolution, 22 programs can fit on the Start panel when the small icons are used. If you have an older computer or just a small display and your screen resolution is set for 800 × 600, you will be able to display only 15 programs on your Frequently Run Programs list.

The resolution settings of your screen determine the maximum number of programs that can be displayed. If you accidentally choose too many programs, Windows will let you know by giving you a friendly pop-up message when you try to click your Start menu after the change.

Now that you have an idea of the number of programs that your computer can display, you are ready to get started. To increase the number of programs, do the following:

1. Right-click the Start button and select Properties to bring up the Taskbar and Start Menu Properties settings.

2. Click the Customize button to show the Customize Start Menu options.

3. On this screen, locate the Start Menu Size section and the Number of recent programs to display box. You can adjust this value by clicking the up and down buttons or just by selecting all the text and entering a new number.

Tip   If you want to save even more room and never use the Internet Explorer and Mail client links on the top of the Frequently Run Programs list, clear all the boxes in the Show on Start menu box on the Customize Start Menu window.

4. After you have entered the number of programs you want displayed, click OK to save your changes.

5. Click OK once more and you are finished.

The best way to set the number of programs is to experiment with several different values until you get your Start panel looking the way you want it. After you find the value that is just right, you will have a much-improved Start panel.

Keeping programs off the list

Say you have a top-secret program that you do not want anyone else to know you have. Every time you run a program on your computer, Windows Vista records it and places the shortcut on your Frequently Run Programs list. Sometimes this is not always a good thing and can cause a privacy or job-security problem.

For example, let's use the situation of a guy named Larry. Larry is a big fan of Purble Place in Windows Vista. It is not the best game, but he likes it because it is an alternative to actually doing work. Every time Larry plays Purble Place, Windows Vista automatically adds the game to the Frequently Run Programs list. In this situation, program tracking creates a big problem for Larry. He is concerned that one of his fellow employees might see his Frequently Run Programs list and ridicule him for playing a children's game or report him to management for not doing work. What should he do? First, Larry should buy a copy of *Hacking Windows Vista*, and then he should follow these steps:

1. Click the Start menu and select Run. Type **regedit** and click OK to start the Registry Editor.

2. Expand the HKEY_CLASSES_ROOT folder.

3. Search through the list of folders until you find the folder called Applications and expand that, too.

4. Now you will see a list of every executable file for the programs installed on your computer. To hide a program from the Frequently Run Programs list, expand the folder that is the executable for the program. To hide Purble Place, expand the PurblePlace.exe folder.

Tip

If you do not know the name of the executable file that a program shortcut points to, you can easily look this up by right-clicking the shortcut and selecting Properties. In the Properties box, you will see a full path to where the file is located and the name of the file. When you right-click the shortcut in the Start menu for Purble Place, you will discover that the name of the executable for the game is PurblePlace.exe.

5. Can't find a folder called PurblePlace.exe? That is because some Windows applications are not listed. If your application *is* listed, skip this step. Otherwise, you need to create a new Registry key. To do so, select the Applications key within HKEY_CLASSES_ROOT. Right-click and select New, and then select Key. Type in the name of the executable for the name of the key. For Purble Place, name the key PurblePlace.exe.

6. Now that you have found the folder for the application or have created one, expand it so that you can see all its values. Then right-click your executable's folder that you just

created or found in the Registry. Select New, and then select String. Type **NoStartPage** as the name of the string variable, as shown in Figure 2-4.

7. Close the Registry Editor and log off and then back in. You will never see Purble Place in your Frequently Run Programs list again.

Now Larry can play as much Purble Place at work as he wants without having to worry about it showing up in his Frequently Run Programs list.

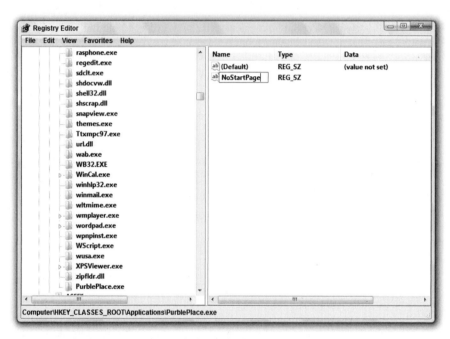

FIGURE 2-4: Using Registry Editor to hide applications from the Frequently Run Programs list

Pinning programs

I use the Calculator application all the time when I am using my computer. My desk calculator is always lost, and I don't want to waste time looking for it when I just need to do a quick calculation. Every time that I want to use the Calculator application, I have to click the Start menu, select All Programs, and then navigate up through the Accessories menu until I finally can click the Calculator app. There is a much better way that I can access this program.

Instead of navigating through the program listings, I can just pin the program to the Start panel. Pinning a program is a simple task that allows the program that you pin to appear on the Start panel just above the Frequently Run Programs list. If you pin a program shortcut, it appears just below the Internet Explorer and e-mail icons in the Start panel.

Navigating through the entire Start menu to launch a program you use all the time is a waste of time. Why waste your time? Pin your most commonly used programs today!

Are you excited yet? No? Okay, well let's get started anyway:

1. Start your pinning adventure by navigating through the Start menu as you normally do to launch a program. Navigate to a program that you use all the time, such as the Calculator application in the Accessories menu.

2. After you have highlighted the item, right-click the item and select Pin to Start menu. That's it. Your program will now appear directly on the Start panel.

Now let's say that you got a little too excited and pinned too many applications and want to remove some. What should you do? Just click the Start button once more to bring up the Start menu and highlight the program you want to unpin from the Start panel. Next, just right-click the item and select Unpin from Start Menu.

Pinning your favorite programs is a simple solution to speeding up your access to your programs.

Customizing the program list and search

The actual program listings are the last component of the Start menu that you can customize. In Windows Vista, users of the new Start panel have a new way of accessing the program list using the search box. These next few sections show you how you can customize the search box feature of the new Start panel and show you tweaks for the way the program list displays in both the new Start panel and the classic Windows Start menu.

Adjusting scope

The new search box on the bottom of the Start panel in Windows Vista is an extremely versatile box where you can do everything from executing programs to searching your entire computer for a specific document. By default, when you search for some text, it will search all the indexed locations. When I am using this feature, I just want it to search for programs in my Start menu, not search all my e-mails and other documents all over my computer. Why? I like a clean-looking Start menu, and when the search scope is set to something very wide, the results can become cluttered with other useless information I don't care about. As I mentioned previously, when I search in the Start panel search box, I expect it to just search the Start menu and nothing more. Thankfully, Microsoft has provided a way for you to customize the scope of where this search box searches. Follow these steps to customize your search scope:

1. Right-click the Start button and select Properties.

2. Click the Customize button on the Taskbar and Start Menu Properties window.

3. Scroll down the list of options until you get to the search settings, as shown in Figure 2-5.

4. Here, I like to uncheck Search Communications and Search favorites and history, and I select Don't search for files.

5. Click OK to save and OK once more to close the Properties window.

After you are finished disabling the extra default search locations, you will notice that your search results are presented faster and are now less cluttered. Keep in mind that you can always still use the Search button on the right side of the Start panel to search for documents, favorites, communications, and files.

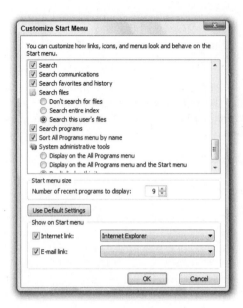

FIGURE 2-5: Start Menu search options

Disabling new program highlights

Program highlights was a great feature when I first started to use Windows XP. This feature will automatically highlight any new programs that you install so that you can easily find them on the Start menu the first few times that you want to run the application. However, after I used this feature for a few months, I started to get annoyed with it. It never seemed to work correctly, and applications that I installed quite some time ago seemed like they were going to be highlighted forever. Unfortunately, it is also included in Windows Vista. So, as soon as I installed Vista on my PC, I was haunted by the return of this once-great feature. Thankfully, Microsoft has made it simple to turn off this feature. Just follow these steps to get rid of those annoying highlights:

1. Right-click the Start button and select Properties.

2. Click the top Customize button for the Start panel.

3. Scroll through the list and uncheck Highlight Newly Installed Programs.

4. Click OK to save your changes.

5. Click OK once more to close the Properties window.

Now you will not have to worry about the programs that sometimes seem to be highlighted randomly.

Disabling pop-up help

Ever notice that when you hover your cursor over a program listing in the Start menu a little help box pops up? This help feature is called Balloon Help. If users do not know what a program does, they can hold the cursor over the program for a second or so and a little message will fade in telling users what it is — if the programmer has set up this feature of the program. For programs that do not have this feature set up for their shortcut, the balloon just tells users where the program is located on their computer.

This feature can be useful for a beginning computer user. However, it can be another annoyance for more advanced users. If you don't need this feature, why not disable it? Follow these steps to get rid of this feature:

1. Click the Start menu and select Run, and then type **regedit** in the box and click OK.

2. After the Registry Editor has been loaded, navigate though HKEY_CURRENT_ USER\Software\Microsoft\Windows\CurrentVersion\Explorer\Advanced.

3. Right-click the entry called ShowInfoTip and select Modify.

4. Set the value to 0 to disable this feature, and click OK.

5. Close the Registry Editor and log off and back on so that the feature can be removed.

You are now finished with the last section on customizing the Start menu and program listing. Now on to customizing the classic Start menu.

Customizing the Classic Start Menu

The classic Start menu, also known as the Windows 2000/98 style, has its advantages and also its share of disadvantages. It provides a clean and small interface to your programs, but does not offer nearly as much access to your computer as the new Start panel does. Some users like the old Start menu and dislike the big bulky Start panel. If you are one of those users, these next few sections are for you.

Activating the classic Start menu

Don't like the new Start menu? The new Start panel can be overwhelming for some users and is just not as clean looking as the old Start menu. Getting the old Start menu back is actually simple. To get started, just follow these steps:

1. Right-click the Start button and select Properties.

2. Select Classic Start Menu, as shown in Figure 2-6, and click OK.

FIGURE 2-6: Turning on the classic Start menu

Now that you have the classic Start menu back, you can begin to customize the way it looks and what it includes.

Customizing classic Start menu icons

Just as it is possible to customize the Start panel, it is possible to make changes to the classic Start menu to make it look the way you want it. Not as many things can be done to customize the classic Start menu as can be done to customize the Start panel, but a handful of features can be customized.

To get started, let's assume that you want to display your expanding Internet Explorer Favorites menu directly on your Start menu. I will walk you though how to turn this feature on or off and then provide you with more information on all the different features available on the same screen. Follow these steps to start customizing:

1. Right-click the Start menu and select Properties. This brings up the Taskbar and Start Menu Properties screen.

2. Click the lower Customize button to bring up the Customize Classic Start Menu Properties screen.

3. Now you will see a list of all the different features available in the Advanced Start menu options box. You can scroll through this box to view all the different features. Locate the Display Favorites option and check it to enable it.

4. Click OK to save your changes.

5. Click OK once more to exit the Properties window.

That's it. As you can see, customizing the Start menu is easy. If you want to disable a feature, just uncheck it.

Table 2-1 shows a list of all the different features and describes what they can do.

Table 2-1   Customizable Features of the Start Menu

Feature Name	Description
Display Administrative Tools	The administrative tools provide users with even more control over their system. I suggest that you enable this feature by checking the box so that you can take advantage of the easy access to your advanced system controls.
Display Favorites	The favorites can be useful depending on how often you use your favorites in Internet Explorer. If you are like me and do not use your favorites often, consider leaving this one off. If you want to add your favorites to your Start menu, this will place an expandable menu that will display all your links.
Logoff	This feature allows you to toggle the Logoff button on the Start menu. You want to leave this one checked in most cases.
Display Run	This feature displays the Run command on the Start menu.
Expand Control Panel	I like this feature the most out of all the features that you can customize. Enabling this feature makes the Control Panel automatically expand and shows you each of the Control Panel applets. This way you can get almost anywhere in your computer controls easily without even having to load the Control Panel first; you can jump directly to where you want to go instead.
Expand My Documents	I personally do not use this feature because I have too many documents in my My Documents folder. Trying to find the correct document is a waste of time when you have to scroll through the list. It is much faster to leave this one alone and then just browse through the icons when you open up My Documents.
Expand My Pictures	As I mentioned before when I covered this option as a feature on the Start panel, this feature is pretty much useless when you have more than a few photos. Because most pictures that you take use numbers or dates for filenames, it is hard to find a particular photo. Instead, don't enable this one. (Leave it alone so that it remains just a link.) That way you will be able to take advantage of the large thumbnail views in Explorer when browsing your photos.

Continued

Table 2-1 *Continued*

Feature Name	Description
Expand Network Connections	I recommend that you enable this feature because it allows you to easily access and connect to your various communications devices. If you use a dial-up connection, your dial-up connection will display, and you can connect by right-clicking the name and selecting Connect. If you have a network adapter, you can access your network properties and status easily from this menu, too.
Expand Printers	Have a lot of printers installed on your computer? Or, do you use a lot of network printers? This is an easy way to access all the different printers that you use. You can view the print queue and delete jobs for a specific printer.
Show Small Icons in Start menu	This is my favorite feature on the list. This basically shrinks your whole Start menu by removing the Windows Vista banner from the left and replaces the large icons with small icons. This allows the Start menu to take up far less space than before. Take a look at Figure 2-7 for a example of small icons in action.

FIGURE 2-7: Start menu with the
Show Small Icons setting enabled

Customizing the program list

The Classic Mode works slightly differently than the Start panel program list. You have fewer features, such as the ability to search through the listing, and have other more annoying features, such as personalized menus. The next two sections will help you disable personalized menus and show you a new way to handle your program list as it grows over time.

Disabling personalized menus

Personalized menus is a feature in Windows that has been around for a little while. It uses your program run history to hide all the other programs in your Start menu program listing that you don't use (or don't use often). After a user has used his computer for a short while, Windows hides all the programs that the user does not run so that he can find his most frequently run programs more easily.

Personalized menus is like a great feature, but really think about it. Why would you have programs in your Start menu that you don't use? If a program is installed and never used on my computer, I uninstall it. You don't need to be wasting your storage space with useless programs.

In addition, sometimes beginning computer users believe that Windows deleted all their programs because those programs no longer appear in the Start menu programs listing. Well, as you probably know, they are still listed; the user just doesn't realize that if you click the down arrow, the Start menu expands back to its original size so that you can view all the programs.

When considering all these issues with personalized menus, I cannot see why you would want to have this feature enabled. Follow these steps to take back your computer:

1. Right-click the Start menu and select Properties.

2. Click the bottom Customize button to bring up the Customize Classic Start menu window.

3. Locate the Advanced Start menu options box, and scroll down all the way to the bottom.

4. You should now be able to see the Use Personalized Menus setting. Just uncheck the box to disable the feature.

5. Click OK to save your changes.

6. Click OK once more to close the Taskbar and Start Menu Properties window.

Now you will no longer have to deal with your programs disappearing. I highly recommend that you disable this feature on any beginner computer user's computer, too, to save yourself the headache of explaining that Windows didn't really delete everything.

Scrolling the Start menu

The scroll feature is a great way to manage a large list of installed programs on your computer. Instead of showing simultaneously all the programs on your list onscreen, it shows only one column of programs that you can scroll through.

Some computer manufacturers ship their systems with this feature enabled, whereas some have it disabled. Follow these steps to modify this feature for your computer:

1. Right-click the Start button and select Properties.

2. Click the Customize button next to the Classic Start Menu.

3. Located the Advanced Start Menu Options box, and scroll all the way to the bottom again.

4. Locate the Scroll Programs feature and check it to enable it, or uncheck it to disable it.

5. Click OK to save your changes.

6. Click OK once more to close the Properties window.

Now your program scrolling is under your control.

Customizing the Taskbar

The taskbar in Windows Vista is the same old taskbar you are already familiar with but with a few new added enhancements, such as animations and preview images. The taskbar is normally used to reach the Start menu and switch between open applications and Windows. This section shows you how to customize taskbar behavior and how you can customize the taskbar's contents to make it much more usable.

Taskbar animations

In Windows Vista when you close an application or window, the buttons on the taskbar gently slide around and resize. This sounds like a great effect, but often on some computers the animation can be choppy and just plain look bad. On my Vista PC, I always disable this option because the animation does not look the best, and the taskbar seems to operate much faster with the animations disabled. I recommend experimenting with this feature to see whether you like the old non-animated taskbar button better.

Follow these steps to disable the sliding taskbar buttons:

1. Click the Start button, type **Performance Information**, and press Enter.

2. When Performance Information and Tools loads, click Adjust visual effects under tasks on the left menu.

3. The Performance Options window opens. On the Visual Effects tab, scroll through the list and clear Slide taskbar buttons.

4. Click OK to save your changes.

Your changes are applied immediately. Close the Performance Information and Tools window now, and you will see the difference. Better? I hope you like it, too.

Program grouping

The program grouping feature can be useful or it can be an annoyance. When you have more than just a few programs open, the taskbar can become cluttered. To fight this, as the taskbar fills up, programs that have more than one window open are grouped together. If you have a bunch of Internet Explorer windows open, they will all be grouped together into one entry on the taskbar. If you want to switch between them or close one, you have to select the entry on the taskbar. A new menu will pop up showing you all the different windows open for the specific application.

One cool feature of grouping is that it enables you to close several windows simultaneously. When all the Internet Explorer windows are grouped together, you can just right-click the entry on the taskbar and select Close Group. Doing so automatically closes all the browser windows simultaneously.

The downside to this is that it takes an extra step to navigate through the grouped program items. Some people do not like this option much and would rather have a taskbar that is more cluttered because they will be able to switch between programs faster.

Depending on your screen resolution and your taskbar size, you might want to consider disabling program grouping. I personally flip-flop on my stance on program grouping. At times, I really appreciate how it neatly organizes my taskbar; at other times, I find it a major inconvenience to have to navigate through the pop-up grouped menus. Typically, I end up disabling grouping because I find it much easier to work without the pop-up grouped application menus. Follow these steps to disable program grouping for your taskbar:

1. Click the Start button and select Properties.

2. The Taskbar and Start Menu Properties window will load. Select the Taskbar tab.

3. Clear Group similar taskbar items.

4. Click OK to save your changes.

Bye-bye taskbar grouping. If you ever change your mind about the feature, just select the Group similar taskbar items box again on the Taskbar tab.

Adjusting Aero preview images

Windows Vista's new Aero glass interface provides many new features to the user interface. One of those new features is the window preview image shown when you hover over the taskbar's open application buttons. If your computer supports Aero glass and you have that visual interface turned on, you will see a live thumbnail preview image of what the window looks like, as shown in Figure 2-8.

FIGURE 2-8: Taskbar live preview images

These live thumbnails are powered by the new Desktop Windows Manager (DWM), a major component of Windows Vista. It works by using DirectX to display the user interface for the end user. When Aero glass is running, all applications are not drawn directly to the screen. Instead, they are drawn to an off-screen location that makes it possible to do cool things such as Flip 3d (the new Alt+Tab switcher) and view live taskbar preview images.

I personally like these new preview images, but I want you to have the opportunity to disable them if you find them annoying. Just follow these steps to disable the Aero preview images for your computer:

1. Click the Start button and select Properties.

2. The Taskbar and Start Menu Properties window will load. Click the Taskbar tab.

3. Clear Show window previews.

4. Click OK to save your changes.

Quick launching your programs

The Quick Launch bar is a great way to start your programs. You can completely bypass the Start menu and launch your programs with just one click. By default, the Quick Launch bar is not enabled. This section shows you how you can enable the Quick Launch bar and how you can make it useful. First, enable the Quick Launch bar, and then customize it by doing the following:

1. Right-click an open space on your taskbar and expand Toolbars, and then select Quick Launch. This makes the Quick Launch bar appear.

2. By default, there are two icons on it: Show Desktop and Switch between windows. You can easily add more icons to the Quick Launch bar by just dragging them onto the toolbar. You can even specify where you want the icon to be placed by dragging the icon between two icons. The best way to add programs to your Quick Launch bar is to browse through your Start menu and drag icons to the bar while holding down the Alt key. Holding down the Alt key ensures that you create a copy of the shortcut in the Start menu to be placed on the Quick Launch bar. Otherwise, when you drag a shortcut from the Start menu, it will be removed from the Start menu and placed only on the Quick Launch toolbar. I like to add my drives from my computer to my Quick Launch bar, too, for easy access. Just open My Computer and drag them down to the toolbar.

3. After you have all the icons set up on your Quick Launch bar, have some fun changing the position of the bar. To do this, unlock your taskbar first. Right-click an open part of the taskbar and select Lock the Taskbar only if there is already a check mark next to it, as shown in Figure 2-9. If there is not a check mark, your taskbar is not locked, and you are ready to proceed.

FIGURE 2-9: Taskbar properties showing the taskbar locked

Now that you made sure that the taskbar is not locked, you are ready to move the bar around. Let's expand the taskbar up so that you can have one row of Quick Launch icons; your open programs will be listed below. To do this, place the cursor (while holding down the left mouse button) on the top of the taskbar, as shown in Figure 2-10, and move the cursor up, while still holding the button down on the mouse, until the taskbar expands upward.

FIGURE 2-10: Expanding the taskbar with your mouse

When the taskbar moves up one notch, you can move the Quick Launch bar up. To do so, grab the left side of the menu on the dotted vertical line with the cursor and move the cursor up while holding down the left mouse button. When you have finished, your taskbar should look like Figure 2-11. Notice that when you have expanded your taskbar up one notch, the system clock expands to show the date *and* the day.

FIGURE 2-11: What the taskbar can look like after you move it to the Quick Launch bar, adjust the taskbar size, and add more programs to your Quick Launch bar

4. When you have the taskbar unlocked, you can easily change the size of the icons that are placed on the Quick Launch bar. To do so, right-click somewhere on the bar that is taken up by an icon and select View. You then see two choices: large and small icons. By default, the small icons are shown. The large icons look pretty cool because they make your taskbar look different. I suggest you play around with this feature and get your icons looking the way you like them best.

5. When you have finished making all your changes to the taskbar, lock it again so that you won't accidentally move things around the taskbar.

Now you have customized your Quick Launch bar and have greatly improved your navigation by creating your own list of programs. This will speed up the amount of time it takes to start any program.

Modifying the taskbar location

You usually see the taskbar appear at the bottom of your screen. That does not always have to be the case. It is possible to move the taskbar to every side of the screen, thus changing the look of Windows Vista. Figure 2-12 shows what your screen might look like if you move your taskbar to the left side of the screen.

FIGURE 2-12: Windows Vista with the
taskbar on the left side of the screen

Moving the taskbar is simple. There are just three basic steps:

1. Unlock the taskbar if it is already locked. Right-click an open part of the taskbar and select Lock the Taskbar, if there is a check mark next to the entry.

2. Click and hold your cursor on any part of the taskbar where there are no icons, such as the system clock, and drag the taskbar by moving your mouse in the general direction of the side you want.

3. When you have the taskbar where you want it, you might want to readjust your toolbars (such as the Quick Launch bar) inside the taskbar. Then lock it back up again by right-clicking it and selecting Lock the Taskbar.

Customizing the system tray

Over the years, the system tray in Windows has remained pretty much the same. In Windows XP, you could hide system tray icons for the first time (icons that were not used frequently, so that your tray did not become overcrowded and consume too much space). In Windows Vista, the system tray remains similar, with the exception of a few noticeable tweaks. One of the first things you will notice when you install Windows Vista is the new Network icon that is there by default. The system tray clock has also been improved in Windows Vista.

Similar to Windows XP, in Vista you can keep icons from displaying and configure which system components (for instance, time and various icons) display. The next few sections show you how to customize these aspects of your taskbar.

Hiding icons

As you install various applications on your PC, you might run into a problem with too many icons causing a space problem in your system tray. Quite often, applications abuse the system tray. It seems that too many developers have applications that add an entry on the taskbar and in the system tray. What is the point of having it in both places? It is just a waste of space. In Windows Vista, you can hide the system tray icon so that you can have a clean and clutter-free taskbar and system tray.

Hiding a system tray icon is easy to do. Just follow these steps:

1. Right-click the Start button and select Properties.

2. Click the Notification tab.

3. Make sure Hide inactive icons is checked.

4. Hit Customize under the Icons section.

5. When Customize Notification Icons is shown, you will see two sections: Current Items and Past Items. To hide an icon, select an icon and change the behavior drop-down box to Hide, as shown in Figure 2-13.

6. When you have finished hiding the desired icons, click OK to save your changes.

7. Click OK once more to exit the Taskbar and Start Menu Properties screen.

Your changes are effective immediately.

Removing system icons and the clock

As I mentioned previously, there are various system component icons and features in the system tray, too. In Windows Vista, there are the clock, volume, network, and power icons (power icon only on laptops). All these system components can be customized and turned off to save system tray real estate. Follow these steps to disable these icons:

1. Right-click the Start button and select Properties.

2. Select the Notification tab.

3. Under the System icons section, uncheck any icons you do not want to display, as shown in Figure 2-14.

4. Click OK to save your changes.

Now you can easily control the state of your system tray by managing the system icons, too.

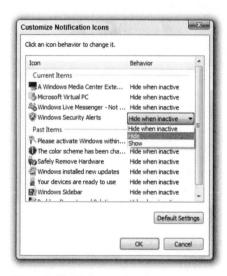

FIGURE 2-13: Hiding system tray icons

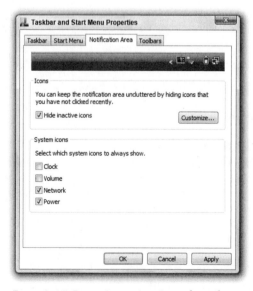

FIGURE 2-14: Removing system icons from the system tray

Using the Group Policy Editor to Customize the Start Menu and Taskbar

The Group Policy Editor is a great component of Windows Vista that enables you to make dozens of advanced settings changes that are hidden from normal users. This works by defining various rules, called the *policy*, that tell Windows how to behave.

The collection of policies is what is known as Group Policy, of which there are two types: local and domain based. Local is when the policy resides in and is controlled on the local computer. Domain-based policy is when the policy resides on an Active Directory domain controller that multiple computers are connected to. Domain policy is primarily used only in businesses that need a way to control multiple computers from a central location. In this book, you use local Group Policy to configure the Start panel because most of you are customizing your home computer and do not have it connected to a domain controller. The actual policies and way you set them are the same for both types of group policies, so you can apply these same techniques to a domain policy if desired.

The policies are set and modified using the, you guessed it, Group Policy Editor. This is the tool that you will be using to set the policies to help you customize the Start panel. First, I show you how to use the policy editor, and then I go over all the policies relevant to customizing the Start panel and explain how to use them.

Setting policies with the Group Policy Editor

Using the Group Policy Editor is a lot like using the Registry Editor. It is based on a hierarchical structure of sections that all policies are organized within. All policies are divided into two sections: Computer Policies and User Policies. Computer Policies are settings that apply to components of Windows Vista such as hardware and global feature settings. User Policies are settings that can vary between users on a computer. This is where most of the policies that you will use to customize the look of your interface are located.

Now that you know the basics of the Group Policy Editor, also known as gpedit, let's dive in and start using the policy editor:

1. Click the Start button, enter **gpedit.msc** in the search box, and press Enter.

2. After the Group Policy Editor has loaded, you will see the hierarchical structure and Computer & User policies sections mentioned previously, as shown in Figure 2-15.

3. Navigate through User Configuration\Administrative Template and then select Start Menu and Taskbar.

4. You will now see a list of all policies that you can configure. Right-click a policy that you want to configure and select Properties.

5. On the Policy Properties screen, select the option to turn on the policy or set the policy value, and then press OK, as shown in Figure 2-16.

6. Exit the policy editor and log off and back on. Some policy changes may require a reboot.

Now that you know how to use the Group Policy Editor, the next section shows you all the policies and briefly describes what they do.

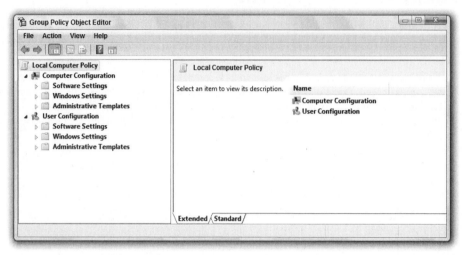

FIGURE 2-15: Using the Group Policy Editor

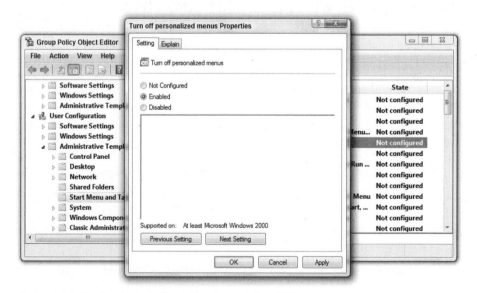

FIGURE 2-16: Configuring a policy in the Group Policy Editor

Start panel (and menu) and taskbar policies

Table 2-2 shows a list of all the group policies that will help you customize the Start panel (and menu) and the taskbar.

Table 2-2   Group Policy Settings to Configure the Start Menu and Taskbar

Policy	Description
Clear history of recently opened documents on exit	Purges document history at logoff.
Clear the recent programs list for new users	Purges program history at logoff.
Add Logoff to the Start Menu	Controls the logoff option in the classic Start menu and Start panel.
Gray unavailable Windows Installer programs Start Menu shortcuts	Provides users with a visual notification of applications that are not available.
Turn off personalized menus	Disables the feature that hides uncommonly run programs from the classic Start menu.
Lock the Taskbar	Controls the locking state of the taskbar. A locked taskbar does not allow any changes to be made to it.
Add "Run in Separate Memory Space" check box to Run dialog box	Adds an additional setting for running programs with the Run box. I recommend enabling this setting.
Turn off notification area cleanup	Disables the ability to hide icons.
Remove Balloon Tips on Start Menu items	Disables pop-up information when hovering over items in the Start menu.
Remove drag-and-drop context menus on the Start Menu	Disables the ability to use the drag-and-drop functionality in the Start menu.
Remove and prevent access to the Shut Down, Restart, Sleep, and Hibernate commands	Disables the user's ability to change the state of the machine. Useful for public computers.
Remove common program groups from Start Menu	Allows only user-specific applications to appear in the Start menu.
Remove Favorites menu from Start Menu	Hides the favorites shortcut.
Remove Search link from Start Menu	Hides the Search shortcut.
Remove frequent programs list from the Start Menu	Hides the Frequently Run Programs list.
Remove Games link from Start Menu	Hides the games shortcut.
Remove Help menu from Start Menu	Hides the help shortcut.

Continued

Table 2-2   *Continued*

Policy	Description
Turn off user tracking	Disables all tracking of user programs and documents.
Remove All Programs list from the Start menu	Removes the ability to search through the main part of the Start menu, All Programs.
Remove Network Connections from Start Menu	Hides the Network Connection shortcut.
Remove pinned programs list from the Start Menu	Disables the ability to pin applications.
Do not keep history of recently opened documents	Disables the tracking of opening documents.
Remove Recent Items menu from Start Menu	Hides the Recent Items shortcut.
Do not use the search-based method when resolving shell shortcuts	Disables the ability to search the computer when a shortcut is broken.
Do not use the tracking-based method when resolving shell shortcuts	Disables the ability to use NTFS tracking to try to fix a broken shortcut.
Remove Run menu from Start Menu	Hides the Run shortcut.
Remove Default Programs link from the Start menu	Hides the Default Programs shortcut.
Remove Documents icon from Start Menu	Hides the Documents shortcut.
Remove Music icon from Start Menu	Hides the Music shortcut.
Remove Network icon from Start Menu	Hides the Network shortcut.
Remove Pictures icon from Start Menu	Hides the Pictures shortcut.
Do not search communications	Disables the ability to search e-mails from the Start menu search box.
Remove Search Computer link	Hides the Search shortcut.
Do not search files	Disables the ability to search for files that are in indexed locations from within the Start menu.
Do not search Internet	Disables the ability to search the Internet from the Start menu.
Do not search programs	Disables the ability to search the Start menu from the Start menu search box. This will not make the search box go away. It just becomes inactive.
Remove programs on Settings menu	Prevents various settings components from running, such as the Control Panel and Network Connections.

Table 2-2   *Continued*

Policy	Description
Prevent changes to Taskbar and Start Menu Settings	Locks taskbar and Start menu settings.
Remove user's folders from the Start Menu	Hides user folders.
Force classic Start Menu	Disables the new Start panel and uses the Windows 2000–style Start menu instead.
Remove Clock from the system notification area	Hides the clock.
Prevent grouping of taskbar items	Disables application grouping on the taskbar.
Do not display any custom toolbars in the taskbar	Disables third-party taskbars or user-made toolbars.
Remove access to the context menus for the taskbar	Disables the capacity to right-click the toolbars in the taskbar.
Hide the notification area	Disables the entire notification area (system tray).
Remove user folder link from Start Menu	Hides the User Folder shortcuts.
Remove user name from Start Menu	Hides the username from appearing on the Start panel.
Remove links and access to Windows Update	Hides the shortcuts to Windows Update.
Show QuickLaunch on Taskbar	Enables the Quick Launch toolbar.
Remove the "Undock PC" button from the Start Menu	Hides the shortcut for undocking a laptop.
Add the Run command to the Start Menu	Provides the Run command on both the Start panel and the classic Start menu.
Remove Logoff on the Start Menu	Hides the Logoff shortcut.
Use folders instead of library	Enables folder view rather than library view.
Remove the battery meter	Hides the power icon in the system tray.
Remove the networking icon	Hides the network icon in the system tray.
Remove the volume control icon	Hides the volume icon in the system tray.
Lock all taskbar settings	Locks the taskbar.
Prevent users from adding or removing toolbars	Disables the ability to add toolbars.
Prevent users from rearranging toolbars	Locks in the position of your toolbars (similar to locking the taskbar).

Continued

Table 2-2 *Continued*

Policy	Description
Turn off all balloon notifications	Disables pop-up help.
Prevent users from moving taskbar to another screen dock location	Locks the position of your taskbar.
Prevent users from resizing the taskbar	Locks the size of your taskbar.
Turn off taskbar thumbnails	Disables the application thumbnails that are shown when you move your cursor over taskbar items when running Aero Glass.

As you can see, there are dozens of useful group policies that will help you customize your desktop more than any other method. Additionally, these policies can be used in a Domain Policy that governs all Windows Vista computers connected to a domain.

Summary

This chapter walked you through the process of customizing the Start menu and then moved on to the taskbar. You customized your Start panel for the way you work and got rid of the extra clutter. In case you are a fan of the classic Start menu, you were shown how you can activate the time machine and bring your Start menu back to the nineties. Then you were shown how you can customize and improve how the taskbar works, followed by advanced tweaking via Group Policy.

The next chapter concentrates on customizing the desktop. You will find out how you can completely change the look of the interface and use other third-party applications to make the interface even better.

Hacking the Desktop

Studies have shown that customizing your desktop will result in a 64 percent increase in productivity as well as a 248 percent increase in happiness levels of computer users. I was unable to contact the institute where these numbers purportedly came from to confirm this information, but even if these numbers are slightly off (or completely made up), customizing the desktop is still very beneficial.

This chapter shows you some cool tricks and tools to make your desktop look and work much better so that you can also benefit from a customized desktop. I show you how to remove icons, customize the size of icons, and replace icons on your desktop. Then I show you how you can customize your desktop way beyond changing your wallpaper. In the second half of this chapter, I show you how you can customize the new Windows Sidebar in Windows Vista as well as how you can create your own gadgets.

Customizing the Desktop Icons

When Windows Vista was in its early stages, Microsoft received a lot of feedback on improving the icons. What were Windows 2000 icons still doing in a modern Windows release? Microsoft took this feedback to heart and spent a great amount of resources on improving the icons in Windows Vista. I think that everyone would agree that the new icons look much better than anything Microsoft ever used in the past. These new high-resolution icons include various sizes, all the way up to 256×256 pixels. This allows the icons to look great at many different sizes and really shows off the quality and time that was spent on creating the hundreds of new icons.

The next few sections are going to show you how to take advantage of the new icons as well as how to trim down icons to use in other areas where they are considered more clutter than eye candy.

Removing all icons from the desktop

No matter how hard I try, I always end up with a lot of junk on my desktop. Programs that I download and documents that I was too lazy to save elsewhere as well as new program links that seem to pop up from nowhere: There is never an end to the war that I fight with my desktop to keep it clutter-free. I like to be able to see my desktop wallpaper and not have my view of the wallpaper blocked by useless icons. One cool way to win the never-ending desktop war is to just disable the desktop's ability to show the icons and instead place the most common desktop icons such as My Computer and the Recycle Bin on the Quick Launch bar.

Disabling the icons on the desktop is actually a very simple task. Most people never know about this feature because it was placed where you would never expect it in previous versions of Windows. In Windows Vista, Microsoft finally got it right. Just right-click your desktop, expand View, and then select Show Desktop Icons. Almost instantly, the icons disappear.

Don't worry; the icons and folder on your desktop were not deleted. If you ever want to turn the icons back on, just repeat the preceding steps once more.

This is a very simple way to quickly clean up the desktop. It's sort of like sweeping the dirt under a rug. The desktop clutter is still there, but you just can't see it.

Customizing the icon drop shadow effect

The drop shadow effect makes the icons stand out from your wallpaper and makes them much easier to read when you are using a background such as a photo that has both light and dark spots. Depending on the wallpaper that you are using, you may like or dislike the feature. I really like the new effect, but if you like having a clean and crisp interface, I recommend disabling it. Perform the following steps to turn the feature on or off:

1. Click the Start button, type **sysdm.cpl** in the Search box, and then press Enter to launch the System Properties window.

2. Click the Advanced tab, and then click the Settings button under the Performance section.

3. While on the Visual Effects tab, scroll down to the bottom of the box.

4. Locate Use Drop Shadows for Icon Labels on the Desktop, as shown in Figure 3-1, and check or uncheck the value, depending on what you would like to do.

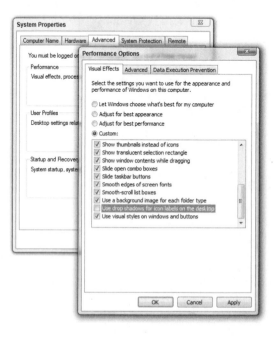

FIGURE 3-1: Turning the drop shadow effect on and off for icons on the desktop

5. Click OK to save your changes.

6. Click OK again to close the System Properties window.

If you enable the effect by checking the box and the effect still does not show up after you reboot your computer, this is a sign that your computer does not support the feature.

Displaying Windows system and user icons on the desktop

In Windows Vista, only one icon, the Recycle Bin, is on the desktop by default. Unlike previous versions of Windows, Microsoft is trying to keep the number of icons on the desktop to a minimum for a cleaner look. However, if you like having the system and user icons on the desktop, such as Computer, Documents, Network, and others for convenience, it is possible to add those icons back to the desktop. Just follow these steps:

1. Click the Start button.

2. Right-click one of the items you would like to add back to desktop, and then select Show on desktop, as shown in Figure 3-2.

3. Repeat Step 2 for each item you want to add back to the desktop.

You will see the icons on your desktop immediately after you complete the steps.

FIGURE 3-2: Adding Computer to the desktop

Adjusting the size of desktop icons

Windows Vista introduces a new desktop icon size that is slightly larger than in previous versions of Windows. This is one of the first things that I disliked immediately after installing Windows Vista on my computer. Why are the icons so large now? Well, everything seems to be bigger in Vista, but thankfully, like other new features and decisions that were made by Microsoft developers, it is very easy to adjust the size of the desktop icons.

You now have a choice between three different icon sizes on the desktop. Figure 3-3 shows the three icon sizes: classic, medium, and large.

Computer   Computer   Computer

FIGURE 3-3: Various desktop icon sizes

You can change the icon size by simply right-clicking the desktop, expanding View, and then selecting the icon size you prefer.

Renaming the Recycle Bin

To give my desktop a personalized touch, I like to rename my Recycle Bin to something different. In previous version of Windows, this was only possible by editing the Registry. In Windows Vista, it is much easier. Just perform the following steps to rename your Recycle Bin:

1. Right-click the Recycle Bin on the desktop and select Rename.

2. Type a new name, such as Trash Compactor, and press Enter.

Removing the shortcut arrow from icons on the desktop

One thing that I always hate about Windows is the shortcut arrow. Sure, it is good to be able to tell if a shortcut is actually a shortcut, but I think that I know that the applications that I put on my desktop are already shortcuts. Also, the shortcut indicator that Windows uses does not look the best in my opinion. With a cool reg hack, it is possible to replace that shortcut icon overlay with any icon. This allows you to create your own icon using any popular icon editor and use it as an overlay on any shortcut.

I created a green arrow that I like to use as my shortcut icon overlay. You can grab it from the Hacking Windows Vista Web site at www.HackingWindowsVista.com/downloads. Use the following steps to change the icon shortcut overlay:

1. Click the Start button, type **regedit** in the Search box, and then press Enter to start the Registry Editor.

2. After the Registry Editor has started, navigate through HKEY_LOCAL_MACHINE\ SOFTWARE\Microsoft\Windows\CurrentVersion\Explorer.

3. Right-click the Explorer folder, expand New, and select Key. Type **Shell Icons** as the name of the new key.

4. Right-click the new Shell Icons folder, expand New, and select String Value. Type **29** as the name of the new value.

5. Right-click the new string you just created and select Modify. Set the value to the path to the icon plus a comma and the icon index number. For example, I use C:\icons\ myshortcut.ico.1, as shown in Figure 3-4. The icon index number specifies which icon you want to use in the file. (Some files can contain multiple icons, such as the shell32.dll file.) Click OK when you are finished.

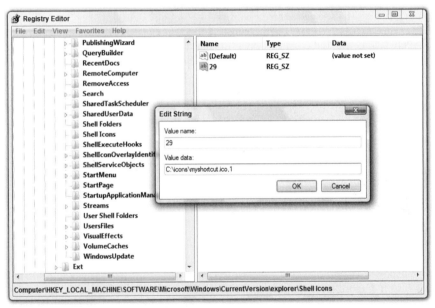

FIGURE 3-4: Setting the shell icon path and index

6. Log off and back on, and you should see you new shortcut overlay. Figure 3-5 shows the before and after look.

FIGURE 3-5: Before and after shell icon overlays

Customizing the icons

Are you starting to get tired of the default icons in Windows Vista? Sure, they are new and improved and have the new Vista look, but they can get old and dull after a while. If you are a hardcore desktop customizer, which you probably are if you have this book, then it is time to customize the Windows icons on the desktop.

To get started, you first need to find some great looking replacement icons. Check out my favorite Web sites and download some icons to use to customize your desktop:

- **Iconaholic:** www.iconaholic.com
- **InterfaceLIFT:** www.interfacelift.com
- **VistaIcons:** www.vistaicons.com
- **VistaICO:** www.vistaico.com

Now let's get started replacing icons on your desktop. Changing application shortcut icons is easier than system icons such as the Recycle Bin or Computer. Changing system icons requires the help of an icon utility. First I am going to show you how to change application icons and then how to change system icons. Perform the following steps to change any application icons:

1. Right-click the item for which you want to change the icon and select Properties.
2. On the Shortcut tab, click Change Icon.
3. While on the Change Icon screen, click the Browse button and navigate to your new icon.
4. Select your new icon on the screen, as shown in Figure 3-6, and click OK.
5. Click OK once more to exit and save your changes on the Properties screen.

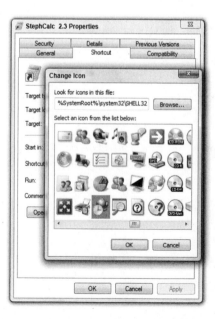

FIGURE 3-6: Selecting a new icon

Now that you know how to change application shortcut icons, let's move on and go over how to change system icons, such as the Computer shortcut or the Recycle Bin. It is best to use an icon utility to make these changes. My favorite utility for this is called Microangelo On Display, developed by Impact Software.

To get started, head over to `www.microangelo.us/free-download.asp` to get a free evaluation copy. After it is installed, follow these steps to customize your system icons:

1. To use Microangelo On Display, you will need to temporarily disable User Account Control because the current version does not work with UAC on. To disable UAC, click the Start button and select Control Panel.

2. Type **user account control** in the Search box and then select Turn User Account Control (UAC) on or off listed under User Accounts.

3. Clear the check from Use User Account Control (UAC) to help protect your computer. You now have to reboot.

4. After a reboot, you will be able to start using Microangelo On Display. Right-click any system icon, such as the hard drive icon in Computer, and select Appearance. This brings up the Appearance window.

5. Under the Display section, switch the option to Custom and press the Change button.

6. Browse and select your replacement icon and press OK.

7. Click Apply to save and see your changes and then press OK.

If you do not like your new icon and want to change it back to the default, just right-click the icon again and this time select System Default under the Display section and press OK.

Also, don't forget to turn UAC back on in Control Panel the same way you disabled it when you are finished customizing all your system icons.

Now that you've finished customizing the look of your desktop and system icons, let's move on to customizing the desktop.

Customizing the Desktop

The desktop is a pretty simple part of Windows. Normally, you can't do much to customize its looks besides changing the wallpaper. However, several different tools are available that you can use to add features to the desktop and take advantage of some of the lesser-known features. The next few sections will show you how you can use these tools to do cool things such as animate your desktop and add cool gadgets with Windows Sidebar.

Animating your desktop

Those who purchase the Windows Vista Ultimate Edition have the opportunity to download free Ultimate Extras that are planned to be released every quarter by Microsoft. One of the Ultimate Extras is a cool application called Windows DreamScene that allows you to use movie files as your wallpaper. Microsoft has released several subtle looped movies that make great desktop backgrounds, such as waterfall scenes and computer-generated animations. Depending on the video file selected, your background can range from absolutely amazing to something that can make you sick because the motion is too much. Overall, this new Ultimate Extra adds a great feature for those who are running Windows Vista Ultimate Edition. Sorry to those of you who are not — you cannot run Windows DreamScene.

To get started, you will need to visit Windows Update to download the Ultimate Extra if you have not already done so. Follow these steps to get it installed:

1. Click the Start button, type **Windows Update** in the Search box, and then press Enter.

2. On the top left of the Windows Update screen, press Check for Updates. Windows will now search online for any security updates as well as new Ultimate Extras.

3. When the search is finished, click View available Extras to see what is available to download.

4. Locate and check Windows DreamScene.

5. Click Install.

After you have Windows DreamScene installed, you will be able to start using it after a quick reboot. After it is restarted, you can turn on Windows DreamScene by going to the same place where you change your background image. Right-click your desktop and select Personalize. Next, click Desktop Background and then change the location to Windows DreamScene Content, as shown in Figure 3-7, to see the stock videos. Simply select the video you want to use and press OK.

FIGURE 3-7: Selecting Windows DreamScene video content for your desktop

To pause the video from playing on your desktop temporarily, simply right-click the desktop and select Pause Windows DreamScene.

Using Windows Sidebar

Windows Sidebar is Microsoft's response to the growing number of available desktop gadget/widget applications. Think of it as a docking station on the side of your screen where various miniature applications, called *gadgets*, reside. These gadgets can do anything from displaying the current time, weather, and system information to offering simple games. The possibilities truly are endless and end users make new gadgets all the time.

So why would you want to use Windows Sidebar? Simple — it is a great way to customize your desktop because you can also drag the gadgets off of the Sidebar dock and place them anywhere on your desktop. Figure 3-8 shows what gadgets look like and how they can be used on the sidebar dock and anywhere on the desktop. Best of all, Windows Sidebar is included in Windows Vista so you can get started using it right away.

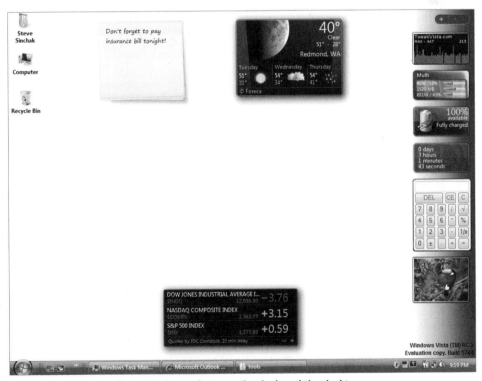

FIGURE 3-8: Using Windows Sidebar gadgets on the dock and the desktop

Tweaking the look of the dock

You can customize the background of the Windows Sidebar dock on the side of the screen, just as you can other aspects of Windows Vista. Hidden inside the Sidebar executable file is a PNG image file that is used for the dock background. With the help of a resource editing utility and an image editor such as Adobe Photoshop, it is possible to create your own background image and then insert it into the Sidebar executable file.

A lot of steps are involved in changing the dock background image, so I am going to assume that you already know how to create a PNG image in an image editor. If you need help creating an image, I suggest you take a look at *Photoshop CS2 For Dummies* (ISBN 0-7645-9969-0) by Peter Bauer to learn about the most popular image editor, Adobe Photoshop.

Before you can get started, you need to download a resource editor. I use a popular free resource editor called Resource Hacker for this section. You can download a copy from www.angusj.com/resourcehacker/. You also need to have your replacement image ready. It must be saved as a 24-bit PNG image and not wider than 150 pixels. The height can vary depending on your screen size. If the image is not tall enough vertically, it will be stretched.

When you have your resource editor and replacement image ready, you are ready to get started:

1. Start Resource Hacker and click File and then Open. Navigate through C:\Program Files\Windows Sidebar and open sidebar.exe. You will see the various resource types that are hidden inside the Windows Sidebar executable.

2. Expand the RCDATA section and resource number 20001. This is where the image is stored for the sidebar background when your sidebar is on the right side of the screen. If you have changed your sidebar properties to show the sidebar on the left side of the screen, select resource number 20000 instead.

3. Right-click the 1033 property and select Replace Resource, as shown in Figure 3-9.

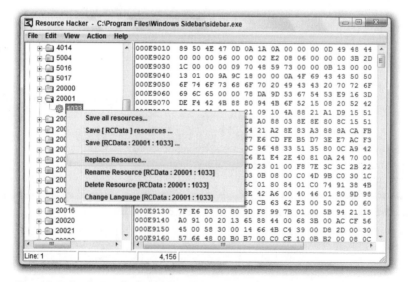

FIGURE 3-9: Replacing the background resource with Resource Hacker

4. On the Replace a Resource screen, press the Open file with new resource button and select your replacement background image PNG file.

5. Type **RCDATA** as the resource type and **20001** as the resource name. Leave the Resource Language box blank.

6. Press the Replace button to insert the new PNG background image. The image has now been replaced.

7. Save the modified `sidebar.exe` as a new file to save the changes. Click File and select Save As. Save the file as `sidebar2.exe` or another filename that is different from `sidebar.exe`. Because of security restrictions in Vista, you will need to save this new `sidebar2.exe` file to your desktop.

8. After you have the new file saved to your desktop, copy and paste it to your `C:\Program Files\Windows Sidebar\` folder. You are now ready to test your new file. First, make sure that the sidebar is currently closed on your computer. Then, just double-click your new file. If your replacement image is successful, you should see your new background when Windows Sidebar starts.

9. If everything is looking good with your new sidebar test, move ahead and set up the sidebar so that your version is loaded instead of the Microsoft version. Once again, close the Sidebar program if it is currently running. Then, in `C:\Program Files\Windows Sidebar\`, rename `sidebar.exe` to `sidebar_old.exe` and rename your new file to `sidebar.exe`. This will make it so that your file runs when Windows starts as well as when you click the various sidebar shortcuts.

Remember that if you ever want to revert back to the Microsoft sidebar backgrounds, just rename your `sidebar.exe` file with your backup called `sidebar_old.exe`.

Adding gadgets

Gadgets are what Windows Sidebar is all about. After all, without them the sidebar is just a waste of space. As I mentioned earlier, gadgets are basically miniature applications that can provide all sorts of information and functions. On my sidebar, for example, I have a calculator, CPU & memory meter, the current weather, a battery meter, and my latest Outlook e-mails. Some of these gadgets came with Windows Vista, whereas others I had to download and add to my sidebar. When you are finished with this section, you are going to know where to download more gadgets and add them to your sidebar so your sidebar can be just as useful as mine.

First let's go over the basics: The process of adding and removing gadgets to your sidebar is very simple. To add, you just press the big + button located at the top of the sidebar on your screen and then drag the gadget you want over to the sidebar into the location you want. To remove, press the little X button on the top-right side of the gadget that is shown when you hover over the gadget with your mouse. Feel like changing the order of gadgets around? Simply drag them into the order you want.

After you use Windows Sidebar for a little while you will definitely want to go exploring and see what other gadgets are online that you can use. There are dozens of high-quality gadgets online that will add a lot of value to your sidebar. Now that you know the basics, let's go online and start downloading some new gadgets:

1. Various sidebar gadget sites are starting to pop up on the Web but the most popular one is Microsoft's own located at gallery.microsoft.com. This is a very comprehensive site that has gadgets and plug-ins for various Microsoft applications including Windows Sidebar. Because the site is so large, I have a trick for you that will help you get right to the Windows Sidebar gadgets section. Click the + sign on the top of the sidebar as you normally add gadgets. Then, just click the link in the bottom right of the window that says Get More Gadgets Online. That will take you right to the correct section of the site.

2. Once you are in the Microsoft Windows Sidebar gadget section, navigate through the pages until you find a gadget you would like to add to your sidebar, and then click Download.

3. Click OK on the third-party warning screen on the web page and the file will begin to download. Click Open on the file download screen.

4. When the gadget is downloaded, press Allow on the Internet Explorer Security screen and then press Install on the Windows Sidebar - Security Warning screen. The gadget will now be installed and will automatically show up on your sidebar.

After the gadget is installed and on your sidebar, you might need to configure settings for it. For example, if you are using a weather gadget, you will probably need to tell it your ZIP code so that it downloads the right weather information for your area. You can do this by clicking the little tool icon located on the top-right border (just under the X that is used to remove a gadget) of the gadget that is shown when you hover over the gadget with your mouse.

Using gadgets on your desktop

Windows Sidebar is a cool little application that can be very helpful, depending on the gadgets you have on your sidebar. One feature of the application that is often overlooked or simply unknown by the vast majority of users is the ability to also use gadgets anywhere on your desktop. Figure 3-8 shows this in action.

How? It is so simple you are going to hit yourself in the head for not trying this before. Simply drag the gadget off the sidebar and onto your desktop. After you release your mouse button, the gadget will be stuck to that location on your desktop. You may even notice that some gadgets expand into a larger form when they are undocked from the sidebar. This is often very useful for some gadgets, such as RSS feed readers, because the expanded version makes it much easier to read the news.

Experiment with dragging your gadgets off the sidebar and onto your desktop and see how your gadgets work. You might find additional features and functionality.

Creating your own gadgets

Now that you are an expert at using gadgets, you are ready to start creating your own. Creating a Windows Sidebar gadget is a lot like creating an interactive HTML web page that uses JavaScript. Those are the same two technologies that are at the core of Windows Sidebar gadgets. A gadget basically breaks down to an HTML page that uses special Windows Sidebar JavaScript APIs (application programming interfaces) to get access to various system information and interact with other Windows components.

Window Sidebar gadgets can be very complex and take a great deal of time to create. You use the expansive sidebar JavaScript APIs and even WMI to access all sorts of information and work with other Windows components. To keep things simple, I am going to show you how to create a simple gadget that will enable you to search a Web site such as TweakVista.com. This gadget will not be the best looking and will not use any of the advanced features of gadgets, such as JavaScript. However, you will have a thorough understanding of creating gadgets and the foundation necessary to start making more advanced gadgets.

Gadget creation overview

The three main steps to creating all gadgets are as follows:

1. You start off by creating an XML gadget information file that tells the Windows Sidebar application information about your gadget, such as what it is called, who created it, and the main files it uses so that the sidebar application knows which files to read.

2. Next comes the most time-intensive part of the creation process in which you actually create the HTML and JavaScript that makes the gadget user interface and adds the interactive element of a gadget. Here you start off creating the interface, usually in plain HTML and with the help of PNG images. Then you add your JavaScript elements to the HTML to bring it to life.

3. The final step in the creation process is packaging the gadget into a Windows Sidebar gadget package. This allows you to easily install and distribute your gadget to multiple computers when you are ready.

Now let's get started making your own gadget with the first step, creating the XML gadget information file.

Creating the XML gadget information file

As I mentioned earlier, the XML gadget file is what tells the Windows Sidebar application what your gadget is called and which files it uses. To start the creation process, create a new folder somewhere on your computer to store all the gadget files that you create. Then, follow these steps to create the XML information file:

1. Open Notepad by clicking the Start button, typing **Notepad** in the Search box, and then pressing Enter.

2. You are now ready to start creating your XML gadget file. The following text shows the basic structure of the XML file:

```
<?xml version="1.0" encoding="utf-8" ?>
<gadget>
    <name>Search Gadget</name>
    <namespace>search.gadget</namespace>
    <version>1.0</version>
    <author name="Your Name">
        <info url="www.YourWebsite.com" />
    </author>
    <copyright>2007</copyright>
    <description>This gadget will search a website</description>
    <hosts>
        <host name="sidebar">
```

```
                        <base type="HTML" apiVersion="1.0.0" src="search.html" />
                        <permissions>full</permissions>
                        <platform minPlatformVersion="0.3" />
                </host>
            </hosts>
        </gadget>
```

The key parts of this XML file are the name, description, and base type sections, where the src (source) is set to search.html (the HTML file that has the gadget code). Type the preceding text into Notepad on your computer and replace the appropriate sections, such as name, description, and author name, with your info. Make sure that you point the base src value to the name of the HTML file that you plan on using to store your gadget code — such as search.html for this example.

3. Once you have your version of the gadget XML file typed into Notepad and you have checked it to make sure you typed it in the correct syntax, as shown in the preceding example code, you are ready to save it as an XML file. Click File and select Save As.

4. In the Save As window, change the Save As type to All Files.

5. Type **gadget.xml** as the filename. Your file must be called gadget.xml.

6. Navigate to the folder that you created to store all of your gadget files in and press Save.

After you have your gadget.xml file saved, you are ready to move on to creating the HTML code file the gadget will use.

Creating the HTML and JavaScript

Now that the XML information file is created, you are ready to create the main part of the gadget. For this step, you are going to use some HTML to create a simple text box and button form that will post back to the TweakVista.com servers to display the search results.

1. Open Notepad again and enter the following HTML code:

```
<html>
<head>
    <style>
        Body
        {
            width:140;
            height:75;
        }
    </style>
</head>
<body>
    <form name="SearchForm" method="get"
action="http://www.tweakvista.com/SearchResults.aspx">
        <input type="text" name="q">
        <input type="submit" name="Search" value="Search">
    </form>
</body>
</html>
```

The preceding code is what draws the text box on the screen and the Search button as well as what creates the form that directs where to send the data when the Submit button is pressed. It starts off with a few formatting HTML commands, such as HTML and HEAD. Then it sets the width and height of the gadget that will be drawn on the sidebar. Finally, you get to the guts of the gadget: the code that specifies that this is a form and where it submits the data to, as specified by the `action` property.

2. After you have entered the preceding code, save it as `search.html` (because that is what you set in the `gadget.xml` file). Click File and select Save As.

3. In the Save As window, change the Save As type to All Files.

4. Type **search.html** as the filename.

5. Navigate to the folder that you created to store all your gadget files and press Save.

When you have your `search.html` file saved in the same folder as the `gadget.xml` file, you are ready for the final step.

Creating the gadget package

Now that you have your XML information file and `search.html` code file, you are ready to package your gadget into a single file format that the Windows Sidebar application can read. This is very easy to do because the gadget package file is just a compressed zip file with the extension changed from `.zip` to `.gadget`.

Perform the following steps to package your gadget so that you can easily install it:

1. Navigate to the folder that you created earlier and saved both the XML information file and the `search.html` code file in.

2. Select both files in this folder.

3. Right-click one of the files while both are selected, expand Send To, and then select Compressed Folder. This will compress the two files into a zip file.

4. Name the file and change the file extension to `.gadget` from `.zip`. This can easily be done at a command prompt with the `rename` command if you have Show known file extensions turned off for Windows Explorer.

5. After you have the zip file renamed as `.gadget`, you will notice that the file icon changes. To test your new gadget, just double-click the new package file. If you properly renamed the extension, you should see an install warning screen. Press Install and your new gadget will be installed and displayed on your sidebar.

You are now finished creating your first gadget!

As I mentioned earlier, this is an extremely basic gadget. However, it gives you an idea how gadgets are made because they are all started the same way. If you have a background in programming and would like to learn how to go to the next level with your gadget creation, check out www.microsoftdgagets.com and press the Build link on the menu. There you will find links to more articles on building gadgets as well as links to the JavaScript Sidebar API.

Keep in mind that you can use various technologies in your gadgets, including CSS, WMI, and VB Scripting (VBS), in addition to the JavaScript APIs. I also recommend looking at some of the other gadgets that were created by Microsoft and other sidebar users; learning by example is very helpful.

Adding a Quick Launch show sidebar button

Since I have been using Windows Vista, I have loaded my sidebar and desktop up with all types of useful gadgets. Unfortunately, quite often the sidebar gets buried behind various open windows and all my useful gadgets are gone. Here is a quick tip that I personally always set up on my computer that will help you in this situation:

1. Click the Start button, type **Sidebar** in the Search box, and then press Enter. This will search your Start menu for the Windows Sidebar shortcut.

2. Drag the shortcut that shows up in the Start menu over to your Quick Launch bar and release. This will create a very useful button on your Quick Launch toolbar that, when clicked, will automatically bring the sidebar and any desktop gadgets you have running to the front of your screen.

3. I like to drag my Sidebar shortcut next to my Show Desktop icon, as shown in Figure 3-10, so that I can easily find it when I have a ton of shortcuts on my Quick Launch bar.

FIGURE 3-10: Showing the Windows Sidebar button
on the Quick Launch bar

Summary

Throughout this chapter you have learned how to customize the icons on your desktop in many different ways to make the desktop much more personalized. I have even walked you though the steps of adding more gadgets to your computer and creating your own from scratch.

The next chapter will be one of the most important customization chapters. I will be showing you how you can change the look of the entire user interface of Windows Vista. The next chapter is a must for anyone who wants to customize the most visible part of Windows: the user interface.

Customizing the Appearance of the Windows Interface

I n the last few chapters, you customized various parts of the operating system, starting with the boot screen. Then you moved on to customizing the Logon screen. After customizing the Start menu and the taskbar, you spent some time customizing the desktop, too. This chapter shows you how to customize what the entire user interface looks like by changing the theme or visual style and fine-tuning settings of both.

In the sections that follow, you learn how to make major alterations in the way your computer looks (much more than you've learned so far). First, I go over the differences between a theme and a visual style, to clear up any possible confusion that you might have. Then you will dive in and create a theme. Finally, I show you how to tweak the new Aero Glass look in Windows Vista. The chapter ends with an easy way to give Windows Vista a completely different look with a third-party skinning utility called WindowBlinds.

Working with Themes

Themes have been a part of Windows for a long time. Ever since Windows 95 was released, themes made it possible to save the configuration of the fonts, colors, visual style, wallpaper, mouse cursors, and even the sounds that are used. Throughout the years, not a lot has changed in the theme world. Originally, you had to have Microsoft Plus to use themes, but now the ability to use themes is included in all the latest Microsoft operating systems. In addition, when themes were first developed, they did not keep track of visual styles (because they didn't exist). Now the theme format has expanded to allow for the new Windows features such as audio and cursor themes.

Why are themes still important to talk about even though they have been around so long? Because they provide a unique way to save all your computer visual settings and audio settings so that you can easily change all of them simultaneously. You don't have to customize each of the different elements such as the font and colors every time you use them. Themes make your life easier. The next few sections explain how you can use themes and make your own so that you, too, can benefit from the convenience they offer.

Changing the current theme

When you install Windows Vista, Microsoft includes two themes: Windows Vista and Windows Classic. By changing the themes, you can turn on and off the new Windows Vista look. Also, remember that you can make your own themes, which I get to in the next section, and you can easily switch between your own theme sets. After you spend some time customizing the look of Vista (for instance, making changes to window metrics, sounds, visual style, cursors, wallpaper, and so on), you can save your changes in a theme file so that you never lose them.

Changing themes is actually very simple. Just follow these steps:

1. Right-click the desktop and select Personalize.

2. On the Personalization screen, select Theme from the list.

3. Expand the drop-down box under Theme, as shown in Figure 4-1, and select the theme that you want to use.

4. When you have selected the theme that you want to use, press OK to save your changes.

FIGURE 4-1: Changing the active theme

After you press OK, the new theme is applied. This process may take a few seconds while the changes are being made.

Now that you know how to change a theme, it's time to make your own.

Making your own theme

Making your own theme enables you to easily back up your visual changes to Windows Vista so that you can distribute your settings to other computers or on the Internet. Making your own theme is actually just like changing the theme. The most difficult part of the process is customizing all the little aspects of the visual elements that make up the user interface. The next few sections walk you through the process of fine-tuning the user interface and then show how you can save your changes and make your own theme file.

Modifying window metrics and fonts

What the heck are window metrics? Well, it is the fancy way of talking about how big everything is. There is a lot that you can adjust that will affect the size of the user interface elements, such as the title bar of a window and other window elements such as buttons. Almost everything on a window has an adjustable size. This section explains how you can alter how your visual style or classic Windows interface looks by fine-tuning the different components of the window.

Another possibility is to fine-tune the fonts used. You can change the size of the font displayed, the style, and even the actual font that is used.

To get started, use Appearance Settings to make the changes:

1. Right-click the desktop and select Personalize.

2. Click Window color and appearance.

3. Select Open classic appearance properties for more color options.

4. When Appearance Settings loads, click the Advanced button.

5. The Advanced Appearance window opens. From here, you can change the size and the font for all the different aspects of a window. You can make changes in two different ways. The first way is to use the Item drop-down box. Just expand it and select the item that you want to modify. The other way is to click the object that you want to customize on the Preview picture. This click automatically selects the item from the Item drop-down box for you. Either way, select an item that you want to change. For the purpose of demonstration, I suggest that you click or select Active Title Bar.

6. After you have selected an object that you want to change, use the Size, Font, and Color settings to customize your window, as shown in Figure 4-2. Keep in mind that most of the color settings here will apply only to the classic Windows interface. If you are running Aero Glass or the non-Glass visual style, the color settings will not affect you.

7. When you have finished customizing your window metrics, press OK to save your changes.

8. Press OK once more to activate your changes and close the Appearance Settings window.

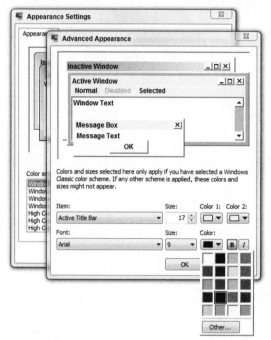

FIGURE 4-2: Customizing the sizes and fonts of the user interface

You have now finished customizing your window metrics. Next you customize the system sounds.

Modifying system sounds

You can attach sounds to many events such as logging on, logging off, minimizing a window, and maximizing a window. Because I am taking you through all the different things that a theme file will save the settings for, I also go over how to change the settings for the sounds that Windows uses so that you can customize this aspect of your computer, too.

Changing the event sounds is simple. Just follow these steps to launch and configure the sound properties:

1. Click the Start button, type **mmsys.cpl** in the box, and press Enter to launch the system Sound properties.

2. After the Sound properties loads, click the Sounds tab.

3. To adjust the sound clip for a specific event, click the event that you want to modify by navigating through the Program list, as shown in Figure 4-3.

FIGURE 4-3: Modifying the sound for the logon event

4. When you have an event selected, the Sounds drop-down list becomes enabled, and you can select the sound clip that you want to use. You can select (None) from the top of the list if you do not want to use a sound for a specific program event. If you cannot find a sound that you like on the list, you can use the Browse button to pick a specific sound file on your computer to use.

5. Here you can also enable or disable the Windows startup sound by clearing the Play Windows Startup sound box.

6. When you have finished with your changes, just press OK to save your work.

You have now finished customizing the sound events on your computer. The next step is to customize the cursors of the mouse so that they, too, are included in your theme file.

Customizing mouse cursors

The mouse cursors are yet another item saved in the theme file. Many different pointer schemes are included with Windows Vista. Although not all of them are the nicest-looking cursors, they can really help out in some situations. In addition, Windows Vista includes special large mouse cursors so that the cursors will be easier on the eyes.

To get your cursors set perfectly for your theme file, follow these steps:

1. Click the Start button, type **main.cpl**, and press Enter to open Mouse Properties.

2. Click the Pointers tab.

3. You have two options to customize the cursors: You can use the drop-down Scheme box to change all the pointers simultaneously to different styles, by selecting a different cursor scheme from the list, as shown in Figure 4-4. When you select the different schemes, all the cursors change automatically. Alternatively, if you do not like the cursor schemes, you can individually select a cursor from the Customize list by scrolling through the list and selecting the cursor you want to change. Then press the Browse button to change it.

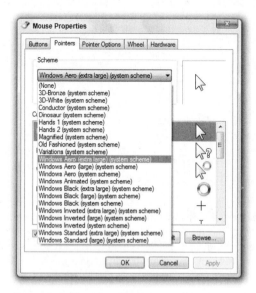

FIGURE 4-4: Changing the pointer scheme

4. When you have finished customizing your cursors, just press OK, and you are finished.

Now you are ready to move on to customizing the visual style that the theme will use.

Selecting the theme's visual style

Windows Vista builds on top of the existing Windows XP visual styles, with the addition of support for the new 3D surface–based desktop powered by the Desktop Window Manager (DWM). Visual styles are basically a skin file for the user interface that allows Microsoft to easily change the look of the entire operating system with just one file. Windows Vista includes only two visual styles: Windows Aero (Vista Glass) and Windows Vista Basic. As you might already know, Vista Glass works only on specific supported hardware; those who do not have the correct hardware can use Windows Vista Basic only. Depending on your personal preferences, you might like the new Windows Vista Basic.

Now that you know the fundamentals of the visual style, it's time to tweak the visual style settings so that when you make your theme file in the next sections it will be included with your sound and mouse settings:

1. Right-click the desktop and select Personalize to bring up the Personalization screen.

2. Click Windows Colors and Appearance.

3. On the next screen, click Open classic appearance properties for more color options. The Appearance Settings window opens.

4. At the bottom of the window, you will see a Color schemes list, as shown in Figure 4-5.

FIGURE 4-5: Adjusting the window style

5. When you have finished selecting the visual style you want to use, press OK to save your changes.

Configuring Windows Aero (Vista Glass) settings

If you have a computer that supports Vista Glass, you can also customize the color and transparency of the Aero window interface. These settings are also saved in your theme file, so it is a good idea to customize these settings, too. With these settings, you can change the color tint of your windows and adjust the transparency of the glass. Some users have found that the interface works a lot better for them if they disable transparency completely because it makes it easier to see and performs better on their hardware.

Customizing the Windows Aero settings is one of the easiest things to do because these settings are set using Microsoft's new-settings window format. Just follow these steps to customize Glass your way:

1. Right-click the desktop and select Personalize.

2. On the Personalization screen, click Window Color and Appearance.

3. You have a couple of approaches you can take to change the color tint. You can select one of eight preset color tints. Alternatively, you can come up with your own by expanding Show Color Mixer and then adjusting the Hue, Saturation, and Brightness sliders, as shown in Figure 4-6.

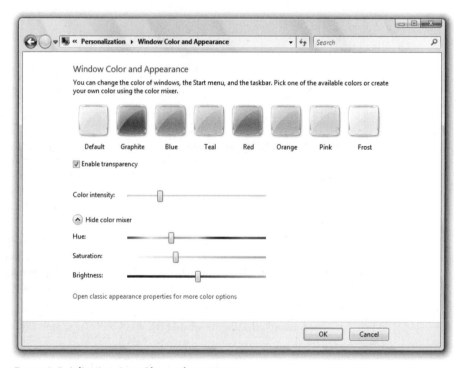

FIGURE 4-6: Adjusting Aero Glass color settings

4. You can also disable transparency completely by removing the check in the Enable transparency box.

5. After you have your color picked, you can fine-tune your selection by adjusting the Color intensity slider.

6. When you're finished, press OK to save your changes.

Setting the wallpaper

Most people know how to change wallpaper on their desktop (right-click the desktop, select Personalize, and then select Change Wallpaper), so I'm going to show you a cool little trick to change your wallpaper even faster. This process also allows you to change the wallpaper on multiple computers without having to go to Personalize on each computer.

The trick? Just create a Registry file that you can import into the Registry that will overwrite your current wallpaper information. Doing so is actually easy. Just follow these steps to create your own file:

1. Open Notepad. (Click the Start button, type **notepad**, and press Enter.)

2. Type the following code:

```
Windows Registry Editor Version 5.00

[HKEY_CURRENT_USER\Control Panel\Desktop]
"Wallpaper"="C:\\windows\\MyWallpaper.bmp"
"WallpaperStyle"="1"
```

3. Replace c:\\window\\... with the path and filename to the bitmap that you want to use. Note that in the path, wherever there is a backslash (\), you have to put two of them in the Registry file you are creating because the Registry Editor requires all paths to be in that format. You can change the WallpaperStyle property that will allow you to control how the bitmap image displays on your computer. Setting the value equal to 0 centers the image onscreen. Setting the value to 1 displays the image as if it were tiled or repeated across the entire screen. Setting the value to 2 stretches the image to fit the entire screen.

4. When you have the text in Notepad looking like the code in Step 2 but with your changes included, you are ready to save the file. Go to the File menu item and select Save As. Then select Save As Type. In the File Name box, enter **wallpaper.reg**. Keep in mind that you need to have the .reg at the end of the filename so that your computer knows to import the file into your Registry using the Registry Editor.

5. After you save the file, just go to the location where you saved it and double-click the file. A screen will come up asking whether you want to import the file into the Registry. Click Yes. Then you are presented with a confirmation screen informing you whether the update was successful.

You must log off and back on if you want to see your changes take effect.

Saving your theme to a file

You have now customized all the aspects that the theme file will keep track of. You are ready to create your own theme file that you can use as backup or give to other people so that they can replicate your changes.

Before I go any further, I want to make it clear what exactly the theme file saves. The theme file saves the configuration of all the different parts of Windows Vista that you just modified; however, it does not save the actual files that you used. For example, if you decide to change the sounds of a program event on your computer, you also have to provide that sound clip to anyone or any computer that you want to apply the theme file that you made. A theme file just saves the settings, nothing else.

Now that you understand what the theme file format is, you are ready to get started. Making your own theme file is just as easy as changing one. To do so, follow these steps:

1. Right-click the desktop and select Personalize.

2. Click theme.

3. On the Theme Settings page, click Save As.

4. Enter the name that you want to save the theme file as and the destination.

You have now created a backup of your theme so that you can easily change back to it when you customize the user interface in the future. Now it's time for you to explore more Aero Glass tweaks.

Customizing Aero Glass

One of the most noticed enhancements in Windows Vista is the sharp-looking user interface. Microsoft invested a lot of time in the new interface, spread across designers and usability studies to find out exactly what works best for users. The end result is a comprehensive user interface overhaul that finally brings Windows up to par with other operating systems in terms of effects and visual appearance.

Powered by the new DWM (Desktop Window Manager), the user interface is drawn on 3D surfaces powered by Direct3D. Essentially, the entire desktop is a collection of 3D surfaces. If Microsoft wanted, it could easily make it so that you could fly through your windows as if you were playing a game by just changing the position and angles of the 3D surfaces your windows are displayed on. In fact, it is this ability that gave birth to the Flip 3D Alt+Tab replacement that we are all familiar with now that allows you to flip through all your open windows.

This new interface is not without its share of problems. Because it is drawn using Direct3D, it requires access to the screen buffer. Older applications that also use components of the Direct3D API sometimes run into problems with Windows Vista and the Aero Glass interface because they often lock the buffer so that only their application can access it. This will not work anymore with Aero Glass because it also needs to use the buffer to display the interface. The solution is to run these applications Vista Glass has to turn off and revert back to the Windows XP visual style called Windows Vista Basic. Essentially, the DWM is turned off so that the older application can run.

Now that you know the brief history of the new user interface in Windows Vista, let's get started tweaking it.

Enabling Aero Glass on slower hardware

Aero Glass can be resource intensive depending on your CPU, amount of RAM, and screen resolution. On top of the speed of your hardware, the DWM has strict hardware requirements, such as a video card that supports DirectX 9 hardware acceleration and Pixel Shader 2.0 support. It also requires new Windows Vista WDDM (Windows display driver model) video drivers to function. Failure to meet the hardware and driver requirements will result in no Glass for you. Back in the beta days, you could trick the DWM into running Glass in a software Direct3D emulation mode and bypassing the hardware checks. This made it possible to run Glass, but so poorly that the operating system was pretty much useless because the frame rate was less than one frame per second. In the final version of Windows Vista, that support was yanked, so you are left with the task of meeting the hardware and driver requirements to run Glass.

Say you have a computer that has a DirectX 9 accelerated graphics card with Pixel Shader 2.0 support and are running WDDM drivers for your card. Aero Glass is going to run, right? Not exactly. The first time that you boot your computer after Windows Vista is installed, Windows will benchmark your computer and all its hardware components during its initial hardware assessment. Based on the results of this benchmark, it automatically fine-tunes Vista settings so that it performs the best on your hardware; at least that's its goal. If hardware assessment finds any thresholds not met, such as not enough RAM, it disables Aero Glass from running on your computer even if your hardware can technically support it. What are you to do? With the help of a useful tweak I show you in this section, you can override the decision and re-enable Aero Glass. If you fall into this situation, I have good news for you. Many users have found that after they override the setting and re-enable Aero Glass, their system performance is just fine. It seems that the Windows hardware assessment might be a little too strict when it comes to deciding whether Aero Glass should be disabled.

Overriding the Windows decision to disable Aero Glass is easy via Registry Editor. Follow these steps to re-enable Aero Glass on your computer:

1. Click the Start button, type **regedit**, and press Enter.

2. When Registry Editor has loaded, navigate through `HKEY_CURRENT_USER\Software\Microsoft\Windows\DWM`, as shown in Figure 4-7.

3. Right-click Composition and select Modify.

4. Set the value to 1 and press OK.

5. Right-click CompositionPolicy and select Modify.

6. Set the value to 2 and press OK.

7. Close Registry Editor and reboot your computer or restart. You can restart the service by typing **net stop uxsms** followed by **net start uxsms** at an administrative-level command prompt.

After you set the two Registry values and restart the service or your computer, you will immediately see Aero Glass running if your hardware truly supports it and you have WDDM drivers for your video card.

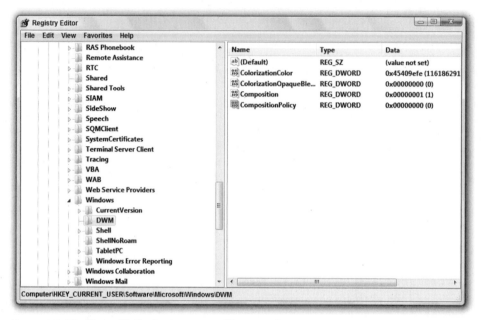

FIGURE 4-7: Working with the Registry to enable Aero Glass

Tweaking the color of Aero Glass

In the preceding section about using themes, I showed you one way to change the color of Aero Glass on your computer. I am now going to show you another way to change the color of Aero Glass using the Registry. This method has its own advantages and disadvantages. It allows you to easily create a Registry file that you can then export to other computers, or you can take what you learn in this section to create a custom group policy (ADM template) that you can use in your domain environment to set the color of Aero Glass. The downside is that you have to deal with the raw hex color format (that is, in ARGB) to set the value of the Registry setting. This can be rather difficult because you need to determine your color (which is usually easiest in a number format) and then you need to convert them to a specially formatted hex value that the DWM can read. This might sound too complex, but don't worry. I created an online converter that makes this easy for you.

Before you get started, I want to go over the basics of the color format and the components of it that you will be working with. As I said previously, the DWM color Registry setting is stored in a hex ARGB format. ARGB stands for Alpha, Red, Green, and Blue. Each of these components has a separate value between 0 and 255, where 0 is off and 255 is completely solid. Red, Green, and Blue are easy to understand. All colors are made up of a mixture of these three basic colors. For example, one shade of orange is Red: 255, Green: 128, and Blue: 64. The Alpha component determines transparency (how well you can see through the color). The value of 0 equates to full transparency; 255 equates to no transparency.

Now that you know the basics of the setting value, let's get started:

1. Click the Start button, type **regedit**, and press Enter.

2. Navigate through `HKEY_CURRENT_USER\Software\Microsoft\Windows\DWM`.

3. Locate ColorizationColor and select Modify.

4. You need to generate your new color value. Open your web browser and head over to `www.tweakvista.com/article39028.aspx`. There I have a useful number (decimal) to ColorizationColor value generator. Enter the Alpha value followed by Red, Green, and Blue numbers, as shown in Figure 4-8, to make your windows orange.

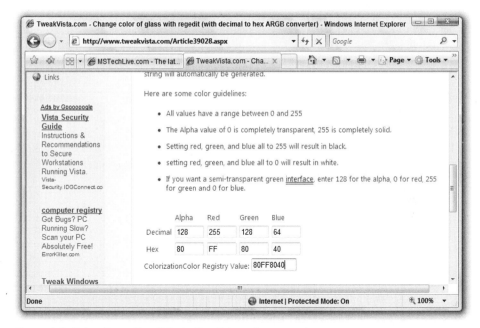

FIGURE 4-8: Using the online ColorizationColor value generator

5. Copy and paste the generated ColorizationColor value from the Web site into the open Registry Editor ColorizationColor value window and press OK.

6. Restart the DWM by typing **net stop uxsms** and **net start uxsms** at an administrative-level command prompt to see your changes.

Changing the Aero Glass borders

Other than changing the color and transparency levels of Aero Glass, you can do one more thing to significantly affect the look of Aero Glass: customize the window border. By default, the window border in Windows Vista is thicker than in previous versions of Windows. This can be nice or annoying depending on your personal preference. With the help of a simple tweak, you can easily customize the border width of your windows and by so doing have a big impact on the look of Aero Glass. Take a look at Figure 4-9 for an example of how you can make major changes to your interface and what your windows can look like when you just change the border size.

FIGURE 4-9: An example of a minimum border and fat border windows

The border setting can be tweaked by modifying a new window padding metric. Follow these steps to adjust this value to customize your window borders:

1. Right-click the desktop and select Personalize.

2. Click Window Color and Appearance.

3. Select Open classic appearance properties for more color options.

4. On the Appearance Settings window, press Advanced.

5. On the Advanced Appearance screen, change the Item to Border Padding, as shown in Figure 4-10.

6. Adjust the size value (default is 4) and press OK.

7. Press OK once more to see your changes.

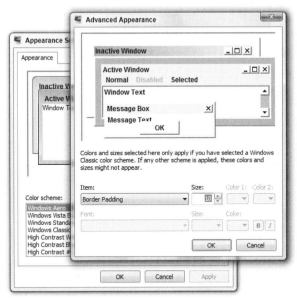

FIGURE 4-10: Changing the window border on the Advanced Appearance screen

Disabling animations

When demonstrating the Windows Vista user interface, I always get a lot of comments about the animations. Some love them, but others hate them and immediately ask how they can turn them off. This section is for all those users who find the minimize and maximize animations annoying and want to turn them off.

I personally like the animations, but I cannot help but notice how much faster my computer feels when they are turned off. There is not really much of a performance increase, but it just feels snappier because the instant I click Maximize or Minimize or even Close, the window instantly changes or is gone. I recommend giving this section a try even if you like the new animations; you might like the feel even better when they are disabled.

You can disable the animations a few different ways. In this section, I show how you can disable the animations using the Registry. Follow these steps to get started:

1. Click the Start button, type **regedit**, and press Enter.

2. When the Registry Editor loads, navigate through HKEY_LOCAL_MACHINES\SOFTWARE\ Policies\Microsoft\Windows\DWM.

3. Right-click the DWM folder, select New, and then select DWORD (32-bit) Value.

4. Name this new value **DisallowAnimations**.

5. Right-click DisallowAnimations and select Modify. Set the value to 1 and press OK.

6. Exit the Registry Editor and open a command prompt with administrative access.

7. You now need to restart the DWM so that it knows to disable animations. Type **net stop uxsms** followed by **net start uxsms** to restart the DWM.

When the DWM restarts, the animations are disabled.

Disabling Aero Glass

Are you one of the few users who prefer the non–Aero Glass look of Windows Vista? Is the new user interface too much eye candy for you? This section walks you through turning off the new Aero Glass interface (in case you answered yes to either of those questions).

Before you proceed, you need to fully understand which features you will lose when you disable Aero Glass. Flip 3D will be replaced with the Windows XP–style tab box. Taskbar preview thumbnails will be gone, and some Windows applications such as Media Player are just not going to look as cool. If you are fine with losing these features and fine with the boring look of non–Aero Glass Windows applications, follow these steps to turn off Aero Glass on your computer:

1. Right-click the desktop and select Personalize.

2. Click Window Color and Appearance.

3. Select Open classic appearance properties for more color options.

4. Change the color scheme to Windows Vista Basic.

5. Press OK.

Skinning Windows Vista

Skinning Windows Vista is all about changing the look of the entire user interface with the help of third-party utilities and visual styles that allow you to make massive alterations to the look of Windows Vista. By skinning Windows, it is possible to completely change the appearance and make it look like a different operating system, such as OS X or something completely different. In the next sections, I show how you can use hacked visual styles as well as the leading skinning utility, WindowBlinds, to customize the look of your computer. This will help you take customization to the next level.

Using hacked visual styles

Windows Vista uses an enhanced skinning engine based on the engine found in Windows XP to display the non-Glass interface as well as the new Glass DWM interface. In Windows XP, the visual style engine used bitmaps stored in a resource file. The visual style's resource file contains all visual elements such as images of buttons and window components as well as some configuration files. In Windows Vista, the resource file has been modernized to include PNG images instead of bitmaps and updated for the new interface structure.

You create visual styles for Windows Visa just as you do for Windows XP. You start with an existing visual style, such as the default visual style that is included in Windows Vista, and use a resource hacking tool to replace the images within the file. After you have replaced all of the resources in the file with PNG replacements and created a new visual style file, you are almost ready to use the hacked visual style.

The last step before you can use any visual style that you downloaded or made yourself is patching the skinning engine files. The skinning engine in Windows Vista will use only visual styles that have a Microsoft digital signature on the file. Visual styles that you make yourself by editing the resources or other visual styles that you download from the Internet no longer have a valid Microsoft digital signature because the file contents changed. In order to use hacked visual styles in Windows Vista you need to patch the system files that impose this digital signature requirement on visual styles files. Thankfully, one well-known skinning engine hacker, Rafael, has been releasing patches for XP for years and has released a patch for Windows Vista as well. Follow these steps to install Rafael's patch:

1. Visit Rafael's Web site at `http://anti-tgtsoft.com` and click the Classic Repository link on the top.

2. You need to download the UXTheme patch. Navigate through `UXTheme\Windows Vista\SP0`. If you have a 64-bit Windows Vista computer, install the AMD64 version; otherwise, download the other file for 32-bit versions of Windows Vista.

3. After you have downloaded the correct patch for your computer, extract it with WinRAR, which can be downloaded from `www.rarlabs.com`.

4. You need to replace your system files with the patched system files. To do this, you need to take ownership of these system files and then give your account access to them. Click the Start button and type **command prompt**. When the Command Prompt shortcut is displayed, right-click it and select Run as administrator.

5. When Command Prompt has loaded, type **takeown /f "c:\windows\system32\ uxtheme.dll"** and press Enter.

6. Type **takeown /f "c:\windows\system32\themeui.dll"** and press Enter.

7. Type **takeown /f "c:\windows\system32\shsvcs.dll"** and press Enter. You have now taken ownership of all three system files that need to be replaced.

8. Now you need to give your Windows account full control over these files. In the same Command Prompt window, type **cacls "c:\windows\system32\uxtheme.dll" /G** *<your account>:F* and press Enter. Replace *<your account>* with your account logon name. I use "Steve Sinchak".

9. Do the same for the other two files. Run **cacls "c:\windows\system32\themeui.dll" /G <your account>:F** and **cacls "c:\windows\system32\shsvcs.dll" /G <your account>:F** for the last file.

10. It is now time to rename these old system files so that you can always revert back to them should you run into problems with the new patched files. Open Explorer and navigate to the `c:\windows\system32` directory and rename uxtheme.dll, themeui.dll, and shsvcs.dll. I like to append "_old" onto the filename to create files like uxtheme_old.dll so I can easily restore the old version if needed.

11. You are finally ready to copy in the new patch files. Copy the three files from where you extracted the patch files to and paste them into `c:\windows\system32`.

12. After you have replaced the system files, reboot.

After your computer has rebooted you can use hacked visual styles that you downloaded from the Internet or made yourself with a resource hacker utility. Be sure to put your hacked visual styles in the `C:\Windows\Resources\Themes` folder so that Windows Vista can use them. After it is in that folder, double-click the visual style file to bring up Appearance Settings so you can enable the new visual style.

Most likely you will want to start with downloading some hacked visual styles from the Internet. The following are some great sites to get hacked visual styles from:

- **AeroXP.org:**

  `www.aeroxp.org/board/index.php?showforum=41`

- **deviantART:**

  `http://browse.deviantart.com/customization/skins/windows/visualstyle/`

- **JoeJoe.org:**

  `www.joejoe.org/forum/index.php?showforum=24`

- **NeoWin.net:**

  `www.neowin.net/forum/index.php?showforum=163`

Make sure that you download visual styles that are made specifically for Windows Vista. Windows XP visual styles will not work in Windows Vista.

Changing the look of Windows Vista via WindowBlinds

Before visual styles were a part of Windows, only one way existed to change the way Windows looked: via the WindowBlinds program from Stardock (`www.windowblinds.net`). WindowBlinds is a classic Windows program. When it first came out, it transformed the boring gray interface of Windows into an attractive and colorful experience. Now that Windows Vista includes its own skinning engine, products that have their own skinning engines, such as WindowBlinds, seem less necessary. So, why am I even mentioning this application? Because the Microsoft engine will only run skins digitally signed from Microsoft unless you use the hacked system files. Additionally, the quality of visual styles available for WindowBlinds has generally been better than the hacked visual styles available in the past.

WindowBlinds has a strong skin base. A lot of talented people have created skins for WindowBlinds that look great. Another benefit of using WindowBlinds to change the way your computer looks is the set of additional features that it provides — one of which is the ability to "roll up" a window so that just its title bar shows. This is a great feature that can be activated by just double-clicking the title bar on skins that support the feature.

Using WindowBlinds is much easier than using hacked visual styles. Just follow these steps to get started using WindowBlinds on your PC:

1. Visit www.WindowBlinds.net and download a copy of WindowBlinds. Install it. Make sure that you reboot after you install WindowBlinds.

2. After a reboot, click the Start menu, type **windowblinds**, and press Enter to start WindowBlinds.

3. After the WindowBlinds Configuration screen has loaded, you will see a list of all skins installed on your computer at the bottom of the screen. Scroll the list horizontally and click a skin that you want to preview. Some skins have multiple versions. Click the drop-down box and select a specific version, as shown in Figure 4-11.

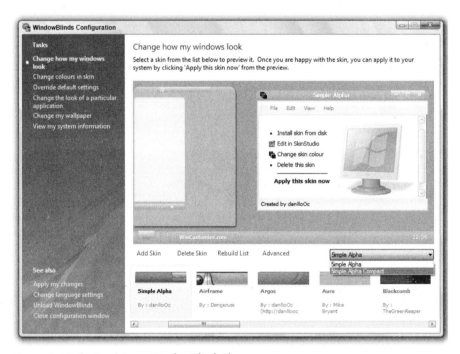

FIGURE 4-11: Customizing a WindowBlinds theme

4. When you have the skin selected you want to use, it is also possible to customize the colors of the skin. Click Change colors in skin to do this and adjust the sliders to change the color of the skin.

5. When you are ready to apply your customized skin, click Apply my changes, and you will see your user interface transformed.

You can always change your skin back to the default Windows Vista look if you do not like any of the skins offered by WindowBlinds by selecting the Windows Aero skin from the horizontal list when you open WindowBlinds. If you want more skins, the next section is for you!

Adding more skins for WindowBlinds

As I mentioned previously, WindowBlinds has a strong skin base of thousands of skins that are easy to install. Stardock operates an excellent Web site for thousands of WindowBlinds skins called WinCustomize, located at `www.wincustomize.com`. To get started, open your web browser and visit `www.wincustomize.com/Skins.aspx?LibID=1` for a list of all the skins available.

From the list of available skins, you can install a skin by clicking the Download link. It should automatically start to download. When the skin has finished downloading, WindowBlinds automatically loads it and prompts you by asking whether you want to apply it. After the skin has been installed, you can go back into the WindowBlinds Configuration screen to browse through the different versions and colors of the skin (assuming, of course, that the skin *has* multiple versions).

Summary

This chapter focused on the most important part of customizing your computer: the user interface. The visual interface is by far the part of the operating system that has the most impact when it is customized. Using the tools and techniques presented in this chapter, you can completely change the way Windows Vista looks.

The next chapter is all about customizing Windows Explorer, which is the program that you use to browse through all the files on your computer. I show you how you can customize the way it looks and works so that you can maximize its functionality to meet your needs.

Hacking Windows Explorer

W indows Explorer is one of the most used components of Windows Vista. Every time you go to My Computer and browse through files on your computer, you are using Explorer. Using the icons on the desktop, right-clicking on files and folders, and copying and pasting files are all examples of using the features that Explorer provides.

Many of the features that Windows Explorer provides can be easily customized to make your Windows experiences even better. This chapter will show you how you can change many of the features and how to take advantage of some of the new, lesser known features. It begins by showing you how you can customize the layout of the new Explorer interface. By the end of this chapter, you will have completely customized the Explorer features that enable you to browse through and create files on your computer.

Customizing Window Layout

Explorer in Windows Vista includes various new panes, including Details, Preview, and Navigation, that provide a wealth of new information that might change the way you use Windows Explorer. By default, all the new panels are turned on, which gives a cluttered feeling to the Explorer interface. Personally, I like to get rid of the panes that I don't use in order to speed up and streamline my Explorer windows. In addition to the new panels, Explorer includes many other new features, such as the Favorites section and the ability to search subfolders. The next few sections will show you how you can customize all of these.

Customizing Panes

The panes on the Explorer window are located on all sides of the window. Figure 5-1 shows a typical Explorer window with all panes visible.

As shown in Figure 5-1, the Navigation pane is on the left, Details is on the bottom, and Preview is on the right. Each pane offers a different array of features that can either help your Explorer experience or clutter it up. Let's dive into customizing each of the different panes and hack up Explorer to make it work the way you want.

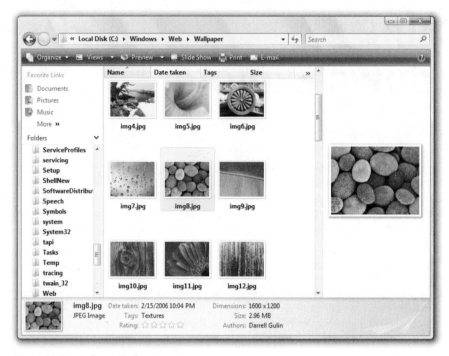

Figure 5-1: Windows Explorer's panes

The Navigation pane

The Navigation pane in Windows Explorer is divided into two key areas of information: Favorite Links and the Folders sections. You can think of the Favorite Links section as a sticky dock that you can drag any folder onto to create a shortcut for accessing it in the future. This allows you to quickly access your common folder very easily at the expense of file browsing space and making your Explorer window look cluttered.

The Folder section, which is collapsed by default, offers a tree-driven interface that resembles the classic Windows Explorer that was in previous versions of Windows. The primary benefit of the Folder section is the ability to quickly jump between locations without having to go all the way back to My Computer to restart your navigation. Now that you know the basics, let's customize everything on the Navigation pane.

Adding and removing favorite links

You can manage your Favorite Links section in two different ways. The easiest is to simply drag and drop folders and saved searches onto the Favorites Links section to add them to the list. You can then remove items by right-clicking them from the list and selecting Remove Link. Alternatively, you can navigate to the Favorite Links folder that is located at C:\Users\Username\Links. There, you can easily copy and paste multiple folders or short-cuts at once to be added to the Favorite Links section.

Using Folders View

The Folders view section is collapsed by default in Windows Vista. You can easily pop it open by clicking the up arrow on the Folders bar or by dragging the top of the bar up. If you do not like the Favorite Links section, you can drag the top of the Folders bar all the way to the top of the window so that it completely covers the entire Favorite Links section. I like to do this because it gives me a lot of extra space to browse through the navigation tree and removes some extra clutter from the interface.

Removing the Navigation pane

If you want to have a super clean interface and have no use for the Favorite Links and Folders sections, you can easily remove the entire pane from view. Follow these steps to disable this view for your windows:

1. While a folder is open and showing the Navigation pane, click Organize on the toolbar.

2. Select Layout and then Navigation Pane. This will remove the entire left-side pane.

When you close the active window, the changes are saved to the Registry.

The Details pane

The Details pane, located at the bottom of the Explorer window, provides information on a file or folder when one is selected. Similar to the classic status bar in Explorer, the Details pane displays common information (such as the size of a file) but goes beyond that by also showing many other file settings. The actual contents of the Details pane depend on the type of file you have selected. For example, if you have selected a Word document, the Details pane will show the date modified, author, tags, size, title, comments, category, number of pages, status, content type, and offline availability. If you selected an image, it will show you a thumbnail preview as well as the date it was taken, tags, your star rating, dimensions, file size, title, author, and even the camera manufacturer.

The Details pane has proven to be a valuable source of information that can really help you tag and rate your personal documents, images, and music. Without the Details pane, setting all these values would be much more difficult.

Now that you know what the Details pane offers, you are ready to customize the look or remove it completely. You can customize the size of the Details pane simply by dragging the top border up or down. You can also right-click it and select Size and then Small, Medium, or Large. If you are not interested in using the Details pane at all, I suggest removing it completely to save screen real estate and create a cleaner Explorer interface. Just right-click the pane and select Hide Details Pane.

If you choose to remove the Details pane, I recommend turning on the original status bar so that you have some indicator of how many items you have selected and a quick and easy way to get file sizes. To do this, press Alt on the keyboard to bring up the classic menu bar, click View, and then select Status Bar.

The Preview pane

The Preview window is the one pane that is turned off by default in most folders but can be very useful for browsing through an image collection or screening your MP3 files. When you are browsing through your music collection and select an MP3 file, the Preview pane shows a picture of the song's album and mini audio controls to play and sample the song. When you select an image file, a large thumbnail of the photo is displayed. Unfortunately, you can't customize much on this pane. You can adjust the width by clicking and dragging the left border left or right when the preview pane is turned on. Turn it on and off by clicking Organize, selecting layout, and then clicking Preview Pane.

Microsoft hopes that over time more companies write preview filters that work with Explorer so that you can see their file contents previewed on the Preview pane.

Hacking Search

One of the most useful new features in Windows Vista is the Search box that is in every Explorer window and many of the other built-in applications. This Search box enables you to easily sort through your files like never before. Looking for all text files in a folder? Just type ***.txt** into the Search box and press Enter. Almost instantly you will begin to see a list of all text files in the current directory you are viewing.

Looking for all Word documents that reference a specific company or person? Just go to your Documents folder and search for the name and press Enter. Windows Search will look at the filenames but it will also search the contents of your files. This is possible because Windows Search has built-in readers for many of the most popular file types.

As you can see, Windows Search is a comprehensive search solution compared to the prior search options in Windows XP. With the addition of this new search system comes the ability to customize searches even more than ever before. Various search settings are hidden deep in various windows and will help you customize the way searching works for you.

Adjusting Scope

Every time you perform a search, the results are based on the scope, the folders, and types of files the search software looks in. Depending on the scope settings you have enabled, the results of your search can be drastically different. These next two settings will help you fine-tune what and how the search software searches, and then you will fine-tune the indexing service to index the files you want to be indexed for speedy searches.

Customizing what and how to search

You can find all the "where to look" settings for Windows Search on the Folder and Search Options window in Windows Explorer. Follow these steps to customize where Windows Search looks:

1. Open Windows Explorer to a folder you want to modify the search settings for, click Organize, and select Folder and Search Options.

2. Click the Search tab, as shown in Figure 5-2.

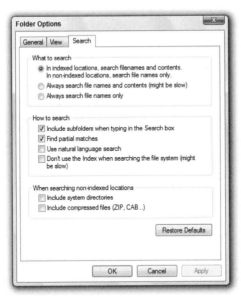

FIGURE 5-2: Windows Explorer search options

3. On the Search tab, you will see three separate sections. First, let's work with the What to search section. Here you can specify if you would like the search software to use the indexing service's data or if you would like it to check all the data it is searching on-the-fly. By default, Windows Search will search both filenames and contents of indexed files and just filenames of files not in the index. This works well for most users but if you don't care about file contents or don't want to use the indexer at all, experiment with the other options.

4. Now let's configure how searches are performed in the next section, How to search. Here you can choose from four different settings: the ability to search subfolders, report results with partial matches, turn on natural language searches, and disable searching from the index.

The two settings here that you really want to pay attention to are the subfolder search and natural language search options. These features are usually the two that I tweak the most. First, to speed up searches, I uncheck searching subfolders. I also turn on the natural language search option so that I can perform easier searches. For example, if I want to find e-mails from a person, I normally have to type **Kind:email from:person** in the Search box. When I turn on natural language search, however, I can type **email from person** instead and get the same results.

5. The final section — When searching non-indexed locations — specifies what to do with compressed files and system folders that are not indexed or when index search is turned off. I leave these blank to speed up searches, but I strongly suggest that you do not turn on the compressed file option; it will cause your searches to take forever and make your hard drive go crazy with activity.

6. When you are finished tweaking the search options, press OK to save your changes. You might have to reboot for all settings to start working.

Customizing the indexing service

The indexing service runs in the background and reads and indexes your files when your computer is idle to speed up searches. This works by reading all the files and storing search keywords and other information in a single database that can be easily read instead of having to read all the file information again every time you perform a search.

In Windows Vista, the scope of the indexing service is limited to the user folders by default. If you use search a lot, you might want to tweak the folders and types of files that are indexed. The following steps will help you customize which folders are indexed as well as the file types so that you can control what is indexed and what is not.

1. Click the Start button, type **Performance Information** in the Search box, and then press Enter. Select Performance Information and Tool when it appears on the top of the list.

2. After Performance Information and Tools loads, click Adjust Indexing Options on the left menu. When Indexing Options loads, you will see all the locations the indexing service is currently monitoring.

3. Now you should see the Indexing Options window. First, tweak where the indexer looks. Click Modify and then Show All Locations on the Indexed Locations window. Next, navigate through the list of your drives and folders and simply check the boxes for the folders you want to be indexed. When you are finished, press OK and the indexer goes to work indexing the new locations.

4. Modify the file types that the indexer indexes. This can be done back on the Indexing Options window. This time, click the Advanced button and then click on the File Types tab.

5. Scroll through the list of file extensions and select the file type that you would like to modify. Then, check the box and pick how the file should be indexed in the section below. If your file type is not listed, type the file extension in the box at the bottom of the window, as shown in Figure 5-3, and press Add new extension.

6. When you are finished, press OK and then Close to exit the indexing options.

Because the indexing service runs only when the computer is idle, it may take up to a few hours before your new files, folders, and file types are added into the index and show up in the search results.

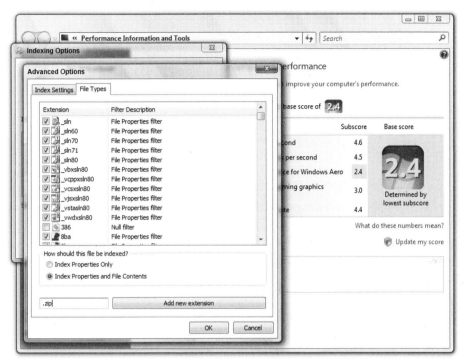

FIGURE 5-3: Adding additional file extensions to be indexed

Hacking File Associations

Every time you click a file, Windows looks up in the Registry the default program to open the file. Then, Windows loads that application and tells the application which file to open. This is something that you encounter almost all the time when you're using your computer. Often, when you install many programs on your computer, programs start to compete over which is going to be the default program to open a file.

One of the most common situations for this is when you install a bunch of similar applications. For example, I primarily use Windows Media Player for playing my music. When Apple releases a new version of iTunes, however, I usually install it to check out the new features. The next time that I try to play a CD or listen to an MP3, the music always opens in iTunes. My file association for my music has been stolen by iTunes. How do I take control over my file associations again? The following two sections show you how you can customize the default launch application for any file type on your computer, as well as how your file types look.

Changing the default launch app

Windows Explorer uses information stored in the Registry to find out what application is used to open a specific file type. This information is stored in the HKEY_CLASSES_ROOT section. With the Registry Editor, it is possible to browse to that key and then find the file type that you want to change and edit some keys. However, there is a better way to do this in Windows Vista.

In Windows Vista's new Default Programs utility lies the ability to easily change file association information without having to deal with the Registry class ID junk. Just follow these steps to change the default launch app for any file type:

1. Click the Start button and select Default Programs.

2. When the Default Programs utility loads, select Associate a file type or protocol with a program.

3. Scroll through the list and select the file type you want to change the default program for, as shown in Figure 5-4.

4. Click Change program.

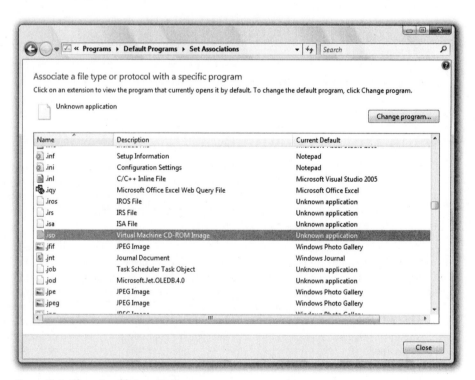

FIGURE 5-4: Changing file associations

5. The program that you want to change the file type to may be on the default Open With list. If not, just click Browse and select the program that you want to use to open the file.

6. Press OK and then Close.

Your changes to file launch apps are activated immediately after you click Close to save your changes. Now you will no longer have to worry about applications taking control over your files because you know how easy it is to fix them.

Hacking the Context Menu

What is the context menu? It's the menu that pops up when you right-click anywhere on your computer. Over the years, these menus have become more and more useful. However, with the extra entries in the context menu, they can become cluttered with options and features that you just don't need. These next few sections will shown you how you can get your menus back under control as well as how you can take advantage of the new features to make your own context menu entries.

I will start off by removing items from the context menus and then move on to adding and customizing the components of the menus.

Removing items from the context menu

Over time, your context menus can become cluttered with program entries from old programs that you may not use any more. You might experience programs that take over all of your context menus. Compression apps such as WinZip or Picozip always end up adding program entries to all the context menus. I have Picozip installed on my computer and every time I right-click any file or folder, I see five entries from Picozip giving me different compression options. This can be a convenient feature, but if you don't compress and extract zip files very often, you might not need the added convenience. Instead, you could remove these entries from your context menu, which will give your system a cleaner interface as well as a small performance boost if you have a lot of extra entries in your context menu.

Removing these programs from your context menus can be a little tricky because they can be spread in different places in the Registry. The only way to remove these types of entries is to edit the Registry directly. Follow these steps:

1. Click the Start button, type **regedit** in the Search box, and then press Enter.

2. When the Registry Editor appears, expand the HKEY_CLASSES_ROOT folder. You will now see a list of every file type that is set up on your computer.

3. If the entry that you want to remove from the context menu appears in all context menus, such as the preceding WinZip example, you will have to expand the * folder. Otherwise, expand the folder with the file extension you want to modify.

4. After expanding the correct folder, expand the Shellex and ContextMenuHandlers folders. Your registry path should be `HKEY_CLASSES_ROOT\*\shellex\ ContextMenuHandlers`.

5. Look through the list until you find the entry that you want to remove. Right-click the entry and select Delete. You will find that identifying some of the programs is easy. For example, WinZip is labeled WinZip, as shown in Figure 5-5. However, you may run into some items that are listed using their application/class ID or a vague name. If so, do a Registry search of the class ID (Ctrl+F), which is formatted as `{XXXXXXXX-XXXX-XXXX-XXXX-XXXXXXXXXXXX}`, to find other references that will give you clues to what the ID belongs to. If that does not work, try doing a search on Google to see if that turns up anything.

FIGURE 5-5: WinZip's context menu entry in the Registry

6. After you are finished removing all the entries from your context menus, just close Registry Editor and you are finished. Your changes will be in effect immediately.

Modifying the Send To menu

The Send To menu is one of the features of my context menus that I use the most. The ability to right-click any file and have a shortcut of it sent to the desktop is invaluable. How would you like to make it even more useful? It is very easy to add your own items to the Send To menu, such as folders that you can send files to. Do you have a folder that you store all your music in? How about a folder that you store all your digital photos in? Just follow these quick steps to add anything you want to your Send To context menu entry.

Tip   If you do not see any of the folders that are required in this section, you might have Hidden Files turned on. Because these folders are hidden by default, you will have to tell Windows to show all files. To do this, refer to the section on working with hidden files toward the end of this chapter.

1. Click the Start button and select Computer.

2. Click on your Windows drive and browse through Users*Username*\\AppData\\Roaming\\Microsoft\\Windows\\SendTo.

3. You will see all the files that appear in the Send To menu. If you want to add an entry to the menu, just copy a shortcut to this folder.

4. Let's say that you want to add your Digital Photos folder to your Send To menu. Navigate to your Digital Photos folder, right-click it, and then select Send To desktop. This will create a shortcut to the folder and save it on your desktop. Next, cut and paste the shortcut that was created from your desktop into the SendTo folder.

5. If you ever want to remove items from the Send To menu, just delete them from the SendTo folder.

It is that simple. You are now finished customizing your Send To menu.

Customizing Your Folders

The folders of Windows Vista can be customized in ways that never were possible before. You can easily change the icon of the folder as well as the way the folder behaves after you open it. These next few sections show you how you can take advantage of the great new folder features of Vista.

Changing a folder icon and picture

Changing the icon that is displayed for a folder is one of the easiest ways to customize the way a folder looks and make it stand out from the rest. This section shows you how to change the way your files and folders look as you browse through them by taking advantage of the high-resolution icons.

You change the folder icon and the folder picture within the folder properties window. To see what you can do with these settings, create a new folder named Downloads on one of your hard drives. You can save all of your downloads to this folder so that they do not clutter up your desktop. Follow these steps to change the way this folder looks:

1. Right-click the new folder that you just created, or right-click on any folder that you want to customize, and select Properties.

2. Click the Customize tab to reveal all your customizing options.

3. First, customize the icon, because that is the most popular way to customize the look of the folder. To do that, click the Change Icon button on the bottom of the window.

4. Now you will be able to browse through the list of available system icons or you can specify your own by clicking the Browse button.

5. After you have selected the icon that you want to use, just click OK to return to the Customize screen. Then click Apply to see your changes.

6. Instead of changing the icon, you can show an image if you are using one of the larger icon views. This will display your image as if it were inside the folder — a cool-looking effect. To do that, just click the Choose Picture button on the Customize screen and specify an image to be displayed on the file.

7. After selecting the image, click OK to save your change. Then click Apply on the Customize screen to see your changes. Remember that you will see your new image only if you are using medium icons or larger. You can change to Thumbnail view by clicking the Views menu item.

When you are finished changing the way your folder looks, just click OK to save your changes and exit the folder properties window.

Changing the template of a folder

Windows Vista uses a few different pre-made templates, depending on the type of content inside a folder. For example, it has separate templates for documents, pictures, and videos, and two for music. Each template will automatically customize the folder view so that it looks best for the type of content that is in it.

You can customize the template that any folder uses so that you can take advantage of the cool new features in Windows Vista's Explorer. This can be done by using the Customize tab in folder properties. Follow these steps to specify the template that should be used for a folder:

1. Navigate to the folder that you want to modify, right-click it, and select Properties.

2. Click the Customize tab.

3. Select the template that you want to use by expanding the drop-down box, as shown in Figure 5-6.

4. If you have a lot of folders within this folder with the same type of content, click the Also apply this template to all subfolders box so that your changes will be propagated to all subfolders as well.

You have now customized the template of the folder and are ready to customize the view.

FIGURE 5-6: Changing the template of a folder

Customizing the folder view

Now that you have a specific template selected for your folder, you will have a more advanced feature list to work with so that you can display a lot of useful information about the files in your folder. First, you need to be aware of the views you can use in Windows Vista:

- **Details view** is the default view of Windows Vista. This view shows all folders or files on a vertical list with the most file details shown compared to any other view.

- **List view** is similar to the Details view size but without the extra file information. List view also scrolls horizontally, whereas Details view scrolls vertically.

- **Small Icons view** is just like List view but scrolls vertically.

- **Tiles view** is similar to the other icon views but icon text is placed to the right of the icon, as shown in Figure 5-7.

- **Medium Icons view** is similar to Tiles view but with icon text on the bottom.

- **Large Icons view** is, well, larger.

- **Extra Large Icons view** is ridiculously large, as shown in Figure 5-8.

FIGURE 5-7: Displaying folders with Tiles view

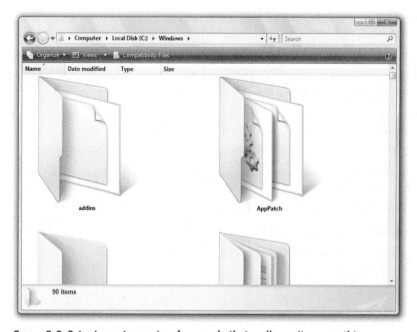

FIGURE 5-8: Extra Large Icons view for people that really can't see anything

The Details view can be customized like no other view can be. All the columns that are displayed can be resized, removed, or rearranged, and more can be added. This can all be accomplished by using some of the lesser-known tricks of the interface. To start off, customize a folder that contains a bunch of MP3 files. By now, you should have already changed the template for this folder to one of the music templates so that you can use the advanced, music-specific features. If you have not already done that, go back to the last section to find out how. When you are ready, follow these steps to customize all the different parts of the Details view:

1. Start off by resizing the columns. To do so, just place the mouse on the vertical line that is displayed between the columns and click and hold the left mouse button while you drag the mouse back and forth.

2. Add some of the new columns that display song information from the ID3 metadata tag embedded in the MP3 files. Just right-click the column heading and select one of the many new options, such as Bitrate. You can even select More from the bottom of the pop-up menu to see a list of even more items that you can add, as shown in Figure 5-9. Repeat this step until you have added all the new columns that you want.

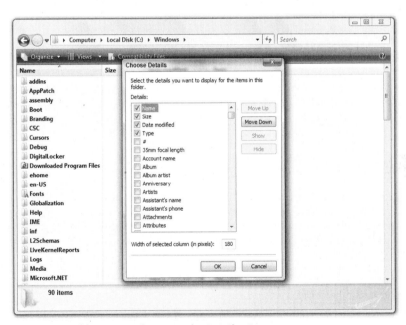

FIGURE 5-9: Adding new columns to the Details view

3. Most likely there will be some columns that you just don't need. To remove these columns from the Details view, just right-click the column heading and select the item once again to uncheck it. This will instantly remove the column from the view.

4. The last part of customizing the view is to set the order of the columns in a way that you like the best. To change the order of a column, just grab the column header and drag it around by holding down the left mouse button and moving the mouse.

If you want to customize the Details view of a folder that contains other multimedia files such as videos or photos, just repeat the previous steps and you will see additional column features with which you will be able to customize your Details view.

Applying your settings to all folders

When you first use Windows Vista, all the folders are configured the way Microsoft wanted them. Personally, I don't always like their decisions and prefer to customize them so they are the way I want and then apply that new default folder setting for all the folders on my computer.

To do this, you could change the settings of every folder, but there is a much easier way. Instead, just customize one folder on your computer as described in the previous sections so that you can get it looking great, and then follow these steps to apply the same configuration to all the other folders on your computer.

1. While the folder that you customized is still open, click the Organize button and select Folder & Search Options.

2. Click the View tab.

3. Click the Apply to Folders button and click Yes on the confirmation screen.

4. Click OK to close the Folder Options window and you are finished.

If for some reason you don't like what you did and want to restore all the folders to the original look, simply click the Reset All Folders button next to the Apply to Folders button to revert back to the Microsoft defaults.

Working with Hidden Files

Just like every other Windows version, Windows Vista likes to hide files. When you are interested in tweaking and customizing your computer, hidden files can become annoying. (Many of the system files with which you want to work are often hidden.) The following two sections show you how to make Windows Vista display all hidden and system files as well as the super hidden files.

Showing hidden files

When tweaking your computer, you often need to edit different configuration files for different applications. This can cause a problem because those configuration files are often hidden. The only way to edit them would be if you knew the exact filename and typed it in the Browse box. Otherwise, you would be out of luck.

Telling Explorer to show hidden files and folders is the only solution to this problem. Making Explorer show hidden files is just a matter of getting to the right place. Follow these steps to show all hidden files:

1. Open a copy of Explorer by clicking the Start button and selecting Computer.

2. Click Organize and select Folder & Search Options.

3. When the window appears, click the View tab to see all the different file display options.

4. Under the Advanced Settings section, scroll down the list until you see the entries for Hidden Files and Folders. Select Show Hidden Files and Folders, as shown in Figure 5-10.

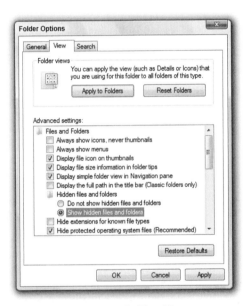

FIGURE 5-10: Revealing hidden files

Tip

While you are on the Folder Options advanced settings list of features, I recommend clearing the Hide extension for known file types box. This is always one of the first things I do right after installing Windows Vista.

5. When you are finished, just click OK to save your changes and exit the configuration window.

You should now see all the files on your computer that are hidden. However, you may notice that some files are still not showing up. These are the system files. To show these files, continue to the next section.

Revealing the super hidden files

Microsoft has added many features to Windows Vista to protect the critical files of the operating system. The new super hidden files feature allows Windows to protect itself even further by hiding some of its most critical files from users. If they can't get to it, they can't hurt it, right?

Revealing the super hidden system files is not very difficult. You can uncheck the box on the list on the View tab of Folder Options that says Hide protected system files, but where is the fun in that? Use the Registry Editor to turn this feature off:

1. Click the Start button, type **regedit** in the Search box, and then press Enter.

2. After the Registry Editor appears, navigate through `HKEY_CURRENT_USER\Software\Microsoft\Windows\CurrentVersion\Explorer` and `Advanced`.

3. Right-click ShowSuperHidden and select Modify.

4. Change the value to 1 and click OK to save your changes.

Now you will be able to see all the files on your computer, including the super hidden system files.

Summary

This chapter has shown you many different ways that you can customize how Explorer looks and works. You discovered how to change file associations as well as how certain file types look when viewed in Explorer. Then, you found out how to customize the context menu as well as how to clean it up. The last part of this chapter showed you how you can customize the different views of Windows Vista and control how and if hidden files are displayed.

The next chapter is all about customizing the next most frequently used program in Windows Vista, Internet Explorer 7. I will show you how you can customize the new features of the latest overhaul of Internet Explorer.

Customizing IE7

Internet Explorer 7 has gone through a major upgrade in Windows Vista. Features include an updated user interface, new tabs, several new security technologies, and RSS, which has taken over the browser. Prior to the release of Windows Vista, Microsoft brought the IE team back together after previously dismantling it. The final result is a complete browser overhaul that adds significant value to Windows Vista.

This chapter is all about taking the new features in Internet Explorer 7 and making the most of them. I show you how you can customize almost every aspect of the browser so that you can get it working the way you work. First, you start with customizing the new search features in IE7, and then you tweak the new tabs. Then you look at ways to customize the RSS features of IE and you add more add-ons to customize it even more.

Customizing Search

Microsoft has introduced a whole new way to search the Web using Internet Explorer 7. Developers have finally added a dedicated Search box directly into the main interface of the browser. This allows you to easily search almost any Web site. I show you how you can customize the new features to work with your favorite sites to search (instead of using what Microsoft wants you to search with). First, I cover the basics of this new feature, and then I show you how you can create custom search entries to search just about any Web site on the Internet that has a Search box.

Adding popular search engines

Before you get started customizing your search engines and developing custom entries, it is useful to go over the basics of adding and changing your default search engines that Internet Explorer uses. Doing so is easy. Just complete the following steps to find out how to add the major search engines through the Microsoft search site so that you have more choices aside from Microsoft Live.com:

1. Open Internet Explorer if it is not already open.

2. Click the down arrow next to the Search box and select Find More Providers, as shown in Figure 6-1.

---

3. When the provider list Web site loads, click the provider title. This opens the Add Search Provider window.

4. If you want to make your new search engine selection the default for the Search box, select the Make this my default search provider box. Click Add Provider when you are ready.

FIGURE 6-1: Adding search engines to Internet Explorer 7

Your new search engine has now been configured. You can switch between active search engines by using the down arrow again next to the Search box in Internet Explorer. If you already have your search engines set up and want to remove or change the default search engine, the next section is for you.

Managing your configured search engines

After you have all the search engines added to Internet Explorer, over time you might want to remove some or adjust your default search engine that IE uses. To do so, go to the advanced search settings found in Internet Options. Follow these steps to change the default search engine or remove a site:

1. Open Internet Explorer.

2. Click Tools and select Internet Options.

3. On the General tab under the Search section, click the Settings button.

4. You will now see a list of all the search engines that you have added to Internet Explorer. Select an entry from the list and click either the Remove or Set Default button to make changes to the search configuration.

Now that you understand the basics of search in Internet Explorer, you are ready to move on to the next section about creating custom search entries.

Adding custom search entries

Do you dislike the set of search engines that Microsoft has available for you on its search Web site or want to be able to search other Web sites that Microsoft does not list? This section shows you how to add any Web site that has a Search box to be searched using the Internet Explorer Search box. You can do so in two ways. Web site owners can add special HTML to their pages that link to an Open Search XML file that allows users to add their site to be searched. Because few Web sites actually support that feature, you can always add a site manually with a few registry hacks. For this section, I show you how to hack the Registry to add a site such as Digg.com to the IE Search box. Just follow these steps:

1. Click the Start button, type **regedit** in the Search box, and press Enter.

2. After Registry Editor has loaded, navigate through HKEY_CURRENT_USER\ Software\Microsoft\Internet Explorer\SearchScopes.

3. Right-click the SearchScopes folder key, select New, and then select Key. Type the name of the site you want to add, such as **Digg Search** for this example, and press Enter.

4. Now you must create two settings for the new key you just created. Right-click the new Digg Search key, select New, and then select String Value. Call this new string value **DisplayName**.

5. Right-click the new DisplayName string value and select Modify. Set its value to the name you want to appear in the Internet Explorer search list. Then click OK to save your change.

6. Now you need to create another string value to store the URL of the search path. Right-click the Digg Search key again, select New, and then select String Value. Name this new string entry **URL**.

7. You are now ready to set the value of the URL string, but first you need to find the search URL that accepts the query in a parameter for the site you want to be able to search. For Digg.com, that URL is http://www.digg.com/?s=. This address can be discovered by simply doing a search on the site and looking at the address bar of the results page. Before you can set this as the value, you need to add the search keywords placeholder to the address. This can be done by appending **{searchTerms}** to the part of the URL where the keywords go. For Digg, the final search URL that IE requires is http://www.digg.com/?s={searchTerms}. Go ahead and right-click the URL string value and select Modify. Then set the value to the search URL like the one for Digg mentioned previously for the site you want to search, as shown in Figure 6-2, and click OK.

You have now added a new site to search with Internet Explorer. Just close and reopen Internet Explorer, and you should see your new site listed on the search provider list.

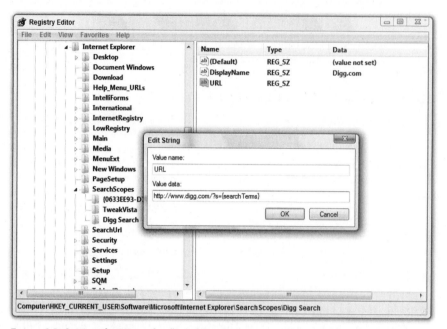

FIGURE 6-2: Setting the URL value for adding Digg.com to the Internet Explorer search provider list

Creating Registry files to import sites to search

Another way to add sites to search in Internet Explorer is to write a Registry file that can be imported into the Registry. This allows you to easily add a site to search to multiple computers without your having to go through the manual step of creating keys and string values on each computer. The following example adds TweakVista.com to your search providers in Internet Explorer. Just follow these steps:

1. Click the Start button, type **notepad** in the Search box, and press Enter.

2. Type the following Registry code into Notepad:

```
[HKEY_CURRENT_USER\Software\Microsoft\Internet
Explorer\SearchScopes\TweakVista]
    "DisplayName"="TweakVista.com"

"URL"="http://www.tweakvista.com/SearchResults.aspx?q={search
Terms}"
```

3. Click File, and then click Save As.

4. Change the Save as type to All Files (*.*).

5. Type **TweakVista.reg** as the filename and click Save.

You have now created a custom search Registry file that you can import into any computer's Registry by double-clicking the file. Keep in mind that this setting is a per-user Registry setting, so every user on your computer who wants to use this must import it under that user's account.

Tweaking the Tabs

Tabs are a great new feature that has finally been integrated natively into Internet Explorer 7. Previously, users had to download third-party add-ons to gain this functionality in IE. Tabs in Internet Explorer allow you to view multiple Web sites in one IE window, enabling you to quickly browse between Web sites. This section shows you how to get the most out of tabs in Internet Explorer. Specifically, I show you how to use keyboard shortcuts and multitab home pages and how to customize the tabs to fit your needs.

Tab keyboard shortcuts

Keyboard shortcuts allow you to get the most out of the new Internet Explorer tab interface by enabling you to do various lesser-known activities that can save time. These keyboard shortcuts require no setup; they are already active on your computer. Table 6-1 lists all the keyboard shortcuts that will help you take control of tabs, and explains how to start the new Quick Tabs feature.

Table 6-1   Internet Explorer 7 Tab Keyboard Shortcuts

Shortcut Keys	Function
Ctrl+T	Opens a new tab.
Ctrl+Shift+Click	Holding these keys while clicking a link will open the link in a new tab.
CTRL+Shift+Wheel Click	Holding these keys while clicking the mouse wheel over a link will open the link in a new tab behind the current tab.
Ctrl+W	Closes current tab.
Ctrl+Alt+F4	Closes all background tabs.
Ctrl+Tab	Move to next tab on right.
Ctrl+Shift+Tab	Move to next tab on left.
Ctrl+Q	Brings up Quick Tabs view, as shown in Figure 6-3.

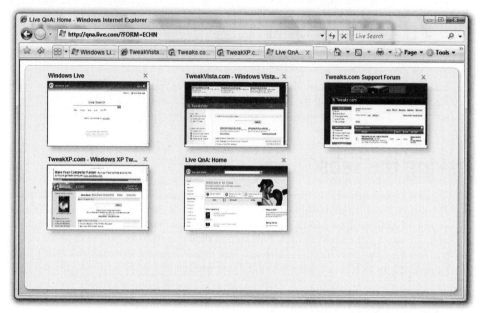

FIGURE 6-3: Quick Tabs view in Internet Explorer 7

Multitab home pages

From older versions of Internet Explorer, you are familiar with the concept of having a home page, a Web site that is displayed when the web browser is loaded. In Windows Vista, that classic browser feature has been mixed in with tabs. Now users can specify multiple Web sites to come up by default when they load Internet Explorer and can display them in different tabs. Although this is not exactly a groundbreaking feature, it is a nice hidden feature that helps you customize your browser.

Using a multitab home page is easy when you know the secret. Just follow these steps to set up your own multitab home page:

1. Start Internet Explorer.
2. Click Tools, and then select Internet Options.
3. When Internet Options loads, you will see the Home Page section at the top of the screen. To use multiple sites as your home pages, just enter each URL on a separate line, as shown in Figure 6-4. When you have finished, click OK to save your changes.
4. Click the Home button to instantly see your changes.

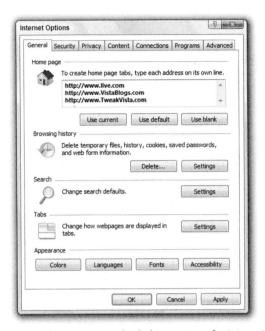

FIGURE 6-4: Setting multiple home pages for Internet
Explorer in Internet Options

Customizing tabs

Now that you have customized your home pages, let's fine-tune the tab settings to make
them work the way you work. Back in Internet Options, it is possible to change the way
the tabs behave. You can alter the order in which new tabs open, specify how pop-ups
are handled, and even customize what happens for various common actions. Follow these
steps to get the Tabbed Browsing Settings, and refer to Table 6-2 for setting details and
my recommendations:

1. Open Internet Explorer.

2. Click Tools, and then select Internet Options.

3. Locate the Tabs section on the General tab and click Settings. This loads the Tabbed
   Browsing Settings window, where you can toggle more than a dozen IE tab settings.
   (Refer to Table 6-2 for setting details.)

4. Click OK to save your changes.

Table 6-2   Internet Explorer 7 Tab Settings

Setting	Function
Enable Tabbed Browsing	Completely disables the tabbed browsing feature.
Warn me when closing multiple tabs	Displays a confirmation box when closing IE with multiple tabs open. I like to have this one disabled.
Always switch to new tabs when they are created	Changes focus to the last tab created.
Enable Quick Tabs	Allows the Quick Tabs feature shown in Figure 6-3 to operate. Keep this one enabled.
Open only the first home page when Internet Explorer starts	Instead of opening all your multitab home pages, it just loads the first one listed.
Open new tabs next to the current tab	Opens a new tab side by side with the current active tab. I like to disable this one.
Open home page for new tabs inside of blank page	Instead of displaying the "You've opened a new tab" screen, your home page is loaded. I suggest leaving this one disabled to increase performance.
Let Internet Explorer decide how pop-ups should open	Allows IE to make pop-up decisions. I recommend picking either of the following two options instead.
Always open pop-ups in a new window	Opens pop-ups in new browser windows.
Always open pop-ups in a new tab	Opens pop-ups in the same browser window but creates a new tab. This works well for most Web sites, but I have found some pop-up windows that contain calendars do not properly close the tab when a date is selected.
Open links for other programs in a new window	This setting opens a link that you clicked in any Windows application, such as your mail client, in a new browser window.
Open links for other programs in the current window	This setting opens a link that you clicked in any Windows application in a new tab. I recommend enabling this one.
Open links for other programs in the current tab or window	This setting opens a link that you clicked in any Windows application in the currently active tab.

Fun with RSS

In recent years, RSS (Really Simple Syndication) has been taking over the Internet. It is not uncommon to see Web sites offering various RSS feeds for their visitors that help them keep up-to-date with what is going on. With RSS, you can be notified when your favorite Web site posts a new article or when there is breaking news from a major news outlet.

RSS is powered by a simple XML file hosted on Web sites that follows the RSS standards. The RSS reader software interprets the XML file and displays it for your viewing. There are two different ways to view RSS feeds in Windows Vista. Internet Explorer 7 includes a new RSS reader, and Windows Sidebar includes an RSS gadget that displays the latest headlines from an RSS feed right on your sidebar.

Adding RSS Feeds to Internet Explorer and your sidebar is a great way to customize your computer and make it work better for you. In this section, I show you how to subscribe to and configure RSS feeds in Internet Explorer and then view those feeds on the Sidebar in the RSS gadget. Then I show you how to fine-tune your RSS settings so that you always have the most up-to-date RSS content.

Subscribing to feeds

Adding feeds, or *subscribing* as it is commonly known, is an easy task when you know the URL of the RSS feed you want to read. Identifying an RSS feed has become easier is recent years because many sites have adopted standard RSS image buttons. Others have simply provided RSS text links that point to their XML file rather than a button.

For this section, you need to find an RSS feed to use. Follow these steps to subscribe to an RSS feed in Internet Explorer 7:

1. Open Internet Explorer.

2. Browse to one of your favorite Web sites, such as TweakVista.com, and click one of the RSS feed links.

3. This causes Internet Explorer to launch into RSS feed reader mode. On this screen, click the Subscribe to this feed button, as shown in Figure 6-5.

4. The Feed Subscription box will pop up on your screen. Type a name for the feed and click the Subscribe button.

You have now successfully subscribed to an RSS feed in Internet Explorer. Now that you have the feed set up in IE, you are ready to configure the RSS reader gadget that is part of the Windows Sidebar.

FIGURE 6-5: Subscribing to an RSS feed with Internet Explorer

Viewing your IE-subscribed RSS feeds on the Sidebar

The Windows Sidebar has a useful RSS reader gadget called Feed Headlines. This gadget uses your RSS feed data from Internet Explorer to display the latest headlines for one of your feeds right on your Sidebar. After you have an RSS feed set up in IE, something you accomplished in the preceding section, you are ready to configure the RSS gadget to consume that feed and display it on your Windows Sidebar.

Before you go any further, make sure that you have Windows Sidebar loaded and visible on your computer. When you are ready, follow these steps to configure the Feed Headlines gadget:

1. On the Windows Sidebar, click the plus button located at the top of the screen to add a new gadget.

2. Locate the Feeds Headlines gadget and drag it to your Sidebar.

3. The new gadget will load with the default Microsoft RSS feed already set up. You now need to change the gadget settings to use your RSS feed subscribed to in Internet Explorer. To do this, click the tool icon while your cursor hovers over the gadget, as shown in Figure 6-6.

4. The option will now display. Change the drop-down box from All Feeds to the feeds you just subscribed to in Internet Explorer. Click OK.

The Feeds Headline gadget is now set up and configured to use your new IE-subscribed feed.

FIGURE 6-6: Opening a Feeds Headlines
gadget's options

Customizing feed settings

Now that you have your feeds set up in Internet Explorer, it is possible to fine-tune the feed
settings (for instance, how often the source is checked for updates, a valuable setting because
it determines how fresh your data is from the feed). You can modify feed settings by using
Internet Explorer again, in much the same way as how you subscribed to the feed. Let's get
started by opening Internet Explorer:

1. After Internet Explorer has loaded, click the Favorites star button and then click the
   Feeds button.

2. Select the feed you want to modify the settings for from the list of subscribed feeds.

3. After selecting a feed, you will notice that it is loaded in the browser RSS reader interface. You can access the feed settings by clicking View feed properties located at the
   bottom of the menu on the right.

4. When the Feed Properties window loads, I recommend that you go to the Update
   schedule section and select Use custom schedule.

5. Select a shorter update, such as 30 minutes, from the drop-down list.

6. When you have finished adjusting all the feed properties, including the archiving settings that specify how many articles of a feed to hold on to, click OK to save your changes.

Using Add-Ons in Internet Explorer

Internet Explorer has a lot of new features but is still behind in some of the features that other
third-party web browsers offer. For one, Internet Explorer still does not have a spell checker
built in to the application. Every time I post a message in a forum or to a Web site, I usually
have to write it in Microsoft Word and then copy and paste the text into Internet Explorer
because I am not the best speller. This can be a hassle; after all, I don't always want to have to
complete this bulky process to ensure my spelling is correct. Instead, I can use an Internet
Explorer add-on that adds spell-check capability within the web browser. In this case, I can

forget about loading up Microsoft Word. I can just initiate a spell check in the browser and let the add-on check my spelling in all text fields.

This section is all about showing you some must-have add-ons for Internet Explorer, such as a spell check component just mentioned. First, I show you how to use the ieSpell add-on to save your web posting from misspelled words. Second, I show you how to use an add-on that remembers all your usernames and passwords and other registration information for you.

Using ieSpell

ieSpell is a great add-on for Internet Explorer that I have been using for years. This useful add-on is available free for personal use and for a small fee if used in a commercial environment. Installing ieSpell and using it in IE is easy. Just visit www.iespell.com and install it just like any other application.

After you have ieSpell installed, restart any open Internet Explorer instances you previously had open; ieSpell will be ready for action. When you need to use it, just right-click any web page and select Check Spelling from the context menu. That is all you need to do to initiate a spell check. Immediately after selecting Check Spelling, you will see a familiar spell-check interface that will help you ensure you have no spelling mistakes.

Using RoboForm

Another great add-on for Internet Explorer is called RoboForm. It is a great little utility that memorizes all your usernames and passwords and other registration information. RoboForm fills in the forms for you so that you don't have to type your personal information when you need to register for a Web site or buy something online. This will save you time and help you remember all your accounts and passwords. Visit www.roboform.com to download and install the add-on.

After you have RoboForm installed, restart IE7, and the new toolbar appears. To get started using it, go to a Web site that you normally sign in to and fill out the fields. When you click the Submit or Login button, you are given the option to save the logon information. The next time you visit that site, you will see a prompt on the toolbar that shows you the button to press so that the form fields are automatically filled in.

Summary

This chapter has been all about customizing one of the most used applications on your computer, the web browser. Internet Explorer has been greatly improved in Windows Vista, and I hope you now understand how you can customize it to fit your specific needs. Earlier in this chapter, I showed you how to customize the search and tab features. Then I covered the new RSS features and how to make them work well with Windows Sidebar. The chapter came to an end with some cool IE add-ons that will help you add more functionality.

The next chapter is all about customizing everything related to media in Windows Vista. I show you how to tweak Windows Media Player and how to build your own media center PC using the upgraded Media Center software included in the higher-end version of Windows Vista.

Customizing Windows Media

Windows Vista is all about improving your experiences with various types of media, including music and videos. The major media components in Windows Vista (such as the sound system) have been completely updated and enhanced to help you experience the very best your hardware can provide. Windows Media Player also received a major upgrade that improved performance and added dozens of cool features to help you browse your music collection. Windows Media Center has undergone a major transformation, adding support for new technologies, such as high definition cable cards, as well as introducing an entirely new high resolution interface that looks amazing on your monitor or a high definition TV.

This chapter shows you how to customize your experience by taking advantage of some of these new features and fine-tuning how they work. To get started, you are going to use some great new audio enhancements to tweak how all types of media sound on your computer.

Adjusting Your Audio Experience

The audio system has gone through a major upgrade in Windows Vista. There are countless new features, such as the ability to control the volume per application, as well as many others that are unnoticed by the end user and hidden away. This section talks about those lesser known features and will show you how to take your audio experience to the next level. To do this, you are going to enable and tweak the new sound enhancements available on all newer high definition audio cards

The new audio enhancements are a collection of effects that allow you to do everything from boosting the bass to optimizing your surround sound using a microphone to get the perfect setup. These audio effects can be found on your output device properties. Follow these steps to get to the Enhancements settings tab:

1. Click the Start button and select Control Panel.

2. Click Hardware and Sound.

3. Click Sound.

4. The Sound properties screen will now load. Select the Speakers playback device and press Properties.

5. After the Speaker Properties window loads, click the Enhancements tab. All the enhancement effects are now displayed, as shown in Figure 7-1.

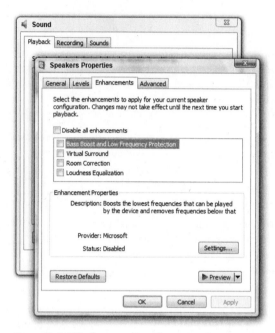

FIGURE **7-1: Windows audio enhancements**

6. Simply check the enhancement that you would like to enable and then click the Setting button to fine-tune the operation.

As you can see, enabling and configuring the settings are easy to do, but before you start using these new enhancements, take a look at the next few sections describing the enhancements in detail.

Bass Boost

Bass Boost and Low Frequency Protection allow you to pump up the bass on your speakers. You can fine-tune the frequency and the level of the boost in dB, as shown in Figure 7-2. Experiment with what is best for your speakers, but I don't recommend setting it higher than 6 dB with most speakers. Otherwise, you might notice some detail lost in your sound.

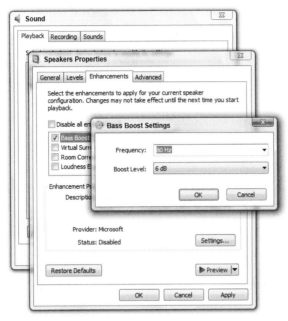

FIGURE 7-2: Using Base Boost

Virtual Surround

Virtual Surround allows you to output surround audio over stereo outputs to a receiver that supports Dolby Pro Logic or another matrix decoder technology to convert the signal into an analog surround sound system. This feature is useful only if you have a receiver that does not have a digital input and are forced to use an analog stereo input. For everyone else, this feature will not help you. Microsoft really should have called this feature something else. It really got my hopes up that it would simulate surround sound using my two stereo speakers the way those old Winamp plug-ins did several years ago.

Room Correction

The placement of your speakers and the size of the room greatly affect the performance of listening to music and watching movies. The Room Correction enhancement automatically calibrates the volume and delay for each speaker for the best possible sound quality. This cool enhancement works by playing various test sounds on all your speakers and using your microphone to record the result. Next, analysis of the results is performed and you are presented with optimal settings for each speaker. Simply OK the calculated settings and your sound is automatically optimized for all applications that run on your computer, including Media Center.

In my opinion, Room Correction is one of the best enhancements because it allows you to optimize your speaker system by just clicking a few buttons. I remember doing this with my surround sound receiver manually when I got a home theater system. This feature would have saved me a lot of time and the end result is better than a human ear could ever do.

Using Room Correction is very simple. While on the Enhancements tab, just check the option to enable it, press the Settings button, and follow these steps:

1. When the Room Calibration Wizard has loaded, click the Next button on the opening screen.

2. Select the microphone input you would like to use for the test. Make sure that you have a microphone plugged in to that input on your sound card. You can use any microphone for the calibration. If you have a studio quality omni-directional microphone, check This is a flat-rate, professional studio microphone. Click Next to proceed.

3. Position your microphone where you sit in your room. Make sure you elevate the microphone to roughly the height of your ears. For example, it is better to place your microphone on the armrest of a chair instead of the seat. Also make sure that your microphone is pointing straight up. When you are ready for the calibration test, press Next. It is best to leave the room when the test is running.

4. When the test is finished, press Next to view the results.

5. The results of the test for each channel will be displayed, as shown in Figure 7-3. When you are ready to apply the settings, press Finish.

FIGURE 7-3: Using Room Calibration

After the calibration wizard is completed, the Room Correction enhancement setup is finished and will be active immediately.

Loudness Equalization

There are many different sources of audio on your computer and among all of these sources, the volume can vary drastically. Even within the sources, the volume can vary. For example, if you are watching a movie in Media Center, there will be times when you can barely hear people talking yet the background music in other scenes is very loud. The Loudness Equalization enhancement helps solve these problems by dynamically adjusting the volume on all the inputs so that they all sound constant.

The Loudness Equalization enhancement has only one setting that allows you to fine-tune the sample period. Click the Settings button to adjust it.

Headphone Virtualization

Available only on Headphone devices listed on the Playback tab, Headphone Virtualization allows you to simulate a surround sound system when using headphones. Say you are watching a DVD on your laptop on a trip; using this enhancement, you can enable special audio effects that simulate a five-speaker surround sound system using only two speakers. If you use headphones often, definitely give this enhancement a try.

Customizing Windows Media Player 11

Windows Media Player has been upgraded and greatly improved in Windows Vista. The interface has been updated and given the new Aero Glass look as well as new ways to browse through your collection of music, movies, and videos with cover art. Similar to Windows Explorer, almost the entire user interface can be customized to your liking. These next few sections are going to show you how you can visually tweak Windows Media Player as well as customize the operation using some lesser known features. Let's get started by tweaking the look.

Tweaking the UI

The user interface can be divided into two separate areas to tweak: the layout of all the different panels and how the information on the different panels is displayed. Depending on your personal taste, Windows Media Player may be too busy for you, so you might want to cut down on the panels that are displayed to make a more slim and streamlined interface. The next two sections show you how to adjust the panels and how the information on the panels is displayed.

Adjusting panels

The various panels in Windows Media Player can be enabled and disabled very easily using the Layout Options button. Toggling the various panels on and off is as simple as clicking the Layout Options button, as shown in Figure 7-4, and selecting the option you would like to adjust.

FIGURE 7-4: Adjusting Media Player layout options

Adjusting views

After you have your layout of the panels set up the way you want, you can also modify the way the information is displayed in the main pane that lists your media. By default, the Icon view is activated. This is a basic view that shows the album cover, title, and artist name. A Tile view is also available that adds the year and your star rating to the screen in addition to what is shown with the Icon view. The Details view provides the classic list view of the media.

You can modify the active view for the main panel by clicking the View Options button, as shown in Figure 7-5, and selecting the new view.

Sharing your library

One of the lesser known but more useful features that I always enable when customizing Windows Media Player is the ability to share my music library with other computers in my home. I have a few different computers and laptops at home that I use for development for my Web sites and other purposes. Instead of loading my personal music collection onto each computer, it is much easier to set it up on just one and then share that music library. Then, on any of my computers also running Windows Media Player, the library is automatically discovered and I can connect to it and easily listen to my music no matter what device I am on.

FIGURE 7-5: Adjusting Media Player view options

Although this feature is easy to use, it is not as simple to set up. Follow these steps to enable it on your computer:

1. Open Windows Media Player if it is not already running.

2. While viewing your library, click the Library heading on the left list view, as shown in Figure 7-6, and select Media Sharing.

3. On the Media Sharing window, check Share my media and click OK.

4. You will have to specify which devices have access to your library. By default, only an entry for "Others users on this PC" shows up. If you want that group of users to have access to your library, you will need to manually select that group and click the Allow button. The same goes for computers connecting to your collection. They will also show up in this box when they try to connect to your library and you will have to select Allow or Deny.

Tip

When other computers connect to your music library, a notification will also show up in the system tray near the clock. Double-clicking this notification can allow you to quickly Allow or Deny them access as well.

5. After approving all groups and computers that have access to your computer, you can fine-tune additional settings by clicking the Settings button. If you are not interested in advanced settings, just press OK to save your changes and activate media sharing.

FIGURE: 7-6: Opening Media Sharing in Windows Media Player

Using audio effects

Windows Media Player has had a long history of supporting various third-party audio and video plug-in effects as well as a collection of built-in effects and features that are often hidden to the normal user. In this section, I am going to show you how you can turn on a few of the best built-in effects that will help you customize and improve your Windows Media experience.

Accessing hidden effects

With the simplification of the user interface in Windows Media Player 11 came the loss of easy access to some of the built-in audio effects. Accessing these effects is still not as easy as it was in earlier versions, but it is not a huge annoyance either, once you figure out how to use them again.

In Windows Media Player 11, the audio effects can be found by bringing up the classic menu by hitting the Alt key. Once the classic menu has appeared, navigate through View and then Enhancements and select Show Enhancements. Alternatively, you can jump to individual enhancements by clicking the name when the classic Enhancements menu is visible.

Using the various enhancements is very simple now that you have them displayed. Take a look at the new few sections for a quick overview of some of the more useful effects to use and customize.

Crossfading

Ever wish that Windows Media Player would gradually fade out of one song and into the next like other popular media players? Windows Media Player has had this feature for quite some time, but it was buried in a horrible UI, so many people never even knew it was there. Using this feature allows you to set a custom period where the end of one song will fade in with the beginning on the new song, creating a smooth transition between songs without any dead air.

When Crossfading is selected, click the Turn on crossfading link and drag the slider toward the right to adjust the time the two songs will be faded together, to a maximum of 10 seconds.

Graphic equalizer

The graphic equalizer allows you to play around with the levels of different frequencies to help you make the song or video sound perfect on your specific speaker setup. Different types of music often require unique levels of values on the equalizer. Experiment with the different sliders or select one of the preset equalizer settings by clicking Custom.

Playback speed

Play speed settings are more of a fun feature than a customization. Still, I figure it is worth mentioning because it can provide hours of fun for the right person, such as keeping your kid busy. When active, slide the slider to the right to speed up play or to the left to slow it down.

Customizing Media Center

Media Center in Windows Vista Home Premium and Ultimate has gone through a total UI upgrade. The graphics look spectacular on a high-definition television. Want to customize the look? Or how about tweaking the operation? I am going to show you how to do all that and more. I start off by going over how to turn your PC that has Media Center but no TV tuner into a fully fledged DVR by adding a TV tuner card. Then, I am going to dive into customizing everything possible followed by cool Media Center add-ons that will enhance your experience. So let's get started!

Turning your PC into a DVR

So, you have Windows Vista Home Premium or Ultimate but do not have a TV tuner card installed? You are missing out on the main Media Center experience. With the help of this section and an inexpensive TV tuner card, I will show you how to turn your PC into a fully functional DVR that will give any TiVo set top box major competition.

Before you can get started, there are some minimum system requirements that I must go over so that you will be able to watch TV on your computer. The most obvious is that you must be running Windows Vista Home Premium or Ultimate edition. The Media Center software is not included in any other version. Second, you will need a video card that has at least 128MB of RAM and supports Aero Glass for the best effect.

The most important aspect of adding a tuner card to your PC is picking one that is compatible with Windows Vista Media Center. Several tuner cards are on the market, so you will want to make sure that the one you buy says it is compatible with Windows Vista. The following are a few models that are known to work well on Windows Vista:

- **ATI TV Wonder 650:** HDTV and analog
- **Hauppague WinTV-HVR-1600:** HDTV and analog
- **Hauppague WinTV-PVR-150:** Analog
- **Hauppague WinTV-PVR-USB2:** External USB 2.0 analog
- **VBOX USB-A 3560:** External USB 2.0 HDTV

As you can see, there are both internal PCI cards and external USB 2.0 devices that can be added to your computer. There are also constantly new cards coming on the market that can be used in Windows Vista Media Center. I recommend checking out the forum at www.TheGreenButton.com to find out about even more compatible TV tuners.

Installing the TV tuner is also very easy, especially if you purchased an external USB tuner. Simply plug it in and install the drivers that came with the device. If you purchased an internal PCI card, just turn off your computer, unplug the power, open the case, and pop the card in an open PCI slot. Make sure to install the drivers after you power your PC back on.

After installing your TV tuner card, you are ready to get started configuring it in Windows Media Center. Follow these steps to get your Windows Media Center up and running:

1. Click the Start button, type **Media Center** in the Search box, and then press Enter.

2. If you are prompted with a setup wizard, cancel out of it. You are going to configure your card a different way. Use the arrow keys to navigate down to the Tasks section. Then press the left key to move over to Settings and press Enter, as shown in Figure 7-7.

3. On the Setting screen, select TV and press Enter.

4. Select Set Up TV Signal and press Enter. At this point, you will get a Tuner Not Found error if your TV tuner hardware is not installed properly. If this happens, make sure that you have the latest drivers for Windows Vista installed.

5. The Set Up TV Signal Wizard will now load. Press Next to continue.

6. Confirm your region by selecting Yes and then press Next.

7. You will now have the option to check online to download the latest options. Check Yes and press Next.

8. Make sure that you have your antenna or cable connected to your TV tuner input before going further. Select Configure my TV signal automatically and press Next. Windows Media Center will now try to auto-detect the type of signal that is connected.

9. The results are presented. If correct, press Yes and then Next. Otherwise, select No, proceed to manual TV setup, and select the type of signal you have attached.

10. Your TV signal is now set up. Now you need to configure your onscreen guide. Select Setup guide listing and press Next.

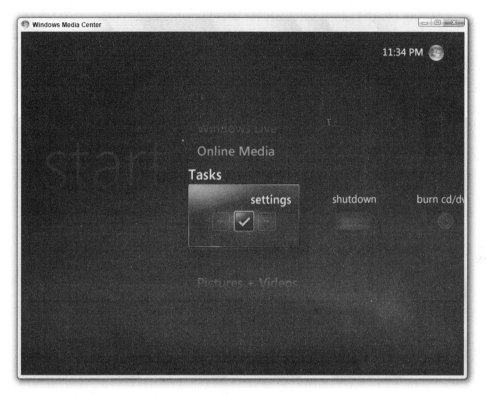

FIGURE 7-7: Configuring Windows Vista Media Center

11. The Guide Wizard starts. Press Next.

12. Press Yes that you agree to the privacy agreement and then Next.

13. Look over the terms of use, and press Agree and then Next.

14. Select your download method. I recommend using Download when connected. Press Next when you are ready.

15. Type your ZIP code and press Next.

16. Select your provider if this is cable and press Next. If you have an antenna, you will be shown this option.

17. The guide will now download. When it is finished, press Next and you are finished.

Your Windows Media Center is now set up. You can begin to watch TV and set up shows to record in the guide. Now you are ready to customize your Windows Media Center even more.

Creating Quick Launch shortcuts for Windows Media Center

Chapter 2 covered how the Quick Launch bar on the taskbar can be extremely useful. Now I am going to show you how to make it even more useful by showing how to make shortcuts that you can put in your Quick Launch bar that will direct to certain sections of Windows Media Center. For example, I am going to show you how to make a shortcut that, when clicked, will open Windows Media Center and go directly to the TV Guide. It is also possible to go directly to other sections, such as Live TV, Recorded TV, Pictures, and Music.

This is all possible with a special /homepage command line argument that the Windows Media Center executable uses. First, right-click your desktop and select New and then Shortcut. Next, enter the location as shown in the following options, depending on what you want to happen. Press Next, name the shortcut, and you are finished. Just drag the shortcut onto your Quick Launch bar and you have a new way to start Windows Media Center.

- **Start Windows Media Center and go directly to the TV Guide:**

  ```
  %SystemRoot%\ehome\ehshell.exe /homepage:videoguide.xml
  ```

- **Start Windows Media Center and go directly to Live TV:**

  ```
  %SystemRoot%\ehome\ehshell.exe /homepage:videofullscreen.xml
  ```

- **Start Windows Media Center and go directly to Recorded TV:**

  ```
  %SystemRoot%\ehome\ehshell.exe
  /homepage:videorecordedprograms.xml
  ```

- **Start Windows Media Center and go directly to Music:**

  ```
  %SystemRoot%\ehome\ehshell.exe /homepage:audio.home.xml
  ```

- **Start Windows Media Center and go directly to Photos:**

  ```
  %SystemRoot%\ehome\ehshell.exe /homepage:photo.xml
  ```

Setting the path where recorded shows are stored

Inside Windows Media Center you can choose on what drive you want to store shows that you schedule to be recorded. However, you cannot choose exactly what folder you want the show to be stored in. With the help of a simple registry hack, you can specify exactly where and on what drive recorded shows are stored. Follow these steps to customize where your shows are stored:

1. Click the Start button, type **regedit** in the Search box, and then press Enter.
2. Navigate through HKEY_LOCAL_MACHINE\SOFTWARE\Microsoft\Windows\ CurrentVersion\Media Center\Service\Recording.
3. Right-click RecordPath and select Modify.
4. Enter the full path followed by a backslash (\), as shown in Figure 7-8, and then press OK. Reboot for the settings to take effect.

The next time you record a show, the new location will be used.

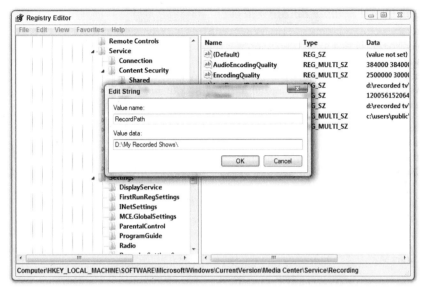

FIGURE 7-8: Modifying the location where recorded shows are stored

Configuring Media Center to look for recorded shows on a network share

Personal network attached storage devices are becoming more and more common in the home environment. I recently purchased a 1TB NAS that I use to back up all my personal documents as well as store recorded TV shows. I have my Media Center recording shows all the time, so the hard drive on my desktop fills up very quickly. For the shows that I want to keep, I move the file from my record folder to a special folder on my NAS that I have configured Windows Media Center to watch and play files from. This is possible with an easy Registry hack.

Follow these steps to configure Windows Media Center to watch for recorded shows in locations other than the main record folder:

1. Click the Start button, type **regedit** in the Search box, and then press Enter.

2. Navigate through `HKEY_LOCAL_MACHINE\SOFTWARE\Microsoft\Windows\`
   `CurrentVersion\Media Center\Service\Recording`.

3. Right-click WatchedFolders and select Modify. If WatchedFolders does not exist, right-click the Recording key folder and select New and then Multi-String Value. Call this new value WatchedFolders. Then modify the value.

4. You can enter as many locations as you want. Just place each location on its own line and make sure that you end each path with a backslash (\). If you want to add your NAS device as I do, make sure that your NAS share is first mapped to a drive letter. Then just enter the path as if it were another hard drive in your computer.

5. Press OK when you are finished and reboot for the settings to take effect.

You are now able to watch recorded shows that are no longer stored on your computer.

Using the MSN Remote Record add-on

MSN Remote Record is my favorite Windows Media Center add-on. It is a free service provided by Microsoft that allows you to browse your local TV listings and remotely schedule a show to record with just a click on MSN's Web site. This is an invaluable service and piece of software that has really helped me make sure I did not miss a show when my plans changed. Instead of calling someone at home and trying to walk them through Windows Media Center to record a show for me, I can do it myself from anywhere in the world.

Getting started with MSN Remote Record is very easy. Just visit `http://tv.msn.com/tv/rr/rrsetup.aspx` and press the Install Remote Record button. After installing and setting up MSN Remote Record on your Windows Vista PC, visit `http://tv.msn.com` when you are away from home and sign in to view your local listings and schedule recordings.

Using third-party Windows Media Center add-ons

There are many very useful and cool third-party add-ons for Windows Media Center that really help you get even more out of it. As Windows Media Center is becoming increasingly popular, even more add-ons are being developed and released. The following is a list of some of the best add-ons available now for Windows Vista Media Center:

- **mcePhone for Skype** (`www.scendix.com/mcephone`): mcePhone is a great add-on for Windows Media Center that allows you to make and receive phone calls using your Skype account through Windows Media Center. This can be very useful and cool because you can use Skype through the Windows Media Center interface while sitting on your couch.

- **mceWeather** (`www.scendix.com/mceweather`): This is a useful add-on that allows you to get the latest weather forecasts and conditions for your area without leaving Windows Media Center.

- **Big Screen Headlines RSS Reader** (`www.mobilewares.net/mce/bshhtm.htm`): Are you a big RSS Feed user? This add-on installs an RSS reader that allows you to easily read your favorite feed through Windows Media Center.

- **MCEBrowser** (`www.anpark.com/MCEBrowser_Screenshots.aspx`): Remember Microsoft's WebTV? Make your own WebTV and browse the Web on your television with this add-on and Windows Media Center.

Most of the Windows Media Center 2005 add-ons also seem to work well in Windows Vista Media Center. Visit `www.benshouse.net/add-ons.php` for even more Media Center add-ons that will work in Windows Vista Media Center.

Summary

This chapter covered almost every aspect of Windows Media. You started with tweaking your audio settings with the cool new features such as Virtual Surround sound and Room Correction. Then you moved on to customizing Windows Media Player 11 and taking advantage of its new features. Finally, I showed you how easy it is to add a TV tuner to your computer and turn it into a full-blown DVR that you can customize in many ways.

This is the last chapter of the first part of *Hacking Windows Vista*. In the next part, I change the topic a bit — to increasing the performance of Windows Vista. You begin by analyzing your system to get a good understanding of your computer hardware capabilities.

Increasing Your System's Performance

part

Analyzing Your System

Did you ever wonder how fast your computer actually is? Sure, you may have an Intel 2.8 GHz Core Duo in your box, but the CPU is not the only factor in determining the speed of your computer. The true speed of your computer is determined by the combined speed of all your hardware, such as the read and write speed of your hard drive, front side bus speed, RAM speed, and even your graphics card GPU. Microsoft has attempted to provide users with a clearer picture of their computer's performance in Windows Vista with the new System Performance Rating benchmarking tool. This chapter will help you understand your Windows System Performance Rating as well as perform a more detailed analysis of the capabilities of your computer, and you learn how you can make your computer faster.

Before you can jump into improving the speed of your computer, it is important to understand the limitations of your hardware and also to identify potential bottlenecks in your system. Using the tools discussed in this chapter, you will be able to run different tests that will help you in the upcoming chapters decide which hacks will work best for your computer.

Monitoring Your System Hardware

Monitoring the status of your system with various tools will help you understand what is going on behind the scenes, much like the instrument panel of a car. If you are driving home and you notice that the temperature gauge is maxed out and the instrument panel is flashing with all sorts of warning icons, it is very easy to understand that your car is not performing at its best. Monitoring your system, for example, will reveal if you are running low on memory, if your CPU is overloaded, or if your system has too many programs running at the same time. These are all useful and important things to know, and having that information available enables you to check your system's operations and to change settings to get optimal performance.

A variety of performance monitoring software is available. Let's get started by using the Reliability and Performance Monitor in Windows Vista.

Using the Reliability and Performance Monitor

Windows has a great diagnostic tool that's built right in called the *Reliability and Performance Monitor*. This cool utility can give you stats on just about every aspect of Windows. Similar to other system monitoring tools, its purpose is to help you diagnose problems and improve the performance of your computer. With the release of Windows Vista, the Reliability and Performance Monitor has been improved and is now even more useful.

To start the application, simply click the Start button, type **perfmon.msc** in the Search box, and then press Enter. The Performance Diagnostic Console requires administrative rights to run. Depending on your User Account Protection settings, you might have to confirm the action by clicking Continue or keying in your admin account password when prompted.

Tip The Windows Performance Diagnostic Console gets the data for the counter from the system registry by default. A special flag for perfmon.msc allows you to change the data source to get the data directly from the Windows Management Interface instead. This is useful if you are getting some strange results and would like to get a second opinion on what is really going on. Simply type **perfmon.msc /sysmon_wmi** in the Search box on the Start panel to use the Windows Performance Diagnostic Console alternate data source.

After the Performance Diagnostic Console loads, you will see the Resource Overview screen that is filled with the most common system stats, as shown in Figure 8-1.

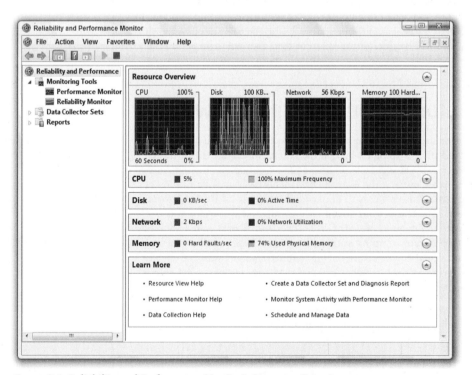

FIGURE 8-1: Reliability and Performance Monitor's Resource Overview screen

By default, you are presented with a moving graph of the CPU, Disk, Network, and Memory usage. Just below the graphs you will find more detailed breakout sections that can be expanded to show exactly how much each process is using the CPU, Network, and Memory as well as which processes and files are using the disk. The Resource Overview screen alone provides a wealth of information that can help you analyze your system, but there are also two more components — the Performance Monitor and the Reliability Monitor — that are very useful. I will get to those shortly; first let's go into more detail on the different detailed component monitors.

Using the detailed CPU overview

Like all the detailed views, the detailed CPU overview view can be expanded using the arrow on the right of the bar, if it is not already expanded. Here you will find a list of all the processes running on your machine, similar to the Processes tab of Task Manager, as shown in Figure 8-2.

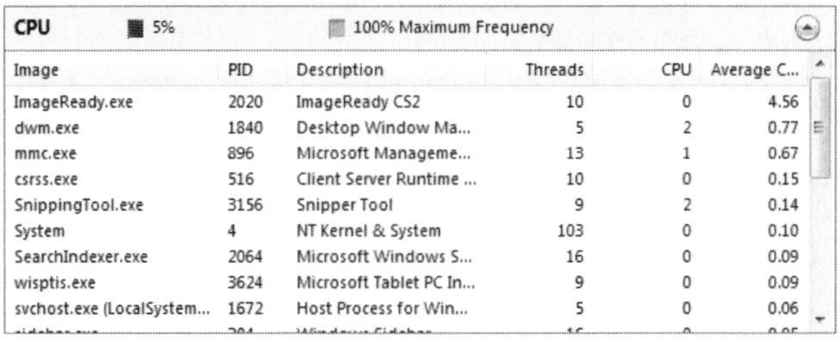

CPU	▇ 5%		▤ 100% Maximum Frequency				⊙
Image		PID	Description	Threads	CPU	Average C...	
ImageReady.exe		2020	ImageReady CS2	10	0	4.56	
dwm.exe		1840	Desktop Window Ma...	5	2	0.77	
mmc.exe		896	Microsoft Manageme...	13	1	0.67	
csrss.exe		516	Client Server Runtime ...	10	0	0.15	
SnippingTool.exe		3156	Snipper Tool	9	2	0.14	
System		4	NT Kernel & System	103	0	0.10	
SearchIndexer.exe		2064	Microsoft Windows S...	16	0	0.09	
wisptis.exe		3624	Microsoft Tablet PC In...	9	0	0.09	
svchost.exe (LocalSystem...		1672	Host Process for Win...	5	0	0.06	
		204	Windows Sidebar	16	0	0.05	

FIGURE 8-2: The detailed CPU overview

On the top of the bar, you will find the current usage of your CPU as well as a maximum usage rate. The list of processes is below, sorted by average CPU usage. Unlike the active process list in Task Manager, this list shows you only the average usage rate. This is very useful when you're looking for an application that has an overall meaningful impact on your CPU usage. Additionally, you are shown the number of threads and CPU cycles the process is currently using.

The information you gain about your computer from the detailed CPU overview will help you identify applications you run that have a big impact on the performance of your computer. If you have a process listed that has a very high average CPU time, try to identify what the process is by using the Description column or even a search engine if necessary. You might find that a simple application such as a desktop weather application that runs in the background is using a big portion of your CPU. With this information, you may decide to uninstall such an application to speed up your system.

Using the detailed Disk overview

The detailed Disk overview shows the read and write speed in bytes per minute of the various processes running, as shown in Figure 8-3. The list of open read and write per processes also shows the file that is in use. The Disk bar shows the total speed of all the disk operations as well as the percent of the time the disk is active.

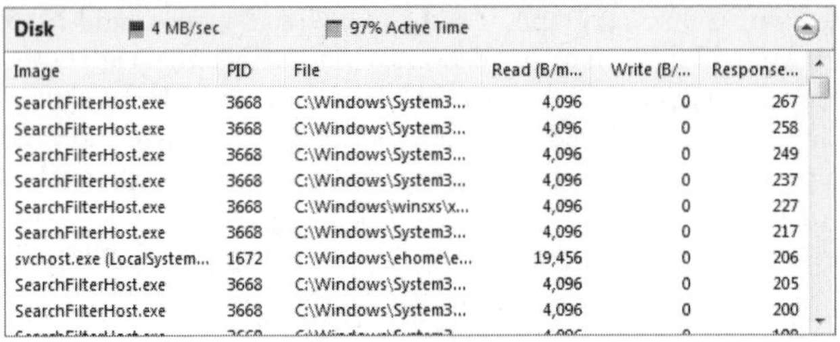

Disk		4 MB/sec		97% Active Time				
Image		PID	File		Read (B/m...	Write (B/...	Response...	
SearchFilterHost.exe		3668	C:\Windows\System3...		4,096	0	267	
SearchFilterHost.exe		3668	C:\Windows\System3...		4,096	0	258	
SearchFilterHost.exe		3668	C:\Windows\System3...		4,096	0	249	
SearchFilterHost.exe		3668	C:\Windows\System3...		4,096	0	237	
SearchFilterHost.exe		3668	C:\Windows\winsxs\x...		4,096	0	227	
SearchFilterHost.exe		3668	C:\Windows\System3...		4,096	0	217	
svchost.exe (LocalSystem...		1672	C:\Windows\ehome\e...		19,456	0	206	
SearchFilterHost.exe		3668	C:\Windows\System3...		4,096	0	205	
SearchFilterHost.exe		3668	C:\Windows\System3...		4,096	0	200	

FIGURE 8-3: The detailed Disk overview

These numbers enable you to see if an application is hogging your disk and slowing down all the other processes on your computer because it is reading and writing so much data. This is especially useful when trying to identify what your hard drive is doing when you hear it going crazy and the hard drive read/write light seems like it is constantly on.

Using the detailed Network overview

The detailed Network overview shows which processes on your system are using the network, as shown in Figure 8-4. The top bar shows you the current network speed and the percent your network connections are utilized. Each open network connection is listed below with the name of the process using the connection. Additionally, you will find the network address the process has connected to as well as the amount of data sent and received in bytes per minute.

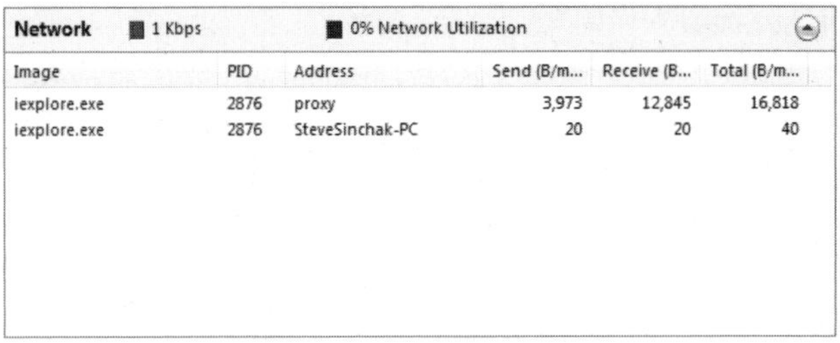

Network		1 Kbps		0% Network Utilization			
Image		PID	Address	Send (B/m...	Receive (B...	Total (B/m...	
iexplore.exe		2876	proxy	3,973	12,845	16,818	
iexplore.exe		2876	SteveSinchak-PC	20	20	40	

FIGURE 8-4: The detailed Network overview

Have a slow Internet connection? Are the lights on your cable or DSL modem going crazy? These network usage stats will help you diagnose a process that is bogging down your network connection, such as a free peer-to-peer VoIP (Voice over IP) application. These applications can use your network connection even if you are not on a call. Other users' calls may be routed through your computer, resulting in your network connection slowing down. Using the information in the detailed Network overview, you can easily identify how much data is transferring both ways for every process on your computer.

Note

With the detailed Network overview, it is easy to find out if your network connection has a high utilization rate by looking at the header bar. Keep in mind that you network card in your computer usually has a greater capacity and is capable of higher speeds than your Internet connection. If you have a 100MB network card in your computer and that is connected to a 10MB broadband Internet connection, when your network card utilization is at 10 percent, your Internet connection is at 100 percent utilization.

Using the detailed Memory overview

The detailed Memory overview shows you how much of the various types of memory each running process is using, as shown in Figure 8-5. The top bar shows the number of hard memory faults per second and the percentage of total physical memory that is in use. The memory overview is one of the most useful overviews in the Reliability and Performance Monitor.

Memory	10 Hard Faults/sec		69% Used Physical Memory			
Image	PID	Hard Fa...	Commit (KB)	Working ...	Shareable...	Private (KB)
dwm.exe	1840	0	73,176	66,256	23,620	42,636
iexplore.exe	2876	0	50,280	57,096	28,532	28,564
explorer.exe	1876	0	43,196	54,508	32,028	22,480
svchost.exe (LocalSystem...	1672	457	23,296	24,956	3,120	21,836
mmc.exe	896	0	19,792	18,908	7,632	11,276
WINWORD.EXE	540	0	10,940	31,612	22,688	8,924
svchost.exe (netsvcs)	1016	1	19,056	20,456	11,868	8,588
sidebar.exe	304	0	27,360	24,356	15,832	8,524
SearchIndexer.exe	2064	10	133,696	16,120	9,016	7,104

FIGURE 8-5: The detailed Memory overview

Take a look at the number of hard memory faults and total percentage of physical memory that is in use. If you are getting any more than a few hard memory faults per second, you might need more memory for your computer. A memory fault occurs when something a program needs is not in memory and the memory manager has to get it and put it there. Usually it has to make room for the new data to be placed in memory by kicking some other processes' data out of physical memory and into the paging file. This can be a slow operation.

Also consider the amount of private memory a process is using. A process that is using a huge amount of private memory can steal your system resources from other processes, which results in more memory faults and a slow-down of your computer.

Using the Performance Monitor to get more system stats

The Performance Monitor is one of the classic features of the Performance Diagnostic Console that has been around since Window NT and has been refined over the years to be a very comprehensive tool. In Windows Vista, hundreds of different monitors are built in that allow you to monitor just about every aspect of the operating system and your hardware. If you want, you can even view information about how fast your laptop's battery is charging or discharging. Similar to other system monitoring tools, the Performance Monitor is provided to help you detect problems and improve your system performance.

Once you have the Performance Diagnostic Console open, click Performance Monitor under Monitoring Tools to use the monitor. When the Performance Monitor loads, you are greeted with a graph of data as well as a list of active counters. You see a graph of the Processor utilization percentage. This is a pretty but rather useless chart because you already have this information on the overview screens. The real power of the Performance Monitor can be found in the performance counters.

To add more performance counters, simply click the icon with the + symbol on it, or press Ctrl+I and the Add Counters window appears, as shown in Figure 8-6.

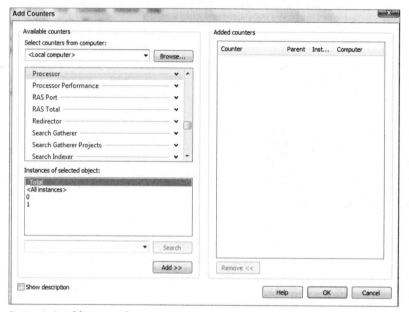

FIGURE 8-6: Adding a performance counter

When the Add Counters window appears, you will notice that the counters are organized in different component categories. Navigate through the list box and click the down arrow to see the individual counters available for the selected subject. Because some of the counter names are vague, you can turn on the bottom description pane to find out more details about a specific counter by checking the Show Description box in the lower-left corner of the window.

Let's say that you want to monitor remote desktop connections made to your computer. You can easily accomplish this with the right performance counter.

1. With the Add Counters window open, navigate through the list of subjects and expand Terminal Services.

2. You will find three counters: Active Sessions, Inactive Sessions, and Total Sessions. Select Active Sessions.

3. Depending on the counter, you may be required to select which instance of the object you want to track. If your computer has a multi-core CPU chip and you were using a CPU Utilization counter, the Instances of selected object list box will display and allow you to choose what core of the CPU you want to track. For the selected Active Sessions counter, there are no instance options, so that box remains grayed out.

4. After you have the counter selected, click the Add button.

5. When a new counter has been added, you can always add more counters on the same screen. Select the Total Sessions counter and click Add again.

6. Click OK to close the Add Counter window and return to the Performance Monitor screen.

Tip

When selecting performance counters, you can hold down the Ctrl key and select multiple counters at once. Then just click the Add button and all of the selected counters are added instead of your having to individually click each counter and then click Add. Additionally, if you want to add all the counters in a category, select the category name and click Add.

Tip

When adding performance counters to the Performance Monitor, it is possible to add counters from a remote computer. If your computer is on a corporate domain and you have administrative rights, or if you have an administrative account on another home computer, you can easily remotely monitor the performance. When the Add Counters window is open, simply type the name of the computer in the Select counters from computer box. Alternatively, you can click the Browse button and select the computer if the remote computer's name is broadcast across your network. After entering the computer name, press Enter to connect. If you get an error, make sure that you have the correct permissions on your domain to use this feature and that your username and password for the account you are currently logged on to is the same on both computers, if this is in a home or non-domain environment.

You will now see the Terminal Services Active Sessions and Total Sessions counters listed on the graph, in addition to the CPU utilization performance counter. However, the line graph makes it hard to read these performance counters. The next section shows you how you can customize the performance counter data display.

Viewing the data

The Performance Monitor allows you to view the data in many different ways. The default screen is the line graph, as shown in Figure 8-7. This display method is adequate for a few performance counters, but when you have more than three or four, figuring out what line is for what counter starts to become a little confusing. Additionally, for certain counters such as Active Sessions and Total Sessions mentioned earlier, the line graph just does not make it easy to understand the data. Fortunately, Microsoft provides two other methods for viewing the data.

Another method of viewing the data is to use the histogram display, as shown in Figure 8-8. To change to this display method, select Histogram bar on the view drop-down list that currently shows Line selected. This method of displaying the data is not much better than the default, but because it relies on one scale, the counters that report large numbers will dwarf counters that report small numbers. This limitation makes it almost impossible to read some of the performance counters.

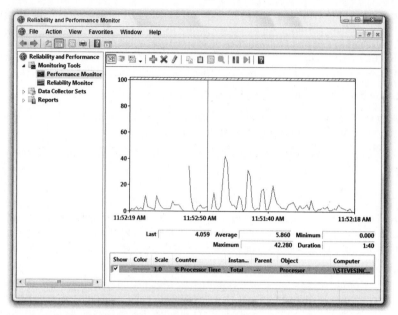

FIGURE 8-7: The default screen of Performance Monitor

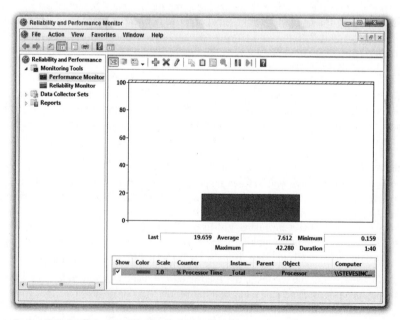

FIGURE 8-8: Performance Monitor's histogram bar view

To make everyone happy, there is also a Report viewing method, which simply lists the counter numbers in text, as shown in Figure 8-9. You can activate this viewing method by choosing Select Report from the View drop-down list or by pressing Ctrl+R.

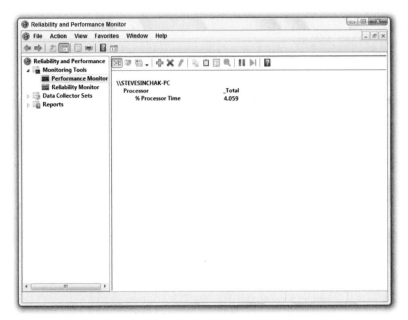

FIGURE 8-9: Performance Monitor's report view

Setting the update interval

Now that you have all your performance counters set up and displaying data, you need to select the interval time of how often the data will be updated. How often you want the counters to be updated depends on your purpose for monitoring your hardware. For example, if you are trying to track how much data your computer is sending through your network adapter every day or hour, it is not necessary to have that counter update every second. You will just be wasting CPU cycles because you are making the computer constantly update that performance counter. However, if you are interested in current memory or CPU utilization, you will want a much faster update time.

To change the update interval, perform the following steps:

1. While in the Performance Monitor section of the Reliability and Performance Monitor, click the Properties button, which looks like a hand pointing to a notebook. Alternatively, you can press Ctrl+Q.

2. After the System Monitor Properties window loads, click the General tab.

3. Locate the Graph elements section and update the Sample Every text box. This number is in seconds.

4. Click OK to close the window and save your changes.

Now Performance Monitor will poll the data sources at your specified interval.

Analyzing and detecting problems

The Performance Monitor and the various performance counters make it possible to detect many problems and shed light on how to make your system run faster. You should familiarize yourself with the following tips that deal with specific performance counters; these will prove to be invaluable in your analysis and decision-making. The following are some of the things to look out for when monitoring your system:

- **Physical Disk: Disk Read Bytes/sec and Disk Write Bytes/sec** — These two performance counters can tell you if your physical disk is set up and functioning correctly. In order to determine this, consult the Web site or the manual of the manufacturer of your hard drive. Look up the range of read/write speeds. If the readings that you are getting are far below what you should be getting, then your hard disk could be damaged or set up incorrectly. Run diagnostic software on the disk and make sure that it is set up properly in Device Manager with the correct transfer mode. Remember that most hard drives read at different speeds when they are reading from different parts of the disk. This is why there may be some discrepancies between your readings.

- **Paging File: % Usage and % Usage Peak** — These two performance counters can tell you how well your system is using the page file. If you set the size of the page file manually, these counters are very critical to deciding what size the page file should be. As a rule, if the page file % Usage is above 95 percent or if the Usage Peak is near 100 percent, consider increasing the size of the page file if you have set the size manually.

- **Memory: Available MBytes and Paging File: % Usage** — These two performance counters help you decide if you should put more RAM in your computer. If the number of your available megabytes is low and your paging file usage percentage is very high, then you should consider purchasing more RAM for your computer.

- **Processor: % Processor Time** — This performance counter monitors the activity and work your processor is doing. If your CPU is consistently working at or above 85 percent, and you are not running any computation-intensive applications in the background, this would indicate that you should consider upgrading your CPU. The CPU is having a hard time keeping up with all your programs. You can also try closing open applications that are running in the background to make your computer more responsive and faster.

Saving your performance counter setup

After you have spent some time adding all the performance counters that you would like to use, it is possible to save this configuration so that every time that you start the Performance Diagnostic Console and use the Performance Monitor, your performance counters are automatically loaded.

To save the performance counters selected:

1. Click the File menu object on the menu bar and select Save As.

2. Type a filename, specify a location, and click Save.

When you want to use your performance counters again, just navigate to the location where you saved the file and double-click it. The Performance Diagnostic Console loads and takes you directly to the Performance Monitor tool.

Using the Reliability Monitor

Like the Performance Monitor, the Reliability Monitor is a system monitoring tool that is designed to help you diagnose problems and improve the performance of your computer. The Reliability Monitor is especially geared to helping you solve various types of system failures that can lead to poor performance in all areas. The Reliability Monitor works by tracking all the software installs, uninstalls, application failures, hardware failures, Windows failures and general miscellaneous failures to compile a System Stability Chart and System Stability Report, as shown in Figure 8-10.

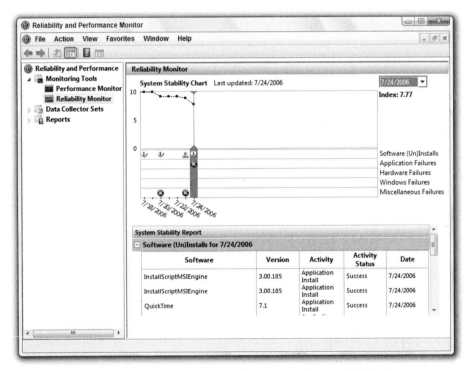

FIGURE 8-10: Reliability Monitor's System Stability Chart and System Stability Report

Any of the icons on the System Stability Chart can be selected to move the scope of the System Stability Report to a specific time period. This is very useful because it allows you to see what happened the same day or just before some kind of failure occurred. Depending on this information, you will have a clue as to what may have been the cause of the failure.

Reading the System Stability Report

Every day your computer is given a system stability index rating based on the system activities of the day. The score is out of a possible 10 points. Depending on what has happened in the past, this score goes up or down. For example, if you have a Windows failure, your score goes down. As days pass, if you do not have any more failures, your score gradually goes back up again. However, if another failure occurs, it drops even more.

I recently had an issue with installing new video drivers for my laptop. I was trying to get the new Glass look in Windows Vista to work and was installing some drivers that were not exactly made for my laptop model. After I installed the new drivers, I had to reboot and was welcomed by the blue screen error. I rebooted again and the same thing happened. These system failures killed my System Stability index. Before I had these problems I had a rating of 9.44; after my driver fiasco, I had an index of 4.78. As you can see, your reliability rating can drop very quickly if you have multiple major errors, such as a blue screen.

When you notice that your System Stability index goes down, you are going to want to know why so that you can fix the problem and get the performance of your system back in line. The System Stability Report is perfect for understanding exactly what happened.

With your mouse, select a time period on the System Stability Chart in which your score dropped significantly. Depending on presence of the information, warning, or error icons in the grid for the specific day, you will be able to know what sections of the report you should expand to see the details of what happened. Figure 8-10 shows a red error icon in the Application Failures grid item on the selected day. This tells you to expand the Application Failures section of the report to see the details. After expanding the section, you will see which application failed and how it failed. Similarly, if this were a hardware failure, you would see the component type, device name, and why it failed. If it were a Windows or miscellaneous failure, you would see the failure type and details of what happened.

As you can see, reading the System Stability Report is a quick and easy way to see what exactly is going on. Next, you are going to use the new Event Viewer in Windows Vista to get even more detailed information on the state of the computer.

Using Event Viewer

Event Viewer in Windows Vista is a centralized source for reading all the system's various log files. When a component such as the Windows Firewall service has an error, a notification, or a warning, it can be viewed in Event Viewer. When a third-party application causes your computer to crash, the details of the event can also be found in Event Viewer. Even when any user logs on to your computer, the details of the event can be found in Event Viewer. As you can see, Event Viewer is the ultimate source to find out what is happening and has happened to your computer.

How can Event Viewer help with increasing the performance of your computer? Event Viewer enables you to identify hardware and software failures that you may not even know have been occurring. If you want to increase the performance of your computer, you need to fix any problems first. Skipping ahead without fixing the problems first is like tweaking your car engine for speed but not fixing the flat tires. Even if you increase the performance of other components of your computer, any errors or failures can offset any improvements in speed.

Using Event Viewer is very easy. Event Viewer is part of every version of Windows Vista but requires an account with administrative privileges to run. To start Event Viewer, click the Start button, type **Eventvwr.msc** in the Search box, and then press Enter.

After Event Viewer shows up onscreen, you will see the Overview and Summary screen, as shown in Figure 8-11. The Summary of Administrative Events section provides an aggregated view of all your events. This groups them together from all your system logs and also gives you time-period stats on the different types of events. Expand the different event types, such as Critical, Error, and Warning, to see a more detailed aggravated view of all events that match that event type. You can also double-click the event types and events to view more details. Doing so will create a custom view for you automatically. I will get into those in more detail shortly. First, let's lay the groundwork for using Event Viewer.

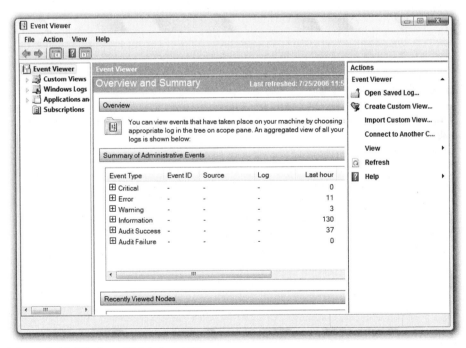

FIGURE 8-11: Windows Vista's Event Viewer

Reading logs and events

The various system logs are organized in two grouping folders:

- **Windows Logs:** Windows Logs enable you to find events covering Windows core applications, security, setup, and the system.

- **Application and Services Logs:** You can find events such as hardware and specific software applications under Applications and Services Logs.

When you expand the top-level grouping folders and select a sub-event topic, you are presented with a list of all the events sorted by date by default. Simply select an event to view the details.

Reading the event log is very easy to do. When an event is selected, you will see details of the event in the bottom pane. The most important pieces of information for each event are the source, ID, and description. If you do not see the description of the event on your screen, expand the Details pane up to review the description. Alternatively, you can double-click the event to bring up the Details pane in a new window.

If you have identified any events that signaled an error or warning, it is a good idea to research the event to find out if it is important to fix or not. The most popular way to investigate an event is to do a search on either Google or Yahoo with the event ID. With the new version of Event Viewer in Windows Vista, you can also click the More Information link on the Details view of an event. This will show you whether Microsoft has any information on the specific event.

Creating custom views

Using Event Viewer can be overwhelming because of the massive amount of data that you have access to. Custom Views is Microsoft's answer to data overload. Instead of looking through multiple log files, you can create a custom view in which you specify parameters for specific types of events. You can use the view to find all events that you specified no matter what log they are in. You first encountered a custom view on the Event Logs Summary screen. All the information in the Summary of administrative events section is populated by a custom view.

Creating your own custom view is easier than manually navigating through all the different log sources, and custom views are more flexible than the Event Log Summary screen. Follow these steps to create your own custom view:

1. With Event Viewer open, click Action in the menu bar and select Create Custom View.

2. The Create Custom View window loads, showing all the parameters of the view. You will see two tabs: Filter and XML. You will use the Filter tab because it automatically produces the XML for you.

3. Select the Time Period for your view. I like to use Last 7 Days for this option.

4. Check the boxes for the Event Levels you want to view, such as Critical, Error, and Warning.

5. Expand the Event Log drop-down box and then select the log sources that you want to search in.

6. You have the option to set a specific object to view events for, such as a specific application or device. Alternatively, you can just leave this setting as <All Event Sources>.

7. To find all the events with a certain ID, enter the Event ID. You can also exclude a specific event from the view by adding a minus sign in front of the ID (for example, –2030).

8. The last few settings are used less frequently. Here you can also specify the Task Category, Keywords for the event, and a specific computer user the event occurred with.

9. After finalizing the settings, click OK.

10. The Save As Custom View screen will pop up. Type a Name and click OK.

After your new custom view has been generated, you can open it by expanding Custom Views and selecting it from the list.

Using Task Manager

The Windows Task Manager is a critical part of Windows that makes it possible for users to have full control over what their system is doing. Providing the ability to monitor individual programs and control any program or process, Task Manager is very useful. No special software must be installed to use Task Manager; just press Ctrl+Alt+Del and then click Start Task Manager. You can also click the Start button, type **taskmgr** in the Search box, and then press Enter.

After Windows Task Manager has started, you will notice a list of active applications running on your computer. Additionally, you will see tabs that list processes, CPU performance data, networking performance data, and active user data.

Monitoring processes

All the applications on the computer that are running under your account, those that are hidden and those that are not, can be found on the list on the Processes tab. On this list, you will be able to see how much memory each process is using as well as how much of the CPU each process is using. By clicking the column headings, you can sort the rows either numerically or alphabetically.

Tip

By default, Task Manager shows you only the processes that were started under your username. When viewing the Processes tab, click the Show Processes from All Users button to view all processes. You will find that there are a lot of processes that run under the System account. Those are primarily system components.

There are many useful columns on the Processes tab:

- The Image Name column shows the name of the process.
- The User Name columns shows who started the process.
- The CPU column shows what percentage of the CPU the process is using
- The Mem Usage column shows how much memory a process is using.

If you find a process that is taking up a lot of your memory or eating up a big portion of your CPU, you might want to consider ending the process if it is not a critical one. Ending a process is very easy. Just select the row of the process you want to end, and click the End Process button.

Viewing performance data

The Performance tab, as shown in Figure 8-12, shows a lot of the same information that the Performance application shows. This tab is another place where you can view memory and CPU information, but in a far less detailed manner.

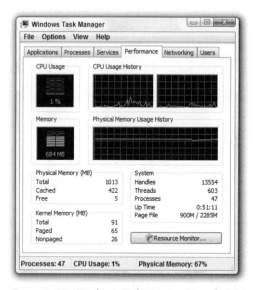

FIGURE 8-12: Windows Task Manager's performance information

The Networking tab is a great way to monitor the network performance. Each networking device on your computer has its own graph showing the percent that it is utilized. Although it does not keep track of bandwidth sent and received, it does show the speed that the hardware is working and if it is connected.

Configuring Task Manager to display CPU utilization

When Windows Task Manager is started, a small histogram is displayed in the system tray that shows the CPU utilization. This little feature can be very useful if you would always like to keep an eye on your CPU utilization but do not want Task Manager always on top of all your windows. With a little bit of work, it is possible to start up the Windows Task Manager automatically on every start and run it minimized and hidden from the taskbar except for the system tray.

1. Click the Start button, navigate to All Programs, and locate the Startup listing.

2. Right-click Startup and select Open. A new window opens with the contents of your personal startup folder. Any shortcuts that you place in this folder will be automatically loaded when Windows starts.

3. After the Startup folder is opened, right-click in the open white space, select New, and then navigate to Shortcut.

4. When the new shortcut wizard loads, type **taskmgr.exe** in the text box asking for the location of the file, and then click Next.

5. Type a name for the shortcut and click Finish.

6. Now you are shown the startup folder again and a new icon for Task Manager. To make Task Manager start minimized, right-click the new icon and select Properties.

7. Change the Run type where it says Normal Window to Minimized, and then click OK.

8. Now the shortcut is all set up. However, there is one last change to make and you will need to open up Task Manager to do this. After you have opened up Windows Task Manager, click the Options menu bar item and select Hide When Minimized so that when the program starts, only the CPU histogram will be shown and the program will not appear on the taskbar.

Your system is now configured to start up the CPU meter on every boot in the system tray. Should you change your mind at a later time and no longer want the Task Manager CPU meter to show up, simply delete the shortcut from the Startup folder.

Other performance monitoring utilities

In Chapter 3 I talked about how you can use the new Windows Sidebar to add all sorts of cool gadgets to the side of your screen. As more and more people begin to use Windows Vista, you are going to see more and more cool performance monitoring gadgets. Already there are several great performance monitoring gadgets that dock on your sidebar that allow you to see all types of performance information, such as drive space and CPU and memory usage. You can find these gadgets on Microsoft's Windows Live Gallery at http://gallery.live.com in the Tools and Utilities section.

Benchmarking Your System

The term "benchmarking" refers to testing your computer and assigning some sort of score to your computer's configuration. The score can be an amount of time, such as the amount of time it takes your computer to solve a complex math problem. The score can also be a calculated point value that is determined by running a variety of tests, such as hard drive transfer speeds. The test can read and write files to your hard drive and then calculate a weighted score depending on how each test goes. The amount of time or calculated point value has very little value on its own; it is when the time or point value is compared to other results of the same test that it becomes valuable.

It is important to get an initial benchmark score for your computer so that you can compare your computer's initial performance to benchmark scores from tests that you may run at a later time. It would be nice to know how much of a difference some of the hacks in this book actually helped your system. Or, if you upgraded the amount of RAM your computer has, it would be helpful to see how it affected your system performance. By running an initial benchmark, you will have a score that you can compare all your benchmarks scores to after you make changes to your computer.

In order to benchmark your system, you will need the help of a benchmarking application. A wide variety of different software programs can benchmark just about every part of your system. If you are interested in benchmarking the abilities of your 3D video card, for example, there is software for that. If you are interested in benchmarking your hard disk speeds, there is special software for that task as well. Next, let's go over three popular benchmarking applications. I am going to start with the built-in Windows System Performance Rating.

Using the Windows System Performance Rating to Buy Compatible Software

In addition to providing a clearer picture of the performance of your hardware with Windows Vista, the Windows System Performance Rating simplifies the process of identifying software that will work with your hardware. Remember the days of having to look at the system requirements on the side of a software box? To make it easier for less technical computer users to select software that will work well with their hardware, there will be a Minimum performance rating on the box. Now even your parents can buy software and easily identify if it will run well on their computer. It sure beats trying to explain why that new computer game that requires the latest video card will not work on the old budget PC they have at home. If it requires a Performance Rating of a 5 and your system is a 2, it just is not going to work well, if it even works at all.

Windows System Performance Rating

Microsoft included this new feature in Windows Vista to make it easier for consumers to understand how powerful the combination of their hardware components actually is. The performance rating application generates an overall score based on the performance and features of your CPU, RAM, hard drive, and graphics card. For example, my computer has been given a score of 3 (see Figure 8-13). In addition to the overall score, you are also provided with individual component scores called the Sub Rating. These scores are useful to get a quick idea of the overall performance of your computer compared to other configurations.

FIGURE 8-13: Windows System Performance Rating

The exact method of scoring different hardware is unknown but is based on support of different levels of features and the performance of your hardware. For example, to get a score of 3, your hardware must support features x, y, and z, in addition to a minimal processor speed and amount of RAM and hardware performance level.

Using and understanding your performance rating

As I mentioned earlier, the overall score of your computer is useful to determine how your hardware compares to other configurations. However, the main purpose of the rating is to determine how well Windows Vista will run on your specific configuration of hardware. The Sub Ratings are the most useful for the purpose of identifying possible bottlenecks and areas that you should investigate further. To get started let's bring up the Performance and Rating Tools window for your computer:

1. Click the Start button to display the Start panel.

2. Right-click Computer and select Properties. This will load the new System Information window.

3. Locate the System section and click the Windows System Performance Rating link next to Rating to open the Performance and Rating Tools window, as shown in Figure 8-14.

4. If your computer does not yet have a rating assigned to it, click Refresh My Rating Now. This will start the rating tool and will take a few minutes while it generates scores based on performance tests and hardware specifications. It is best to not use your computer until the tests have completed to ensure accurate readings.

Tip   If you ever change or upgrade the hardware in your computer, you should refresh your ratings after every change. The score will not refresh automatically.

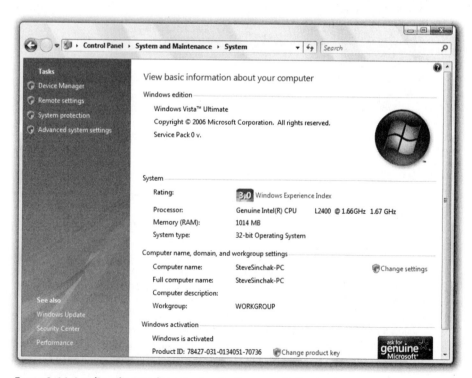

FIGURE 8-14: Loading the Windows System Performance Rating tool

Now that the Performance and Ratings Tools window is loaded and populated, you can analyze the results. I like to see if any of the numbers stand out as lower than my overall rating and may be holding back a higher overall score. For example, if all my Sub Ratings are between 3 to 5 except my Ram Sub Rating is much lower at a 1.2, then it becomes very clear that I should concentrate on determining if I should buy some more RAM.

Depending on your results, if you get a low score in the CPU, RAM, Hard Drive, or Graphics ratings, you should be able to determine what areas to focus on as you explore other more detailed monitoring tools next.

Benchmarking with PCMark05

PCMark05 Basic Edition, from Futuremark Corporation, is one of the most popular benchmarking programs for power users. PCMark05 has a cool online component that allows you to view your benchmark data and compare it to other users' computers. Additionally, the application generates an overall score that can be used to compare your system to other systems. The comprehensive score that is assigned to your system is the result of numerous test results testing various parts of your computer.

You can download a copy of PCMark05 from www.futuremark.com/download/.

The user interface of PCMark05 is very simple and is easy to use. Simply click the Run PCMark button to start the tests. The free version includes only basic tests that simulate various computer usages to come up with your overall score. The basic system tests include the following:

- **HDD XP Startup:** This test simulates Windows starting up.

- **Physics and 3D:** This test analyzes the 3D physics calculating capabilities of your system by running a simulation of a 3D game. A scene is played with falling bricks in a real-time 3D rendered environment. The test results are measured in frames per second.

- **2D - Transparent Windows:** This test measures the operation of application windows on your hardware. Various windows are drawn on the screen and are then faded in and out. The test measures the windows drawn per second.

- **3D Pixel Shader:** This test measures frames per second while doing a real-time 3D rendering of a rock surface using vertex lighting. This is another 3D game simulation to measure your gaming performance.

- **Web Page Rendering:** This is a 20-second test that calculates how many test web pages can be rendered during the test period. This test does not test your Internet connection.

- **File Decryption:** This test uses the Rijndael/AES encryption algorithm to test how fast various file types can be decrypted. The result is measured in megabytes per second.

- **2D Graphics Memory:** This test measure the performance of your graphics adapter memory and the subsystems that data travels through, such as the AGP bus. The test draws on a surface off-screen and then copies frame by frame to an onscreen surface. The result is measured in frames per second.

- **HDD General Use:** This test simulates common activities such as opening Word documents, compressing files, viewing pictures, and playing music.

- **Video Encoding and Audio Compression:** These are the first tests that measure how well your computer can do multiple things at once. The Video Encoding test measures the time it takes to encode a Windows Media Video (WMV) on your hardware, whereas the Audio Compression test compresses a music file into the Ogg Vorbis music format.

- **Text Edit and Image Decompression:** Wordpad is used to test primarily the CPU by performing search and replace operations on a text file. The result is measured in kilobytes per second processed. The Image Decompression runs at the same time and tests the performance of decoding compressed JPEG images. The result is measured in millions of pixels decompressed per second.

- **File Compression, Memory Latency, HDD Virus Scanning, and File Encryption:** File Compression tests the performance of using the Zlib compression library to compress various sizes and types of documents. The result is measured in megabytes processed per second. Memory latency tests measure the amount of time it takes to access data stored in memory. HDD Virus Scanning tests the hard drive performance by simulating an antivirus application. The File Encryption test uses the Rijndael/AES encryption algorithm to encrypt various file types. The encryption result is measured in megabytes per second. All these tests are run at the same time to test multitasking.

After you click the Run PCMark button, the system tests will begin, as shown in Figure 8-15.

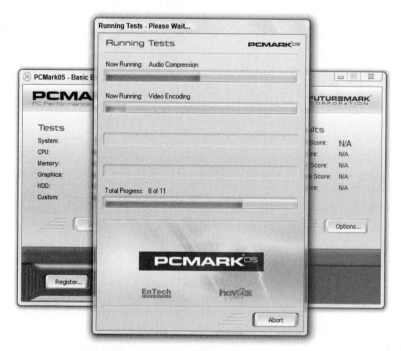

FIGURE 8-15: PCMark05 running the system benchmark test

After the benchmark tests have completed, you will be shown your system's overall score. To view the detailed scores of the different tests, you will have to register on Futuremark's Web site via the link on your results window. This is a slight letdown, but registering on the site enables you to compare your system against other systems. You can find out what hardware really performs and what hardware you should avoid. Overall, the PCMark05 Web site adds a great amount of value to the application.

Summary

This chapter offered an introduction to the world of performance monitoring and benchmarking. Before you can make your computer faster, it is very helpful to know what your computer doesn't perform well with. This chapter showed you how to discover bottlenecks using applications such as the Performance Diagnostic Console, Event Viewer, Task Manager, Windows Performance Rating, and PCMark05. Use the information that you gained in this chapter in the upcoming chapters. For example, if you have a lot of applications that are using a ton of memory, pay close attention to the recommended applications and services to disable in the upcoming chapters.

The next chapter will start to optimize the speed of your computer from the very beginning, the system boot.

Speeding Up the System Boot

When I installed Windows Vista on my computer, I noticed that it did not boot up as fast as Windows XP did. Now I understand that Windows Vista has higher system requirements than XP and during the boot it is loading a lot of new system components and driver models. However, that doesn't justify how slow it boots on my midrange hardware that satisfies all the new higher system requirements. The trend before Vista came along was a constant decrease in booting time. Windows XP booted up much faster than Windows 2000 did. Why is Vista not booting up faster than XP? Despite the Vista boot slowdown, this chapter guides you through the steps of getting it up-to-speed and shows you how to make Windows Vista boot up faster than XP.

Now don't get me wrong: Windows Vista has a lot of great new features and visual enhancements that make it the most feature-rich, stable, and pretty-looking version of Windows from Microsoft to date. However, with all the new features and attractive effects, the operating system has a higher system overhead, which means your hardware has to work even harder. If you are like me, and do not always have the fastest hardware, this chapter will help you get the most out of your current hardware by reducing the heavy workload put on it during the boot process.

Working with the BIOS

Every personal computer has a system *BIOS* (basic input/output system), which is what takes control of your computer the moment that you turn it on. The screen that you first see when you turn on your computer is called the *power on self-test screen*, better known as the *POST screen*. If you purchased your computer from one of the major computer manufacturers, this screen is often hidden by the manufacturer's logo. To get rid of this logo from the screen, just press the Esc button on your keyboard; you'll then see what is going on in the background. At this stage in the system boot, the BIOS is probing the hardware to test the system memory and other device connections. After the POST has completed, the BIOS proceeds to look for a device to boot from. When it finds your hard drive, it begins to load Windows.

☑ Changing the boot order of your drives

☑ Enabling quick boot BIOS features

☑ Modifying the system boot menu

☑ Disabling unneeded drivers and system services

☑ Removing unneeded fonts

☑ Defragmenting boot files

The BIOS also acts as a main hardware component control panel, where low-level settings for all your hardware devices are made. The device boot order, port addresses, and feature settings such as plug and play are all found in the BIOS setup screens. For example, if you want to change the order of the drives that your computer checks to boot from, you want to modify the device boot order. I have to modify this setting almost every time that I install Windows because I want my computer to boot off of the CD-ROM to launch the install DVD instead of booting off the operating system on my hard drive.

BIOSs on each and every PC may be made by different companies or accessed by a different method. Nevertheless, the most common way to access the setup screen is to press F2 or the Delete key when the POST screen is displayed. Some computers even tell you which key to push to access the setup screen, as my notebook does. If your PC doesn't allow you to access the setup screen in this way, consult your computer documentation or contact your computer manufacturer for instructions.

Caution While you are making changes in the system BIOS, make sure you do not accidentally change any other settings. If you accidentally change a value of a setting and do not know what to change it back to, just exit the BIOS setup screen as the onscreen directions indicate and select Do *Not* Save Changes. Then just reboot and reenter the setup screen and continue hacking away at your system.

Changing the boot order of your drives

Most computers are set up so that when you first turn on your computer it checks to see whether you want to boot from drives other than your hard drive. The BIOS automatically checks to see whether you have a bootable CD in your CD drive. If your computer has a floppy drive, it checks to see whether you have a bootable disk in the floppy drive, too. Then, after it has checked all possible locations for a boot disk, the system defaults to your hard drive set in the BIOS and starts booting Windows.

What is the benefit of changing the boot order of your system devices? If you modify the order of the boot devices so that the hard disk with Windows installed will be searched first by the BIOS, the system does not have to waste time checking other devices for boot records. Just by changing the order of the devices, you can shave anywhere from one to several seconds off of your boot time, depending on the speed of your hardware and number of drives your system has installed.

To change the boot order (or sequence, as some call it), you have to enter the system BIOS setup screen that was mentioned previously:

1. Press F2, Delete, or the correct key for your specific system on the POST screen (or the screen that displays the computer manufacturer's logo) to enter the BIOS setup screen.

2. Look for where it says Boot, and enter the submenu.

3. Select Boot Sequence, and press Enter. Figure 9-1 shows an example of the boot sequence screen.

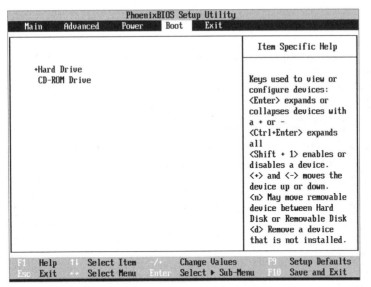

FIGURE 9-1: The boot sequence setup screen

4. If your screen looks similar to Figure 9-1, you are in the right place. Navigate to where it states "first device" and cycle through the list to where it states "Hard Disk Drive" or "IDE0" (assuming that your hard drive is connected to IDE0). If your setup screen does not specifically state "first device" but rather just a list of all the devices, simply select the hard disk and move it to the top of the list. That can be done by using the Change Values keys (which for my BIOS, which is made by Phoenix, is the spacebar to move an item up and the minus symbol key to move an item down). The specific keys differ on almost every system, but the basic concepts are the same. You want to get your hard disk to the top of the list or listed as the first device from which to try to boot. If you do not know the keys for your BIOS, there are usually instructions located on either the bottom or right side of the screen where you will be able to find the correct keys for your system.

5. After you have made the changes, exit the system BIOS by pressing the Escape key, and make sure that you select to save your changes upon exit. After you reboot, the new settings will be in effect.

What are the consequences of changing the boot order? Changing the boot order will not hurt your system in any way if you do it correctly. If by accident you remove your hard drive from the list and save the BIOS settings, you will get an unpleasant surprise when your computer reboots and tells you that it cannot find any operating system. If you happen to get that message, don't worry; you did not just erase your operating system. Just reboot by pressing Ctrl+Alt+Delete at the same time and go back into the BIOS settings and make sure that you select your hard drive as a boot device. After you have done that, your system will be back to normal.

Another possible issue that you might encounter is just a matter of inconvenience. After you change the boot order of the system devices so that the hard drive is listed first, you can no longer use system restore CDs or floppy boot disks. If something has happened to your computer and you need to boot off of those drives to restore your system or run diagnostics, just go back to the system BIOS and lower or remove the hard disk from the first boot device and replace it with either a floppy or CD as needed.

Using the Quick Boot feature of the BIOS

All systems initialize in more or less the same way. During the POST mentioned earlier, the BIOS checks the hardware devices and counts the system memory. Out of all the different types of system memory, the random access memory, better known as RAM, takes the longest to be checked. Checking the RAM takes time, and on a machine that has large amounts of RAM, this calculation can take several seconds. For example, a machine that has 512MB of RAM may take up to 3 seconds just to check the memory. On top of the RAM counting, a few other tests need to be done because your computer wants to make sure that all the hardware in your computer is working properly.

The complete version of these tests is not needed every time that you boot and can be turned off to save time. Most system BIOSs offer a feature called *Quick Boot*. This feature enables the user to turn off the full version of the test and sometimes enables you to run a shorter quick check test instead. Other BIOSs allow you to turn off the Memory Check only, which will still cut down on a lot of time.

To turn on the Quick Boot feature or to turn off the Memory Check, just do the following:

1. Enter the system BIOS again by pressing F2 or the correct system setup Enter key on the POST screen for your system.

2. After you are in the BIOS setup, locate the text "Quick Boot" or "Memory Check," as shown in Figure 9-2. Navigate with the arrow keys until the option is highlighted.

3. Use the Change Value keys to cycle through the options and select Enable for the Quick Boot feature or Disable if your system's BIOS has the Memory Check feature.

4. After you have made the change to the setting, exit the system BIOS by pressing the Escape key. Make sure you save the changes upon exit.

Use of the Quick Boot feature or the disabling of the Memory Check will not do any harm your system. In fact, some computer manufacturers even ship their computers with these settings already optimized for performance. The only downside to disabling the tests is in the rare situation in which your RAM self-destructs; the BIOS will not catch it, and you might receive errors from the operating system or your system could become unstable. If you notice that your system becomes unstable and crashes frequently or will not even boot, go back into the BIOS and re-enable the tests to find out whether your system's memory is causing the problems.

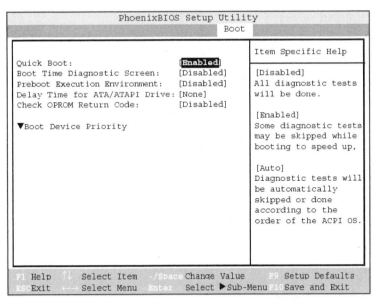

```
                    PhoenixBIOS Setup Utility
                                    Boot

                                          ┌─────────────────────────┐
                                          │  Item Specific Help      │
  Quick Boot:                  [Enabled]  │                          │
  Boot Time Diagnostic Screen: [Disabled] │  [Disabled]              │
  Preboot Execution Environment: [Disabled] │ All diagnostic tests   │
  Delay Time for ATA/ATAPI Drive: [None]  │ will be done.            │
  Check OPROM Return Code:     [Disabled] │                          │
                                          │  [Enabled]               │
  ▼Boot Device Priority                   │  Some diagnostic tests   │
                                          │  may be skipped while     │
                                          │  booting to speed up,    │
                                          │                          │
                                          │  [Auto]                  │
                                          │  Diagnostic tests will   │
                                          │  be automatically        │
                                          │  skipped or done         │
                                          │  according to the        │
                                          │  order of the ACPI OS.   │
                                          └─────────────────────────┘

  F1 Help    ↑↓ Select Item   -/Space Change Value     F9 Setup Defaults
  ESC Exit   ←→ Select Menu    Enter  Select ▶Sub-Menu F10 Save and Exit
```

FIGURE 9-2: BIOS setup screen displaying the Quick Boot feature

Modifying the Operating System Boot

You can use several different tricks to shave a few more seconds off the boot time. For example, you can reduce Timeout values and slim down the system to get rid of all the extra features and services that you do not use or need. Check out the following ways to do so.

Windows Boot Manager

If you have more than one operating system installed on your computer, you'll have to deal with the Windows Boot Manager installed by Windows Vista. By default, the Windows Boot Manager gives you 30 seconds to select an operating system before it reverts to the default operating system. The only way not to wait 30 seconds is to select the operating system you want to use right away. If you use one operating system the majority of your time, you will definitely save time if you set that operating system as the default and lower the Timeout value to 1 or 2 seconds. That way, you will not have to select an operating system every time you turn on your system or wait 30 seconds before your computer actually starts to load the operating system.

Tip

Before you make any changes to the Windows Boot Manager (WBM), it is a good idea to back it up using the Boot Configuration Data Editor (bcdedit.exe) so that you can easily revert back to an earlier version should you have any problems. At a command prompt running under an administrator account, type **bcdedit /export "C:\Backup File"**. This will save the WBM to a file that you can use to import using the /import flag.

Lowering OS Timeout values

As mentioned earlier, if you have multiple operating systems installed on your computer and the Windows Boot Manager is installed, the default selection timeout is often way too high. It is much better to set a lower timeout so that if you do not make a selection, it quickly reverts to the default OS, making your boot time much faster.

Changing the Timeout value is simple with the System Configuration utility. Follow the steps here to use the System Configuration utility to lower the OS Timeout value:

1. Click the Start button, type **msconfig** in the Search box, and press Enter.

2. When the System Configuration utility loads, click the Boot tab.

3. Locate the Timeout box and replace 30 with a much lower value, as shown in Figure 9-3. I recommend you use between 2 and 5. I use 2 because that gives me just the right amount of time to press a key on my keyboard when the Windows Boot Manager is displayed on the screen.

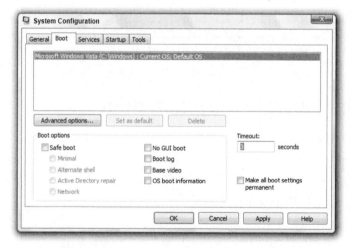

FIGURE 9-3: Setting the Boot menu Timeout value with the System Configuration utility

4. After the value has been updated, click OK to exit.

Now that the Timeout value has been updated, the Boot menu will no longer increase your system startup time. Even though this is a simple tip, it really helps a lot on systems that have multiple operating systems installed. Now let's look at setting the default operating system on the Windows Boot Manager.

Setting the default OS

In the preceding section, I set a new Timeout value that will cut down on the amount of time that is wasted before the operating system starts to load. That works great when your primary operating system is the default; but if it is not, you must remember to press a key at the right moment on every single boot. There is a much better way to handle the situation. Just make your primary operating system the default operating system in the Windows Boot Manager. This will allow you to benefit from the lower Timeout value and speed up the overall boot time.

Setting the default operating system is a little more difficult because you need to use the command-line Boot Configuration Editor, bcdedit.exe. The Boot Configuration Editor is part of Windows Vista, but it requires an account with administrative rights to run. Even if you are logged in with an account that has administrator rights but have user account control enabled, by default the tool will not run as administrator. Follow these steps to use the Boot Configuration Editor to set the default operating system:

1. Click the Start button and navigate through All Programs and Accessories.

2. Locate the Command Prompt shortcut and right-click it to bring up the context menu.

3. Select Run as administrator from the context menu.

4. When the command prompt has loaded, you are ready to use the bcdedit.exe command. First, you need to get the ID of the operating system that you want to set as the default. To do this, type **bcdedit /enum all** in the open command prompt window. Scroll through the list of different entries and look for the one with the description matching "Microsoft Windows" for Windows Vista.

5. After you have found the correct entry, note its identifier. That is used in the next step.

6. While still at the command prompt, run **bcdedit /default (entry identifier)**. For example, I ran bcdedit /default {b2721d73-1db4-4c62-bf78-c548a880142d}.

The default operating system on the Window Boot Manager is now set. The next time you reboot, your changes will be in use.

Tip The Boot Configuration Editor is a powerful utility that you can also use to change many other settings of the Windows Boot Manager. Experiment with bcdedit.exe by running `bcdedit /?` from command prompt. This will show you all the other available options and flags that you can use with the Boot Configuration Editor.

Disabling the system boot screen

Windows Vista has a new high-resolution boot screen that looks much better than the previous Windows boot screens. The aurora look sure is a nice loading screen but is it really worth an extra fraction of a second when your computer is loading? Disabling the boot screen can cut down on your boot time. Keep in mind that every fraction of a second counts. And when you apply all the performance hacks listed in this part of the book, you will see a definite performance increase.

Using VistaBootPro to Edit the Windows Boot Manager

VistaBootPro is a cool and easy-to-use front end to the Boot Configuration Editor. Instead of using the command-line interface, you can use this free utility written by Mahmoud H. Al-Qudsi, also known as Computer Guru at pro-networks.org. With VistaBootPro, you can change the Timeout value, default selection, description, and even the boot order, as shown in the accompanying figure. Download a free copy of VistaBootPro at www.pro-networks.org/vistabootpro/.

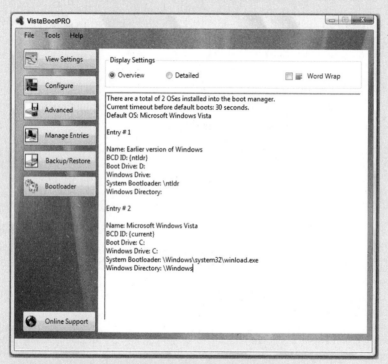

Using VistaBootPro to edit the Windows Boot Manager

This performance improvement works on a simple principle. It takes time for the computer to do anything. Taking away some work the hardware has to do, such as loading the boot screen, frees time that it can spend loading your system files instead.

The process for disabling the system boot screen is similar to the process for modifying the default operating system timeout. For this change, you need to start up the System Configuration tool:

1. Click the Start menu, type **msconfig** in the Search box, and press Enter.

2. When the System Configuration tool loads, click the Boot tab.

3. Locate the No GUI Boot check box and check it, as shown in Figure 9-4.

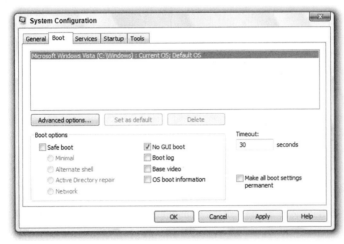

FIGURE 9-4: Disabling the boot screen with the System Configuration tool

4. Click OK to close the System Configuration tool.

5. A small window will pop up and ask you if you would like to reboot your computer now or reboot later. Make sure you have any open documents closed, and click Restart.

6. After your computer has restarted, the System Configuration Tool is going to load automatically, notifying you of the change. Check the box that says Don't show this message or start System Configuration when Windows starts and click OK.

After you close the System Configuration tool and reboot, the boot screen will be gone and you will have saved your computer from doing extra work while loading Windows Vista on your computer.

Disabling unneeded hardware devices

One of the most time-consuming portions of the boot is loading all the hardware drivers for your specific system setup. Every driver for each installed hardware device must be loaded and then initialized by the operating system while the system is starting up. Keep in mind that your computer has a lot of devices that you do not always use. When Windows has to load all the extra hardware on your computer, its performance is slowed down.

Although Windows Vista is more intelligent than previous versions on how it loads drivers and devices, loading those devices and initializing them still takes time. In previous versions of Windows, the system would load one hardware device driver and then load another device driver in a series. The problem with loading the hardware this way was that it could slow down the boot dramatically if one hardware device was taking a long time to initialize.

Windows Vista is similar to Windows XP in the way it loads device drivers and initializes the devices. Instead of loading the hardware device drivers in series, it now loads some of them in parallel. This allows the boot to be much faster. Although the hardware devices are loaded in parallel instead of series, the addition of more devices that the system has to load drivers for has the potential to, and most likely still will, slow down the boot.

Using Device Manager to disable hardware

Getting rid of extra hardware with Device Manager is an easy way to speed up your boot. Follow these steps to disable your extra hardware devices:

1. Click the Start menu, type **devmgmt.msc** in the Search box, and press Enter.

2. After the Device Manager loads, you can browse through your devices that are connected and currently running or disabled by browsing though the device type sections. To disable a device, right-click the device name, and then select Disable.

3. To re-enable a device, right-click the device name and select Disable, as shown in Figure 9-5. This removes the check mark from the menu and re-enables the device.

Tip To quickly determine the status of a device, check out the icon next to its name. All devices that are disabled have a down arrow over the icon. All devices that have a question mark or an explanation point on them are not set up correctly or are having problems. All devices with none of these additions to the icon are running — and doing so without any problems.

Which hardware devices should you disable?

Each user uses (or doesn't use) devices differently depending on the system setup. Nonetheless, some classes of devices are more commonly disabled than others. Knowing which ones will help you make your decision as to which devices you should disable. The following classes of devices are frequently disabled:

- **Network adapters:** Especially on notebook computers, there is often more than one network device. Disabling the network devices that you do not use will definitely save you some booting time.

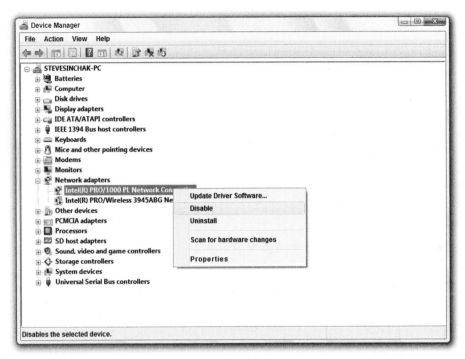

FIGURE 9-5: Disabling hardware with Device Manager

- **FireWire:** If you have 1394 connections, otherwise known as FireWire, you might consider disabling them. Unless you are using your FireWire port to connect your digital video recorder to your computer, or have other external FireWire devices, you have no need to have this device enabled.

- **Biometrics:** Some of the latest computer hardware includes biometric sensor equipment such as a fingerprint scanner. If you do not use these security features, you can save time by disabling these devices, too.

- **Modems:** Do you have a broadband connection? If so, consider disabling your modem. If you rarely use it, why not disable it? If you ever need to use it again, just re-enable it.

- **TPM security chips:** Does your computer have a Trusted Platform Module (TPM)? These chips are typically used as a secure place to store an encryption key that would be used for something such as hard drive encryption. If you are not using any of these advanced security features of Windows Vista, disable these devices, too.

- **Multimedia devices:** Your computer has lots of multimedia devices. Take a look at the "Sound, video, and game controllers" section in Device Manager. You will find a lot of device drivers that are loaded during your boot. Some are used by all users, but you will find a few that you do not use. For example, I do not use my game port or my MIDI device, so I disabled both of those.

- **PCMCIA cards:** If you are a laptop user, consider disabling your PCMCIA card controller located under "PCMCIA adapters." The PCMCIA (Personal Computer Memory Card International Association) slot is a special expansion slot that is rarely used today on laptops except for wireless and wired network cards and card reader attachments for compact flash and other solid-state memory cards. Most laptops now have built-in network adapters, and some even have built-in wireless adapters. If you do not use your PCMCIA adapter, it is yet another device you can safely disable.

Do not disable any hardware devices located under the Disk Drives, Computer, Display Adapters, IDE Disk Controllers, and the System sections (except for the system speaker). These hardware devices are critical to the operation of your system.

Removing extra fonts for speed

Windows Vista has more than 200 different fonts and variations that it loads for use when the system boots up. Of these 200-plus fonts, only a handful are used on a regular basis. Every single font that Windows loads increases the amount of time the operating system takes to boot. If you are like me and have installed one of those font CDs that add hundreds of additional fonts to your system, you will notice that your computer does not boot up as fast as it once did. Simply put, systems with a lot of fonts will take more time to load because the system has to load and index each font. Thankfully, there is a very simple answer to this: Just remove the fonts that you do not use from your font directory.

You can go about removing the unneeded fonts from your font directory in a number of different ways. The best way is to move the unused fonts to a separate folder on your system so that in the event that you ever want to use one of those extra fonts again, you just have to copy it back to the Fonts folder.

When you remove fonts from your computer, you will no longer be able to use them in any software application, including Adobe Photoshop, Microsoft Word, and Excel.

Before you start removing fonts, take at look at Table 9-1. These fonts are commonly used, for reasons that the table explains. Be careful not to remove any fonts on which the system normally depends.

Now that you know which fonts you should not remove, you also need to be aware of one more thing before starting your adventure in the Fonts folder. Inside the Fonts folder are several fonts with similar names. The fonts are broken up not only by font name but also by the type style. For example, there is an Arial Bold, Arial Bold Italic, Arial Italic, and so on. When sorting through the fonts to delete, you also can choose to delete only specific types of fonts.

Table 9-1   Commonly Used Windows Fonts

Font Name	Reason
Segoe	The variations of this font can be found in elements of the Windows interface.
Verdana	This font is often used on web pages and applications.
Arial	Another common web page font, and used in applications.
Trebuchet	Common application font and used in some web pages back in XP days. Some older applications may still require it.
Tahoma	Common Windows font that you may want to hold on to for application and web page compatibility.
Times New Roman	The default font for web pages and word processing applications such as Microsoft Word.
MS Sans Serif	Default font for Visual Studio applications that is now required for a lot of legacy and newer applications.

Deleting fonts is fairly easy. But removing the fonts is a little trickier because the Fonts folder is not like a normal folder. To remove the fonts, you need to start off by creating a folder to put the old fonts in:

1. Click the Start button and select Computer. Navigate to the Local Disk (C:) or where you have installed Windows.

2. Navigate to the Windows folder and create a folder to store the fonts that you are going to remove from the Fonts folder. Right-click the white space that lists the folder and files, select New, and then select Folder. Call your folder **Fonts Backup** or some other name so that you will be able to identify that this is the place where your old fonts are.

3. After you have created the new folder, open it.

4. Without closing the new folder you just opened, click the Start button again and select Computer. Navigate to the Local Disk (C:) drive again and to the Windows folder, and then to the Fonts folder.

5. Now that you have both the Fonts folder open and your backup folder open, arrange the two windows on your screen so that they look like the two windows in Figure 9-6.

6. Now that the two font folders are side by side, drag the fonts you want to back up to your backup folder while holding the Ctrl key down on your keyboard.

7. After you have backed up the fonts you want to delete, right-click the font files in the Fonts folder and select Delete.

FIGURE 9-6: The Windows Fonts folder and a backup folder are arranged side by side on the screen

In the event that you want to reinstall a font, all you have to do is drag the font file from the backup folder back to the Fonts folder. An installation dialog box will flash just for a second as it adds the font back to the library. After you drag the file back to the Fonts folder, the file will still remain in the backup directory because it just copies it there. After you have confirmed that it was actually installed again, feel free to delete the font file from the backup folder.

Disabling unneeded services

A *service* is a software application that runs continuously in the background while your computer is on. The Windows operating system has numerous services that run in the background that provide basic functions to the system. Network connectivity, visual support, and external device connectivity such as printer services are all examples of the types of services that the Windows services provide. Each service that is running in the background takes up system resources, such as memory and CPU time. Also, during the booting of the operating system, the service has to be loaded. On most computers, there are nearly 20 services that are loaded upon startup. Of these 20 services, only a handful are system-critical services; all the others can be disabled.

To disable a service, you first need to know more about what the services in Windows Vista do. Table 9-2 will help you understand what the most common services are, what they do, and whether they can be disabled. The services marked in bold are started by default in Windows Vista.

Table 9-2   Common Windows Services in Use

Name	Use
Net Runtime Optimization v2.0	Increases the performance of applications written in the .Net 2.0 Framework. It is run only when needed.
Application Experience	Provides a compatibility cache for older applications that cache requests when they are run. This service can be disabled, but I recommend leaving it started for application compatibility with the new architecture of Windows Vista.
Application Information	Allows you to run applications with all administrative rights. Keep this service running.
Application Layer Gateway	Provides support for additional protocols for the Internet Connection Sharing service. This service can be safely disabled.
Application Management	Used for software deployment and management through Group Policy. If you do not use Group Policy for software, you can safely disable this service.
Background Intelligent Transfer	Transfers data in the background when the connection is not in use. One use of this service is to download updates automatically in the background. This service is not system critical but can impair other services such as Windows Update if it is disabled.
Base Filtering Engine	Provides support for the firewall, IPsec, and filtering. I recommend keeping this service running.
Block Level Backup Engine	Provides support for data block–level backups.
Bluetooth Support	Provides support for Bluetooth wireless devices. Disable this service if you do not use Bluetooth devices with your computer.
Certificate Propagation	Utilizes certificates from smart cards. Most users have no use for this service.
CNG Key Isolation	Isolates cryptographic operations to protect the cryptographic key. I recommending leaving this service as is because it runs only when needed.
COM+ Event System	Provides event notification to COM objects. Some applications depend on this service. I recommend experimenting with your applications to see whether you can disable it.
COM+ System Application	Used to configure and monitor COM object components. Leave as manual because it is started only when needed.
Computer Browser	Responsible for keeping the list of computers on your network and updating the list. If you have no need for this information, you can safely disable it if started.

Continued

Table 9-2 *Continued*

Name	Use
Cryptographic Services	The main provider of all encryption and encryption operations for all types of applications. It manages private keys, certificates, and other encryption operations. I recommend leaving this service running.
DCOM Server Process Launcher	Starts DCOM processes. Several other system-critical services use this service to start, so I do not recommend disabling it.
Desktop Windows Manager Session Manager	This service is behind the new Windows Vista "glass" look and enhanced desktop features. If your hardware does not support the new "glass" look, I suggest disabling this service.
DFS Replication	In charge of file replication as part of the Distributed File System framework. If you use offline file replication, do not disable this service.
DHCP Client	Provides automatic network address configuration. If you set a static IP address, gateway, and DNS servers, disable this service.
Diagnostic Policy	Provides automatic problem monitoring and troubleshooting of components. If this service is disabled, automatic diagnostics and searching for resolutions will be stopped. If you are an advanced user, you might be able to get away with disabling this service.
Diagnostic Service Host	Diagnostic Policy service helper service that is run only when necessary.
Diagnostic System Host	Diagnostic Policy service helper service that is run only when necessary.
Distributed Link Tracking Client	Used with NTFS file links across networks. If you have no need for this service, and not many do, you can safely disable it.
Distributed Transaction Coordinator	Provides support for managing transactions generated by applications. Some applications use this service, but it is not running unless it is in use.
DNS Client	Provides the computer the ability to resolve a DNS address such as www.TweakVista.com to an IP address as needed by web browsers and other Internet tools. Unless your computer is not connected to the Internet or any other type of network, you should keep this service enabled.
EapHost	The Extensible Authentication Protocol Host provides authentication support to the Wired AutoConfig and WLAN AutoConfig services. Unless you use all manual network configurations, leave this service enabled.

Table 9-2   *Continued*

Name	Use
Fax	Provides support to send and receive faxes. No need for faxes? Disable this service.
Function Discovery Provider Host	Hosts other services that search the network for other devices such as the Media Center Extender service. If you have no need for these services, disable this service.
Function Discovery Resource Publication	Allows this computer and devices connected to it to be published over the network so that other computers on your LAN can share them.
Group Policy Client	Responsible for applying local and domain-based group policy settings and restrictions. This service cannot be disabled in Windows Vista.
Health Key and Certificate Management	Manages the keys used by Network Access Protection. Disable this if your network is not using any sort of authentication-based access.
IKE and AuthIP IPsec Keying Modules	Manages the keys used by IP Security (IPsec) network access. Disable this if your network is not using any sort of authentication-based network access.
Interactive Services Detection	Provides notification and access to interactive dialog boxes. Do not disable this service.
Internet Connection Sharing (ICS)	When started, this service allows you to share your Internet connection among other computers with Network Address Translation (NAT).
IP Helper	Provides IPv6 (Internet Protocol version 6) connectivity over an IPv4 network. Disable this service if you have no use for IPv6 network connections.
KtmRM for Distributed Transaction Coordinator	This is a helper service that aids in the communication between the Distributed Transaction Coordinator and the Kernel Transaction Manager.
Link-Layer Topology Discover Mapper	Provides a generated network map of all computers and other connected devices.
Media Center Extender	Allows Media Center Extender hardware and software devices, such as an Xbox 360, to connect to your computer and share the Media Center features if installed. Disable this service if you have no use for this scenario.
Media Center Receiver	Provides the Media Center application with TV and radio reception.

Continued

Table 9-2   *Continued*

Name	Use
Media Center Scheduler	Provides the Media Center application with notification of when to start and stop recording an application.
Media Center Service Launcher	Launches the Media Center Receiver and Scheduler service when the Media Center application is started. All the Media Center services remain disabled when the Media Center application is stopped.
Microsoft Digital Identity	Provides Windows with the ability to manage digital user identity cards.
Microsoft iSCSI Initiator	Manages connections to iSCSI-connected network devices.
Microsoft Software Shadow Copy Provider	Provides Shadow Copy file operations when needed by applications such as Explorer.
Multimedia Class Scheduler	Helps multimedia applications by prioritizing CPU loads of various system-wide processes and tasks.
Net. Tcp Port Sharing	Allows Windows to share TCP ports over the network. This service is disabled by default in Windows Vista.
Netlogon	Responsible for the connection between the domain controller and your computer if your computer is on a domain. Disable this service if your computer is not on a domain.
Network Access Protection Agent	Primary service for supporting the NAP (Network Access Protection) services.
Network connections	Provides the user with the graphics interface to manage all network connections. If this service is disabled, Network & Sharing Center will not work. I recommend against disabling this service.
Network List	Manages a list of networks the computer has connected to and their individual settings and properties.
Network Location Awareness	Manages a list of networks the computer has connected to and their individual settings and properties.
Network Store Interface	Provides notification of network interface changes. This service is critical to network operation but can be disabled if you do not use a network.
Offline Files	Provides file operations for the offline files feature of Windows Explorer. Feel free to disable this service if you do not use this feature.
Parental Controls	Provides parental rating controls on games, software. and other aspects of Windows Vista. Disabling this will shut down any parental controls.

Table 9-2   *Continued*

Name	Use
Peer Name Resolution Protocol	Allows your computer to resolve names using peer-to-peer connections. This is required by applications such as Windows Collaboration.
Peer Networking Grouping	Provides peer-to-peer networking services. Depends on the Peer Name Resolution Protocol service.
Peer Networking Identify Manager	Provides peer-to-peer identification services for application and Windows peer-to-peer applications. This service also depends on the Peer Name Resolution Protocol.
Performance Logs & Alerts	Collects performance data for use in Windows Diagnostics and other troubleshooting utilities.
Plug and Play	Allows the computer to automatically detect and configure computer hardware. Several other services depend on this service to be running to operate.
PNP-x IP Bus Enumerator	Detects devices on the virtual network bus. It runs only when the service is needed.
PNRP Machine Name Publication	Broadcasts the computer name using the Peer Name Resolution Protocol.
Policy Agent	Responsible for enforcing IPsec policies. You can safely disable this service if your network does not require IPsec authentication.
Portable Device Enumerator	Provides support for portable storage devices, such as USB devices and MP3 players, to communicate with other Windows components such as Windows Media Player. You can safely disable this service if you do not use any such devices.
Print Spooler	Allows you to save your print services to memory to allow for faster printing within your Windows applications. This service can be disabled but may impair printing in some situations.
Problem Reports and Solutions Control Panel Support	Provides support in the Control Panel to view and delete problem reports generated by the Diagnostic services.
Program Compatibility Assistant	Aids in application compatibility. When this service is disabled, you can no longer run applications properly in Compatibility mode. This service is not system critical.
Protected Storage	Provides secure storage support to protect data.
Quality Windows Audio Video Experience	Provides support for audio and video streaming over home networks with traffic prioritization. This service runs only when it is needed by an application.

Continued

Table 9-2 *Continued*

Name	Use
ReadyBoost	Allows you to use USB storage devices to increase the performance of your computer. If you do not want to use this feature of Windows Vista, you can safely disable it.
Remote Access Auto Connection Manager	Automates the creation of connections when applications attempt to access remote computers.
Remote Access Connection Manager	Provides support for modem dial-up connections and VPN connections made through the Windows Networking features.
Remote Procedure Call (RPC)	Responsible for communication between COM components. It is not system critical but is used by dozens of other Windows services. I do not recommend disabling this one.
Remote Procedure Call (RPC) Locator	A helper service for the Remote Procedure Call service that manages connections and lookup of components in its database.
Remote Registry	Provides remote access to your computer's registry when running. It is safe to disable this service.
Routing and Remote Access	Provides network traffic routing to incoming and outgoing traffic. This service is disabled by default.
Secondary Logon	Allows you to run applications using a different account. This is often used when it is necessary to start a program with an administrator account. I recommend leaving this service running.
Security Accounts Manager	Acts as a database of account information that is used for authentication and validation. This is a system-critical service that should not be disabled.
Security Center	Monitors of all your security applications such as antivirus and malware protection. This service is also responsible for notification messages that can drive advanced Windows users crazy. Feel free to disable this service.
Server	Allows you to share files, printers and other devices over your network. This is not a system-critical service but is often useful in a home network environment and in the enterprise.
SL UI Notification	Software Licensing and Activation service. This service is run only when needed.
Smart Card	Keeps track of smart cards that your computer has used.
Smart Card Removal Policy	Provides the ability to monitor your smart card and lock your computer when your smart card is removed.

Table 9-2   *Continued*

Name	Use
SNMP Trap	Processes messages received by the Simple Network Management Protocol.
Software Licensing	Provides support for the digital licenses for software that are downloaded. The SL UI Notification service depends on this and on ReadyBoost.
SSDP Discovery	Looks on your network using the SSDP protocol to detect other compatible networked devices such as game consoles and extender devices. This service can be disabled but will affect Media Center Extenders in addition to other PnP network devices.
Superfetch	Provides caching of application information to speed up application loading. This service can be disabled, but its benefits outweigh the initial performance decrease of loading the service.
System Event Notification	Monitors system events and reports back to other COM components.
Tablet PC Input	Provides software support for Tablet PC's pen device and the use of ink in Windows applications. Disable this service if it is running and you do not have a Tablet PC.
Task Scheduler	Allows you to schedule processes to run at specified intervals. Windows Vista uses this service for all background maintenance, which will stop if this service is disabled. I do not recommend disabling this service.
TCP/IP NetBIOS Helper	Provides NetBIOS protocol support over a TCP/IP connection. This is primarily used for machine name resolutions over a LAN.
Telephony	Provides support for applications to interact with the modem.
Terminal Services	Enables you to remotely connect to your computer using a remote desktop connection. If you do not use this feature, this can be safely disabled. However, disabling this will also disable any Media Center Extender devices you may have.
Terminal Services Configuration	A helper service for Terminal Services that is run only when needed.
Terminal Service UserMode Port Redirector	Another helper for the Terminal Services service. It provides the ability to share files, printers, and the Clipboard between the remote computers. Like the other helper service, this service is run only when needed.

Continued

Table 9-2 *Continued*

Name	Use
Themes	Provides support for visual styles that enable the non-classic Windows look. Disabling this service will result in the entire interface reverting to the classic Windows look.
Thread Ordering Server	Provides thread management and prioritization for Windows applications and components. Disabling this service may break applications and will also disable the Windows Audio service.
TPM Base Services	Provides access to the Trusted Platform Module used to store encryption keys and other important authentication information. It is run only when needed and is not available on computers that do not have a TPM chip.
UPnP Device Host	Provides the ability to host UPnP devices on your computer for use on your local network. This service is required for Windows Media Player library sharing.
User Profile	This is a system-critical service that loads your user profile when you sign on.
Virtual Disk	Responsible for managing your drives and file systems. Do not disable this service; it is required for many operating system requests. In addition, it does not run when it is not needed.
Volume Shadow Copy	Provides support for Shadow Copy hard drive data used by backup applications.
WebClient	Provides support for the WebDAV protocol for accessing remote servers over the Internet through Explorer. If you have no need for this protocol, this service can be safely disabled.
Windows Audio	Provides audio to Windows Vista. I do not recommend disabling this unless you do not like audio. But who doesn't like audio?
Windows Audio Endpoint Builder	A helper service for Windows Audio that manages the various audio-related hardware in your computer.
Windows Backup	Part of the Backup application in Windows Vista that allows you to easily back up your documents and other important data.
Windows Color System	Allows other applications to configure your monitor color settings in Windows Vista.
Windows Connect Now - Config Registrar	Part of the Windows Connect Now feature that lets you automate the addition of other computers on your wireless network by saving the configuration of one machine to a USB flash drive and then using it to set up new PCs.

Table 9-2   *Continued*

Name	Use
Windows Defender	The new spyware protection application in Windows Vista. If you have a different anti-spyware utility that you use, feel free to disable this service.
Windows Driver Foundation	Supports drivers in the User mode.
Windows Error Reporting	When things go bad, this service lets you check with Microsoft to see whether it has a solution for you and to notify Microsoft of what is happening to your computer. Don't feel like notifying Microsoft about your error messages? This service can be safely disabled.
Window Event Collector	Provides the ability to subscribe to remote event sources to monitor activity and store the data.
Windows Event Log	This is the primary source of all local event management and collection. This service can be stopped but is used by a lot of the performance enhancements in Windows Vista so stopping it would result in a negative performance benefit.
Windows Firewall	Provides network security by blocking inbound and outbound network access based on the firewall rules applied. Unless you have a third-party firewall application that you use, do not disable this service; the benefits outweigh any performance decrease.
Windows Image Acquisition (WIA)	Provides an interface used by applications to work with various types of scanners and cameras. This service is run only when needed.
Windows Installer	Allows applications packaged into MSI files to be installed and uninstalled from your computer. Do not disable this service unless you do not want any software to be installed, uninstalled, or modified.
Windows Management Instrumentation	Provides an interface for scripts and other applications to control various components of Windows Vista. Disabling this service will result in the Internet Connection Sharing, IP Helper, and Security Center services stopping, too. If you do not use these services, feel free to safely disable this service.
Windows Media Player Network Sharing	Provides the ability to share your music collection with other computers running Windows Media Player. This service requires the UPnP Device Host service to be running to function.

Continued

Table 9-2 *Continued*

Name	Use
Windows Modules Installer	Allows Windows components and security updates to be installed and uninstalled.
Windows Presentation Foundation Font Cache	Similar to the .Net Optimization service in that it is designed to increase the performance of Windows Presentation Foundation applications.
Windows Remote Management (WS-Management)	Provides support for the WS-Management protocol to remotely manage your computer.
Windows Search	Provides the ability to index your various files on your computer. This service can be disabled, but it will slow down any searches in your computer because the entire drive must be searched every time instead of just the index.
Windows Time	Responsible for syncing up the time on your computer. It can be safely disabled.
Windows Update	Provides the ability to detect and download new updates for your copy of Windows Vista. Disabling this service will stop both automatic updates and the ability to manually update Windows. Because security patches and automatic updates have been so critical to Windows in the past, I suggest keeping this service started.
WinHTTP Web Proxy Auto-Discovery	Provides an API for applications both to make HTTP connections and to auto-detect connection settings. This service is not system critical and can safely be disabled if you do not use the auto-detect connection feature in Internet Explorer and none of your applications use its API.
Wired AutoConfig	Manages your wired NIC connections, including support for 802.1X authentication. The Network and Sharing Center in Windows Vista may malfunction if this service is disabled. This service can be disabled if you do not use the Network and Sharing Center.
WLAN AutoConfig	Manages your wireless network connections and settings. The Networking Center in Windows Vista may malfunction if this service is disabled. This service can be disabled if you do not use the Network and Sharing Center.
WMI Performance Adapter	A helper service for the Windows Management Instrumentation service that runs only when requested.
Workstation	Provides support for creating network connections using the SMB network protocol (a.k.a. Lanman). Disabling this service disables Windows File Sharing.

Disabling services with the Services utility

Now that you have an understanding of the dozens of services in Windows Vista, you can start disabling the services that are not needed for your computer usage and that are slowing down your computer boot process. To do this, you will use the Services utility that enables you to start, stop, and configure Windows Vista services.

Tip   Before you begin changing your service setup, set a system restore point to easily restore your system to an earlier configuration. However, be careful when you restore from restore points. Any applications or files that were created after the system restore point will be deleted when reverting back to an earlier restore point.

The Services utility is included in all versions of Windows Vista, but is hidden away. Disabling a service with the Services utility is easy. Just complete the following steps:

1. Click the Start button, type **services.msc** in the Search box, and press Enter. This will start the Services utility, as shown in Figure 9-7.

2. When the Services utility has loaded, you will see a list of all the services available on your computer and which ones are started. Before you can disable a service from starting up, it is best to stop it first. Scroll through the list of services until you find the name of the one you want to disable. Right-click the service name and select Stop.

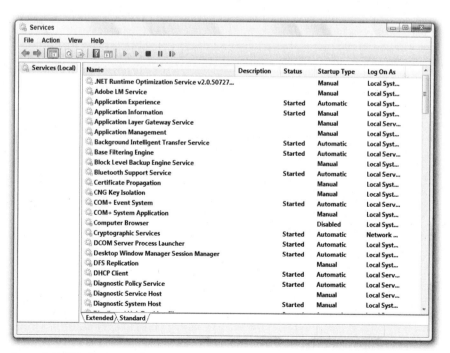

FIGURE 9-7: The Services utility

3. When the service is stopped, right-click the service again and select Properties. On the General tab, look for the Startup Type drop-down box. Click the arrow on the drop-down box and select Disabled.

4. Click OK. From now on, the system will not start the service any more during boot, which should speed up your system start.

Bare-Bones Service Configuration

To get the maximum performance out of your system, you have the option of disabling all the services on your computer that are not critical to the system. This will take away a lot of the nice features and conveniences of Windows, but you would have a much faster machine. The following is a list of all services that started by default in Windows Vista and can be safely disabled:

Application Experience

Application Information

Background Intelligent Transfer

Base Filtering Engine

Bluetooth Support

Desktop Window Manager Session Manager

DHCP Client

Diagnostic Policy

Diagnostic System Host

Distributed Link Tracking Client

EAPHost

Function Discover Provider Host

Group Policy Client

IKE and AuthIP IPsec Keying Modules

IP Helper (if you are not connected to an IPv6 network)

Multimedia Class

Network Connections

Network List

Network Location Awareness

Offline Files

Policy Agent

Portable Device Enumerator

Program Compatibility Assistant

ReadyBoost

Routing and Remote Access

Security Center

Server

SSDP Discovery

Superfetch

Tablet PC Input (if you do not have a Tablet PC)

TCP/IP NetBIOS Helper

Terminal Services

Themes

WebClient

Windows Audio

Windows Audio Endpoint Builder

Windows Defender

Windows Error Reporting Service

Windows Firewall

Windows Management Instrumentation

Windows Search

Windows Time

Windows Update

WinHTTP Web Proxy Auto-Discovery

Workstation

Recommended service configuration

The barebones system service setup is great for optimal performance, but you are eliminating a lot of the cool new features that make Windows Vista new and cool. Check out my list of recommended services to disable:

- Bluetooth Support
- DHCP Client (assign yourself a static IP address)
- Diagnostic Policy
- Diagnostic System Host
- Distributed Link Tracking Client
- EAPHost
- Function Discovery Provider Host
- Group Policy Client
- IKE and AuthIP IPsec Keying Modules
- IP Helper (if you are not on an IPv6 network)
- Offline Files
- Policy Agent
- Routing and Remote Access
- SSDP Discovery
- Tablet PC Input
- WebClient
- Windows Search
- WinHTTP Web Proxy Auto-Discovery

Disabling these least commonly used services provides a good balance between saving boot time while keeping the cool new Windows Vista features and application compatibility.

Optimizing the location of the boot files

The speed at which your files are read depends on your physical hard drive access speed and where the files are located in your hard drive. To increase the speed of your boot, you want to have the files used to boot your computer in a location that will allow the fastest read speed possible.

Windows Vista does a good job of this from a fresh install, but over time as your hard drive fills up and you make changes to the configuration of Windows, some of your boot files can become scattered all over inside the hard drive, resulting in a slower possible read speed. In addition, adding new applications and new hardware can contribute to this even further. Over time, your original boot optimization fades away as your internal hard drive data makeup changes.

Using Windows Vista Disk Defragmenter

Starting with Windows XP and continuing in Windows Vista, the Prefetcher service will automatically optimize the location of the boot files in your hard drive using Windows Disk Defragmenter. However, this occurs only after a certain number of boots and when it gets around to it (because it runs only when your computer is idle).

Microsoft has a talented team working on the Prefetcher service that even took into consideration your system boot changes. For example, you might install an updated device driver or add new hardware. To solve this problem, the systems will re-defragment the boot files every three days.

Windows keeps track of the last time that it has optimized the boot file so that it can calculate how often it should run the boot defrag. If you are interesting in finding when the last time was that the boot defrag was run, open regedit and navigate to HKEY_LOCAL_MACHINE\ SOFTWARE\Microsoft\Windows NT\CurrentVersion\Prefetcher, and then look for the key named LastDiskLayoutTimeString.

An operating system that takes care of itself? Yes, Windows is getting smarter and smarter. However, there is still one problem: There is no possible way to directly initiate a boot defrag. The only way is to leave your computer on for a little while without using it at all. If you are impatient and do not want to wait, I have a solution for you.

As I mentioned earlier, the system will initiate the boot defrag only when the system is idle. Typing in a command that will start the boot is not possible. However, you can tell your computer, even when it is not idle, to process the idle tasks. This will indirectly start the boot defrag. Because the boot defrag is most likely not the only idle task waiting to be run, other processes will be run, too, which can cause your computer to appear to be doing a lot of hard work — from a few minutes up to half an hour — as it completes all tasks. During this time, your computer should not be used for any intensive activities such as playing games. If you try to use your computer while the idle tasks are being processed, you will notice slow performance until the tasks are completed.

Perform the following steps to process all idle tasks:

1. Click the Start button, type **cmd** in the Search box, and press Enter.

2. When the command prompt opens, type **Rundll32.exe advapi32.dll,ProcessIdleTasks** and press Enter. Your computer will now work on the tasks.

Performing these steps will allow your system to defrag the boot files; however, the boot defrag is done every three days. Processing the idle tasks more frequently will do nothing to help you boot because the boot defrag will not be on your idle tasks lists all the time.

Using other third-party boot defrag programs

The built-in boot defragmenter is pretty darn good. However, a few third-party defrag utilities think they can do it better. To name a couple, Diskeeper and O&O Defrag both offer boot defragmentation support. Third-party defrag utilities often use different defrag algorithms that they believe work best. In the next section, I show you how to use Diskeeper to run a boot defrag.

Boot-time system defrag with Diskeeper 2007

To defragment system files, and other files that are normally in use, the defragmentation must be run during the early stages of system boot. This will allow the defrag program to have full access to all files so that it can place them together on the disk. One programs that allows this to be done is called Diskeeper, which was developed by Executive Software. A trial copy of Diskeeper 2007 can be found on Executive Software's Web site (www.Diskeeper.com). If you have not already installed Diskeeper, do so now before proceeding any further. After you have it downloaded and installed, follow these steps:

1. Click the Start Button, type **Diskeeper**, and press Enter.

2. When Diskeeper 2007 loads, click Action, expand Volume Properties, and select Boot-Time Defragmentation.

3. Boot-Time Defrag Properties will now load. Select the drive where your OS is installed, usually C. You can also select multiple drives by holding down Ctrl and clicking them. This is useful if you may have applications that are stored on a drive different than where your OS is stored.

4. Under the Boot Time Defragmentation section, select Enable boot-time defragmentation to run on the selected volumes, as shown in Figure 9-8.

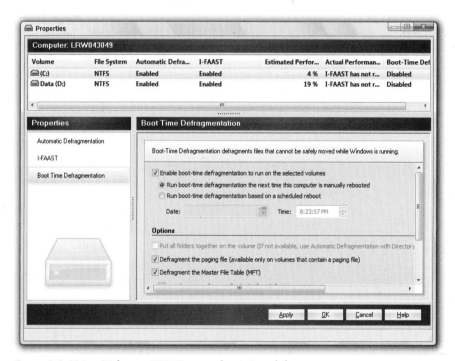

FIGURE 9-8: Using Diskeeper 2007 to run a boot-time defrag

5. Check Defragment the Master File Table (MFT), too.

6. Press OK and reboot your computer.

Caution

If you have enabled the alternate book screen, as shown in Chapter 1, you may have issues with running a boot-time defrag with Diskeeper. In current versions, the defrag status will be hidden from view behind the alternate boot screen. If you want to see the status of the defrag, disable the alternate boot screen, as shown in Chapter 1.

When you reboot your computer, you will notice that instead of loading into Windows all the way, Diskeeper will run in a pre-Windows environment so that it can have full access to your disks before any system files load. Depending on the size of your hard drive, the defragmentation process can take hours. It is best to do a boot-time defrag overnight.

Summary

This chapter showed you many ways to reduce the amount of time it takes your computer to boot. First, you worked on changing some of the BIOS settings that would optimize your computer for maximum boot speed. Then, I showed you how you can remove your boot screen to shave off some more time. After that, I went over how you can disable other parts of Windows, such as hardware, fonts, and services that you may never use, which all take up time when your computer starts up. To wrap up the chapter, I showed you how you can optimize the placement of the files used when your computer boots using the Prefetcher service and a third-party disk defragment tool.

This chapter showed you how to speed up the first half of your computer's startup. The next chapter picks up on the second half, the system logon. I show you some cool tips on how you can speed it up, too.

Making Your Computer Log On Faster

E ver wonder why it takes your computer so long to start up after you log on? After all, the system already loaded the majority of the operating system components. Does your computer take longer to load after you sign on than it used to take when you first brought it home? These are all questions that you will find the answers to in this chapter. You can make your system load faster by using a number of cool tweaks and hacks. The last chapter touched on how to make the system boot faster. This chapter concentrates on how to make the system load faster after the operating system has loaded and you are presented with the welcome sign-on screen.

After you turn on your computer, it goes through the boot-up process, which loads the main system components and drivers. Eventually, when those are finished loading, the Windows shell is started and you are presented with the sign-on screen. After the welcome screen is displayed and you sign on, the system begins to load your user profile settings and the rest of the Windows shell. After that is finished loading, the system runs your applications that are in the startup folder as well as other sneaky Registry startup programs. When these applications are finished loading, your mouse will no longer display the hourglass and you are set to do whatever you want with your computer.

This chapter begins by examining ways to speed up the logon process. Then it discusses how to get rid of all those extra applications that run at startup that further slow down your computer. When you have finished reading this chapter, your system will have a much faster loading time.

Speeding Up the Logon

As I just mentioned, a lot occurs when you log on to your computer. Windows has to validate your password, load your profile settings, apply the settings, and then launch any additional applications that are registered to start automatically. That's a lot of areas to fine-tune to allow for a faster logon. To get started, let's take a look at automatic logon.

Enabling automatic logon

If you are the primary user of your computer and you do not have any other users, or if everyone in your household uses the same username, you are the perfect candidate for enabling automatic logon. Automatic logon is a great technique that will save you time that is often wasted when your computer is waiting for you to type your password. Even if you do not have a password assigned to your account, you are still required by the logon welcome screen to click your name to sign in. Having to do these tasks yourself is unnecessary and a waste of time if you are a candidate for automatic logon.

Caution

Automatic logon can be a great feature but it can also create a security problem for your computer. If you use your computer for business, if you have data you prefer to keep safe from others, or both, I strongly recommend that you do not enable this feature. If you happen to step out of your office or if your laptop is stolen, you have left the door to your computer wide open. By enabling automatic logon, you are trading convenience for physical access security. However, you are not changing your network security, so your data is still safe from network attackers. The risk of someone remotely connecting to your computer is the same as if you did not have automatic logon enabled.

Enabling automatic logon is a quick and easy Registry hack. Follow these steps to speed up your sign-on with automatic logon:

1. Click the Start button, type **regedit** in the Search box, and then press Enter.

2. After Registry Editor has started, navigate through HKEY_LOCAL_MACHINE\SOFTWARE\ Microsoft\Windows NT\CurrentVersion\Winlogon.

3. Locate the AutoAdminLogon entry. If the key does not exist, create it by right-clicking the Winlogon folder and selecting New and then Registry String.

4. Right-click the AutoAdminLogon entry and select Modify. Set the Value to 1, as shown in Figure 10-1. Then press OK to save the new value.

5. Locate the DefaultUserName entry or create it if it does not exist.

6. Right-click DefaultUserName and select Modify. Set the value to the username that you primarily use to sign in to Windows. Press OK.

7. Locate the DefaultPassword entry or create it if it does not exist.

8. Right-click the DefaultPassword entry and set the Value to your password.

9. Close Registry Editor and restart your computer.

After you reboot your computer, Windows Vista should automatically sign on to your account. You will notice that your computer will now get to the desktop much quicker than before. If you ever want to disable automatic logon, just go back into Registry Editor and set the AutoAdminLogon entry to 0.

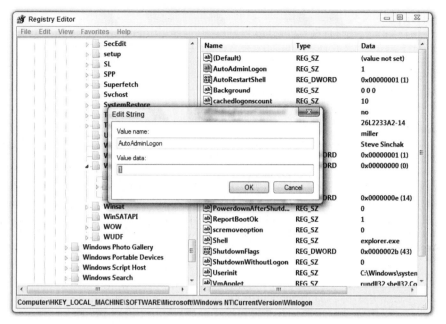

FIGURE 10-1: Setting AutoAdminLogon to 1 to activate automatic logon

Adjusting the startup programs

After you sign on, the system loads your profile, finishes loading the Explorer shell, and then begins to load the startup programs. If you have ever purchased a computer either online or from a retail store, then I am sure that you have noticed all the annoying software programs that automatically load right after you sign on. Some computer manufacturers go so overboard with startup applications that Windows has to automatically hide them from appearing in the system tray so that your taskbar has enough space to show open windows. If you are like me and have built your own computer, you do not have to deal with all that preloaded junk that comes from the big computer manufacturers. However, you are still vulnerable to auto-start programs that get installed by many of the popular applications you use. Over time, as you install more applications, the automatic startup applications can get out of control and defi-nitely slow down your logon.

Popular applications such as Adobe Photoshop, AOL Instant Messenger, iTunes, Windows Live Messenger, and many more install auto-start components. Consider all the extra auto-start components these applications add on top of the auto-start applications already installed on your computer, such as antivirus and anti-spyware applications. Your logon can easily become slowed to a crawl by dozens of applications that load once you sign on. This section helps you see what programs are starting automatically and then will show you some great tricks to stop them all from starting up.

Identifying and disabling auto-start applications

The first step in stopping the auto-start applications is to identify exactly what is starting up and if it is needed. You can use two different utilities to find this information. The first is the System Configuration utility that comes with Windows Vista. System Configuration enables you to easily see which applications start on logon. Another great utility is called Autoruns by Sysinternals. Autoruns is a more comprehensive utility that allows you to see all applications that run on logon as well as other types of auto-starts such as browser or shell plug-ins.

First I cover using Windows Vista's System Configuration to identify and disable unneeded auto-start applications. Then I dive in to using Sysinternal's Autoruns to disable auto-start applications as well as other auto-start components.

Using System Configuration to identify and disable unneeded startup applications

The System Configuration utility included in Windows Vista is very easy to use. First, you need to get a list of all the applications and components that are automatically starting up when you sign in. Follow these steps to discover the applications that are automatically starting up on your system:

1. Click the Start button, type **msconfig** in the Search box, and then press Enter.

2. After the System Configuration Utility has loaded, click the Startup tab, as shown in Figure 10-2.

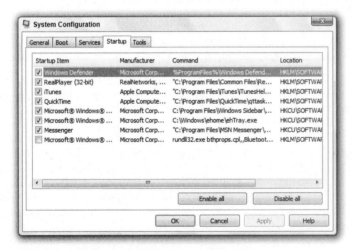

FIGURE 10-2: The System Configuration utility's Startup tab

3. Now that the list of the active startup programs is visible, make a list of all the items listed with the name as well as the file that is loaded, which is listed under the Command column.

4. After making your list, you can start researching which programs should be removed and which programs should stay. Because almost every computer has different programs starting up after logon, it is best to search the Web to find out if the service can be safely removed from the startup. One cool site to visit is a database of common startup programs called AnswersThatWork, located at `www.answersthatwork.com/Tasklist_pages/ tasklist.htm`. At that site, you will find a recommendation for each of the programs listed. If you cannot find one of your programs listed, just do a quick search on Google and most likely you will find several Web sites showing what the program does and what removing it will do.

It's easy to remove the automatic startup applications with the System Configuration tool. When you have the System Configuration tool open, follow these steps:

1. Locate the item you would like to disable from starting up and clear the box to the left of it.

2. When you are finished unchecking all the applications that you no longer want to auto-start, press OK to save your changes.

3. You are asked if you would like to Restart now or Exit without Restarting. I recommend that you restart now instead of waiting.

4. After you restart, you are reminded by the System Configuration tool that you have just made some changes to your startup. Check the box that says Don't show this message or start System Configuration when Windows starts.

After removing some of the automatic startup applications, you will notice that you can sign on much faster. If you have any problems after disabling a startup application component, you can always enable it again by checking its box in the System Configuration tool.

Using Autoruns to identify and disable auto-start components

Autoruns by Sysinternals is a more comprehensive tool to identify and disable unneeded auto-start applications, components, and plug-ins. Similar to the System Configuration tool, Autoruns operates in the same way but also shows the auto-start components of other items such as browsers and the system shell.

Autoruns is also easy to use. To get started, you need to download a free copy of the Autoruns software from `www.microsoft.com/technet/sysinternals/utilities/Autoruns.mspx`. After you have Autoruns downloaded and extracted to a folder, follow these steps to get started:

1. Go to the directory where you have extracted Autoruns and run autoruns.exe.

2. After Autoruns has started, click the Logon tab, as shown in Figure 10-3.

3. You will see all the automatic start applications, as you would if you were using the System Configuration tool. Identifying an unneeded service is even easier in Autoruns because of the right-click Google search feature. Right-click any entry and select Google. This automatically opens your web browser and searches Google for the process name. Simply selecting the entry will also provide more information on what it is.

4. Disabling a process is also similar to the method used in the System Configuration tool. Just clear the box to the left of the process name and it will no longer start after a reboot.

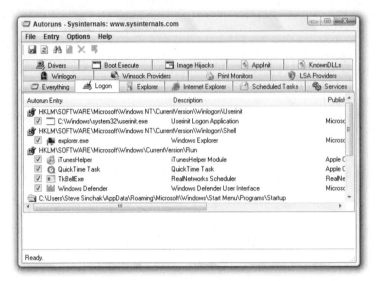

FIGURE 10-3: Using Autoruns

The power of the Autoruns software lies in the ability to control other automatic starting components such as browser add-ons and Explorer shell plug-ins. Check out the following list of the additional useful tabs available in Autoruns:

- **Explorer:** This tab will help you get your shell extensions under control as well as see all the applications that tap into Windows Explorer with DLL files.

- **Internet Explorer:** This tab lets you find applications that hook themselves into IE.

- **Boot Execute:** This tab enables you to find applications that have integrated themselves into the system boot.

- **Print Monitors:** Use this tab to get rid of extra print monitors for features that you don't use.

- **Drivers:** This tab provides another way to disable drivers for your hardware devices.

- **Winlogon:** This tab lets you find all the applications that run on your logon screen.

After you uncheck any options, simply restart your computer for them to take effect.

Controlling auto-start applications that keep coming back

You may experience some applications that you have previously disabled automatically starting up again. Software developers often use various techniques to check to make sure that their application is registered to auto-start when you log on. If it is no longer set to auto-start, it will automatically set it up again to do so. The software developers may be trying to make sure you use their application by making it difficult to disable auto-start or sometimes applications are just trying to make sure that other programs are not disabling their program or taking over their turf.

Software applications can often conflict and compete with each other for use on your computer. This occurred when I installed several media players on my PC. After installing the programs Winamp, iTunes, RealPlayer, and Windows Media Player, I noticed that they would fight for my music file associations (that is, which application would open the file). Every time I would run RealPlayer, it would change all my music files over to be played in their player by default. The same thing happened when I would try to play my music files in other players. From this experience, I found that it was not uncommon for an application to install a program to be run at system startup that would check and take over (or preserve, as the developers call it) itself from other applications.

Getting rid of these applications from your startup is much trickier than unchecking a box in the System Configuration utility or Autoruns. It involves digging into the preferences of each application and changing several options. In the paragraphs that follow, I will show you how to disable two of the most popular and most difficult applications from starting up automatically. Additionally, the methods used can be applied to disable other sneaky applications from starting up.

Getting a handle on RealPlayer

Real Networks, the developers of RealPlayer, could have made it a little easier for users to disable some of the extra program features. RealPlayer is a good application, but it comes bundled with so much extra junk that knowing how to disable all the extra features becomes a necessity.

Tip   RealPlayer does not come preinstalled with Windows Vista. If you did not download and install this application yourself, and it cannot be found on the Start menu, then you do not need to worry about taming RealPlayer.

One of the features of RealPlayer that I find the most annoying is the Message Center application that is automatically set up and starts when you log on. When you least expect it, no matter what you are doing on your computer and after you have run the RealPlayer program, you get a little pop-up message (see Figure 10-4) that alerts you to some random information or advertisement.

FIGURE 10-4: RealPlayer Message Center alert

You can do two things to get RealPlayer under control. First, you need to stop the scheduler from starting up every time you start Windows. You will recognize this application in the System Configuration utility as realsched.exe. No matter how many times you uncheck this item in the System Configuration utility or Autoruns, it will keep coming back. The only way to stop it is inside the RealPlayer application. Follow these steps to stop it for good:

1. Start the RealPlayer application by clicking the Start menu, selecting All Programs, and then selecting the RealPlayer icon.

2. After RealPlayer has loaded, click the Tools menu bar item and then select Preferences. This loads the program preferences.

3. Expand Automatic Services and then select Automatic Updates.

4. Clear the Automatically download and install important updates box, as shown in Figure 10-5.

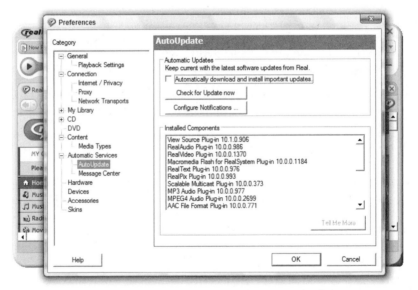

FIGURE 10-5: Disabling RealPlayer's automatic updates

5. Make sure that you will never again see a message from the so-called Message Center. To do so, select the Message Center entry listed under Automatic Services.

6. Click the Select Message Topics button on the right side of the window.

7. When the Message Center window is displayed, uncheck Product News and Real Exclusives located at the bottom of the screen. Navigate through the categories of messages and uncheck those as well. When you are finished, press the Save Changes button.

8. Close the Message Center window so the Preferences window can be viewed again.

9. After you are back to the Preferences window, press the Configure Message Center button.

10. Clear all the boxes on the screen.

11. Press OK to close the Configure Message Center window.

12. A warning window displays informing you that you are disabling the Message Center. Click Yes to proceed.

13. Close the Message Center window again so that you can view the Preferences window.

14. Press OK to save your changes and close the Preferences window.

That's it. RealPlayer is now under your full control and will not be starting up automatically any more and will not be sending you advertisements. As you can see, it is more difficult than just unchecking one box in the System Configuration Utility, but it is not that much more complex when you know what boxes to clear.

Disabling Windows Vista security alerts

Windows Vista security alerts are not only an annoying feature for advanced users but they also slow down your logon time because they have to automatically start when you log on. Disabling this feature by clearing a box is simply not an option using the System Configuration utility or even Autoruns. Security alerts are deeply embedded into Windows Vista and can be turned off only from within the Windows Security Center application, similar to what you had to do with RealPlayer.

If you are unfamiliar with security alerts, these are the little boxes that pop up from your system tray that inform you that you are missing antivirus or other types of computer protection. Figure 10-6 shows an example of a security alert. If you are an advanced user, you do not need to be reminded all the time that your security settings may be insecure.

Figure 10-6: A Windows Vista security alert

In Windows Vista, Microsoft made it easy to disable security alerts from starting automatically. Just follow these steps:

1. Click the Start button, type **Security Center** in the Search box, and then press Enter.

2. After Security Center loads, click Change the way Security Center alerts me.

3. Select Don't notify me and don't display the icon, as shown in Figure 10-7.

4. Close Security Center and you are finished.

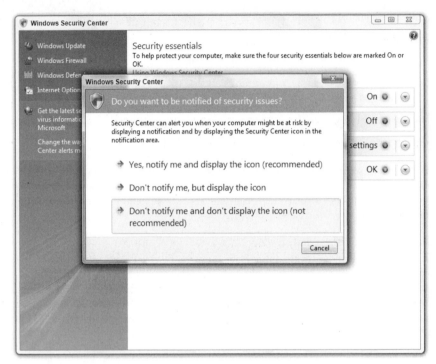

FIGURE 10-7: **Disabling security alerts in Security Center**

Tip   Interested in more security-related tweaks and tips? Check out Part III of this book to learn how to fine-tune Windows security and your Internet settings, and how to protect your privacy.

As you can see, stopping sneaky programs from starting automatically requires you to go into the program's options/preferences/settings. When you are inside a program's settings, you have to uncheck any options of features that start up automatically. Most programs such as Windows Security Center alerts are easy to disable from starting up automatically from within the preferences. However, other programs, such as RealPlayer, require a little more work because you have to disable automatic updates and several Message Center features.

The best way to stop other sneaky programs that keep starting up automatically after you try to remove them using the System Configuration utility is to dig through the program's settings. Look in the program's help file for information on how to disable automatic startup if you are stuck. If you cannot find any information, try searching on the Web for information, or post a request for help on one of the various computer support Web sites, such as the TweakVista.com forum at www.TweakVista.com.

Customizing auto-start programs for other users

Each user account on your computer can have different auto-start applications associated with it. Certain programs may start up for one user but not for another. All these settings are stored in the system registry. With the help of the Registry Editor utility, you can manually change these entries.

But first, let's go over where Windows Vista stores the auto-start information in the Registry. Windows stores auto-start information in two places for every user. It stores which programs will start for a specific user under the user's Registry hive/location. It also stores a list of programs that will start automatically in the local machine hive. Registry entries in the local machine hive will start up for all users of the computer. Removing these entries will remove it for all users of the computer.

Now that you know the two different types of startup items, user-specific and all user entries, you can begin hacking the Registry to change the startup programs. First, you will find out how to modify the startup programs for all users, and then you will learn how to modify the startup programs for individual users.

To modify the startup programs for all users, follow these steps:

1. If you have not already done so, start Registry Editor by clicking the Start button, typing **regedit** in the Search box, and pressing Enter.

2. After Registry Editor has loaded, expand and navigate through HKEY_LOCAL_MACHINE\ SOFTWARE\Microsoft\Windows\CurrentVersion\Run. You will see a list of all the auto-start applications in the local machine context, as shown in Figure 10-8.

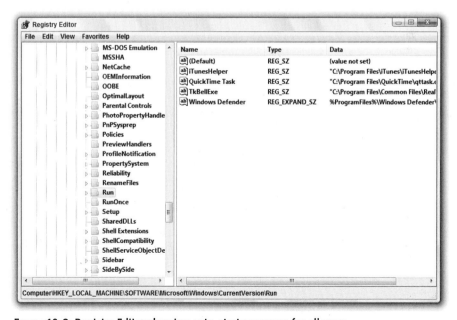

FIGURE 10-8: Registry Editor showing auto-start programs for all users

3. If you want to remove a startup program, just right-click the name and select Delete. Alternatively, if you want to add a new entry, right-click the white space and select New and then String value. Right-click on your new entry and select Modify so that you can edit it and set the value to the path to the executable you want to run.

That is it. You now know how to add and remove programs that will start up for all users on the computer. The steps for modifying the startup programs for individual users are very similar. The only difference is you have to go to a different place in the Registry.

Instead of navigating in the Registry under HKEY_Local_Machine, you have two options. You can log on to an individual's account and then go to HKEY_CURRENT_USER followed by the same navigation path used earlier. Alternatively, you can go to HKEY_USERS, expand the account SID (Security Identifier) key, and then follow the path used earlier.

Either method will result in the same outcome. However, if you don't have access to a user's account, you can still modify his or her auto-start applications by going to HKEY_USERS.

Other Time-Saving Tips

The preceding paragraphs covered the largest contributors to a slow logon, but there still are a few other tips that can save you additional time. These tips, individually, do not save a lot of time, but when they are applied in combination, they can really add up. Additionally, if you are running Windows Vista on older hardware, these tips will help you significantly decrease your logon time even further.

Assigning alternative IP addresses

Over the years Microsoft has experimented with changing when the network devices are initiated to make sure that the boot is not held up by a slow DHCP server. Windows XP made big advances in this area and Windows Vista has an entirely new TCP/IP stack that is optimized for performance. However, assigning an alternative IP address to your network cards is something that can only help because it saves your computer from an outgoing network request to the DHCP server to get an IP address. No matter where Microsoft moves the network initiation in the boot, it cannot eliminate the need to get an IP address.

To review, every time that you turn on your computer, it has to set up the IP configuration for your network card. Often, this setup can result in your computer pausing for moments during the loading process. The delay occurs because the PC is waiting for the DHCP server (a DHCP server dynamically assigns addresses to computers connected to a network), which is the provider of the network information, to respond. In other situations, a user can experience a delay when a DHCP server is not present on the network.

One easy solution to this problem is to assign alternative information to your network card. This task is actually pretty easy, as it does not require any major tampering. Follow these steps to specify an alternative IP configuration for your computer:

1. Click the Start button and select Computer.

2. When Explorer loads, type **network connections** in the address bar, as shown in Figure 10-9.

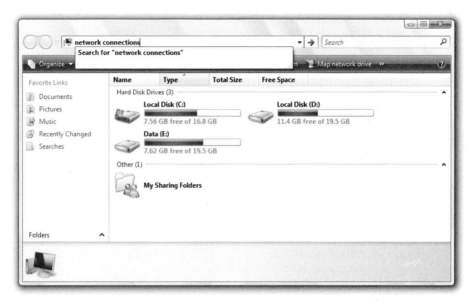

FIGURE 10-9: Accessing network connections using any Explorer window

3. Now that you are in the Network Connections window, you will see a list of network adapters on your computer. Right-click your wired network card adapter and select Properties.

4. Click the Internet Protocol Version 4 (TCP/IP) to select it. Then click the Properties button.

5. When the Internet Protocol Version 4 (TCP/IP) Properties window is displayed, click the Alternative Configuration tab. This is where you will enter your alternate network information.

6. Click the User Configured radio button to allow the text boxes to be edited.

7. Type an IP address for your computer that will be used as a default in the event that your computer cannot get a DHCP address. I recommend using 192.168.1.X. Replace X with any unique number for each computer between 2 and 254.

8. Type **255.255.255.0** as your Subnet Mask.

9. Your Default Gateway should be set to 192.168.1.1 because that is a valid gateway address. As I mentioned earlier, the exact numbers do not matter. You just want to have the computer assign some value instead of spending time searching when it will not find a DHCP server.

10. Enter what your DNS servers should be. You can get this from your ISP. But this information really isn't that essential because this configuration will almost never be used to connect to the Internet. It is just a default fallback in the rare case that you are having networking trouble. Feel free to leave these fields and the WINS fields blank.

11. Click OK and then click OK for the network properties screen.

Your network adapter is now optimized for the fastest possible logon time in all scenarios. For more network-related tweaks, check out Chapter 13, "Speeding Up Your Web Browser and Network Connection."

Turning off the logon music

The music that Windows Vista plays every time the logon screen displays and then again when I log on is something that I can do without. Hearing the tunes was really cool back when most people didn't have soundcards in their computers. But nowadays everyone has a sound card and the cool new Windows Vista logon music is starting to get old. Less is more, and when your computer has to load a 500KB media file to play, it slows things down. I highly recommend that you disable the logon music. To do so, follow these steps:

1. Click the Start button and then Control Panel.

2. Click Hardware & Sound followed by Change System Sounds.

3. Locate the Program Events box, scroll through the list, and select Start Windows, as shown in Figure 10-10.

FIGURE 10-10: Audio Devices and Sound Themes

4. Locate the Sounds drop-down box and scroll to the top of the list and select (None).

5. Click OK and you are finished.

Now that was not too bad. Plus, you just shaved another second or two off your loading time. If you want to save even more time in Windows, you can experiment with turning off all sounds by changing the Sound Scheme on the Audio Devices and Sound Themes screen to No Sounds from Windows Default.

Summary

Throughout this chapter, you found out how to remove unnecessary steps from your logon to cut the fat from the system load and make your computer load faster. You have learned how to remove auto-start programs as well as how to master the tricky programs that are hard to disable. The chapter also covered other ways to get that loading time down.

The next stop on our performance makeover is speeding up Windows Explorer. I will go over a few cool ways to speed up the most popular program in Windows: the shell.

Speeding Up Windows Explorer

N ow that you have optimized the boot startup and your logon, let's speed up the most used application in Windows Vista: Explorer. Windows Explorer is responsible for almost the entire GUI that you normally interact with in Windows Vista. The Start menu, taskbar, and file exploring windows are all part of the Explorer shell. As you can see, Explorer is a very expansive application that is a major part of the operating system.

This chapter shows you how you can use some cool hacks to increase the performance of Explorer. First, you will improve the speed of browsing and accessing files on your computer. Then you will go over how to adjust the visual effects of Windows Vista so that it performs better on your computer hardware and finish off with tweaking Windows Search for optimal performance.

Speeding Up File Browsing and Access

Browsing through lists of files and reading and writing files are the most basic operations that your computer performs. All the other operations that your computer performs build off of these common tasks. If you are launching an application or playing a game, no matter what you are doing, it all breaks down to the simple process of reading a file from a device at some point. Windows Explorer is no exception. The speed of Windows Explorer is greatly influenced by the performance of these basic operations. Therefore, the performance of Windows Explorer, as well as all other applications, can be improved by optimizing these basic operations.

How can you speed up these basic operations? All these basic operations have to do with interactions with your file system. Using various tweaks to the file system settings and using performance utilities, you can improve the performance of your file system, resulting in an increase in performance of the basic file operations.

Before you go any further, be aware that the following speed tips for the file system will work only for the NTFS file system. If you do not know what file system your computer is using, you can go to Computer in the Start menu, right-click your hard drive, and select Properties. This will bring up the Local Disk (C:) Properties window, which will tell you the type of file system your hard drive is running. If your hard drive is running FAT32, these tips will not work for you.

In my opinion, NTFS is the best file system for Windows Vista. It has many advanced security features and also performs better on many machines. If you are still running FAT32, or for some odd reason your computer came preinstalled with FAT32, consider converting your hard disk to NTFS.

Tip

Converting your drive to NTFS is a snap. Click the Start button, type **Command Prompt** in the Search box, and then press Enter. Then, right-click on the Command Prompt shortcut that shows up at the top of the Start menu and select Run as Administrator. Command Prompt will now load with the administrator access that is needed to run the convert tool. Next, at a prompt, type **convert c: /fs:ntfs** and press Enter to start. If you want to convert a different drive letter, just replace the c: with the drive letter that you want. For example, if you want to convert your D drive, then you will have to type **convert d: /fs:ntfs**. The actual conversion process will take a little while, especially on large drives. Keep in mind that once you convert to NTFS, you cannot convert back to FAT32.

Now that the requirements are cleared up, you are ready to get started.

Disabling legacy filename creation

Legacy filename creation is a feature of the NTFS file system that is included in Windows for backwards compatibility with older applications. Over the years, the file system in Windows has changed dramatically. One of the first things that changed was the limitation of the old MS-DOS 8.3 file naming standard. The old MS-DOS file system limited filenames to a maximum length of 8 characters plus a 3-character extension. As Windows became more advanced, this needed to be changed to allow for greater flexibility. Eventually, this limitation was expanded with the release of Windows 95, which bumped up the maximum filename limit to 255 characters. However, there was a hidden price to pay that affects Windows Vista, too.

Microsoft has always believed that backwards compatibility contributes to the success of Windows because it enables users to easily upgrade to a new version and their older applications will still work. However, that mentality often results in performance reductions caused by code that had to be tweaked to allow for new functionality while preserving existing functionality. The legacy filename creation is a perfect example of this scenario. In order for Windows Vista to be able to support older Windows applications, the NTFS file system has to support both the old MS-DOS file naming standard as well as the new updated standard that allows for longer filenames. How do they do it? It's rather simple. When a file is created, the file system creates two names for it: one name in the MS-DOS 8.3 standard and another in the latest filename standard.

Creating two filenames for every file is not the kind of buy-one-get-one-free situation that is good. Creating the second filename takes more time and slows down the performance of the file system. Although this legacy feature has good intentions, it causes the performance of file creation to decrease by 200 percent. Disabling this legacy feature will help you get that lost performance back.

Disabling legacy filename creation will kill any application you have that needs the 8.3 filename standard. If you try to run an application that requires 8.3 filenames, you will get various error messages. Even though this technology is more than 15 years old, there are some major software developers, mentioned in the following paragraphs, that still write code that requires the ancient 8.3 standard. Unfortunately, in the software world, some companies don't bother fixing things if they are not broken to simply increase the performance of the user's computer. For the most part, they do not have to worry about it because Microsoft supports the lazy programmers by leaving these old, inefficient features in the operating system.

Even though some applications will fail when this feature is disabled, I highly recommend trying to disable this on your computer. In the worst case scenario, you would have to turn the feature back on again. However, you will discover that almost all your programs will work just fine. For those that don't, try to download a new version from the company's Web site, or perhaps use this as an excuse to buy a version of the product from this century.

One type of program that has the most problems when the 8.3 standard is disabled is the installer application that many software developers use to get their programs up and running on your computer. For some reason, a few installers are still programmed using the old 16-bit technology that depends on the short filename compatibility feature to function.

Users frequently run into this error with Symantec's AntiVirus software. According to Symantec, users may receive a 1639. Invalid command line argument error when they install certain versions of Symantec's software. For users of Symantec software who want to disable the old support for greater performance, the company recommends that they enable the 8.3-standard filename compatibility support when the software is being installed and then disable it after the software is installed. The software should then work fine.

That basic Symantec approach can be applied to any situations that you may run into when applications are being installed and errors received. Just enable the 8.3-standard filename compatibility support during the install, and then disable it after the install is complete.

Now that you are aware of the possible problems that can be caused by disabling the legacy filename standard, and also know what to do if you experience any, you are ready to try to disable the feature. Follow these steps:

1. Click the Start button, type **Command Prompt** in the Search box, and then press Enter.

2. Command Prompt appears at the top of the list in your Start menu. Right-click the shortcut and select Run as Administrator, as shown in Figure 11-1.

3. After Command Prompt has loaded in the Administrator context, you will be able to access the NTFS configuration utility. At the prompt, type **fsutil behavior set disable8dot3 1**, as shown in Figure 11-2.

4. Close Command Prompt and restart your computer for the change to be activated.

Enabling the legacy filename feature is also very easy. Just repeat the preceding instructions and run **fsutil behavior set disable8dot3 0** instead and restart.

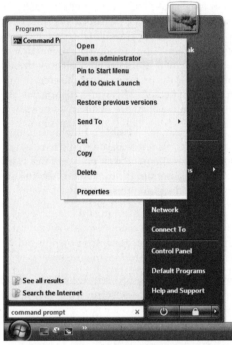

FIGURE 11-1: Running Command Prompt as administrator

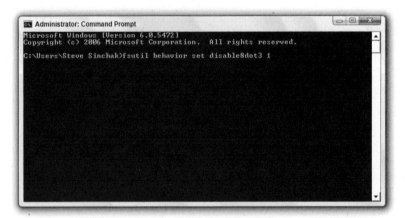

FIGURE 11-2: Disabling legacy filename creation with the file system utility

Disabling the file access timestamp

Every time you or an application accesses a file on your computer, the file system records the date and time the file was accessed and stores the timestamp in two locations. Simply accessing a file requires the system to write to the master file table (MFT) and the directory the file is located in, which results in two writes for every file read. Windows Explorer is one of the most read intensive applications on your computer. Nothing requires more reads to your file system than browsing through your files. In Windows Vista, Explorer has a number of new file previews that require even more file reads. All these file reads add up to extra timestamp writes, resulting in slower performance.

The Microsoft NTFS file system engineers were smart enough to realize that all this timestamp logging can get out of control very quickly, resulting in an even greater performance slowdown. Applications usually open only a small chunk of a file at a time and then repeat the small chunk reads until the entire file is open. This can generate hundreds and maybe even thousands of file reads, depending on the file size and application. As you can imagine, that many file reads in a short amount of time can put a lot of extra work on the file system. To handle this problem, Microsoft designed NTFS to update only the last access timestamp about every hour, which breaks down to just one two-step timestamp update, for each file per hour. This solves the preceding problem but it still has to do two writes for every file; it just limits the need to update the same file over and over again.

Disabling the file access timestamp is a great way to speed up Windows Explorer, but it is not without any side effects. Often backup applications utilize the file access timestamp to determine which files to back up when performing a sequential backup operation (a backup operation that copies only the files that have newer timestamps since the last backup date). Check with your backup application's Web site to find out if it will be affected. If it is, consider doing full backups instead of sequential backups. Full backups are not affected by the lack of a last access timestamp.

The process for disabling the file access timestamp is very similar to disabling MS-DOS filename support. Just follow these steps:

1. Click the Start button, type **Command Prompt** in the Search box, and then press Enter.

2. Command Prompt appears at the top of the list in your Start menu. Right-click the shortcut and select Run as Administrator.

3. After Command Prompt has loaded in the Administrator context, you will be able to access the NTFS configuration utility. At the prompt, type **fsutil behavior set disablelastaccess 1**.

4. Close Command Prompt and restart your computer for the change to take effect.

If you run into any problems with this change in your backup application or any other applications, you can easily undo the tweak. Just type **fsutil behavior set disablelastaccess 0** at the command prompt instead.

Adjusting NTFS memory allocation

The NTFS file system likes to cache files that are open in physical memory for the fastest possible access to the raw data. This is accomplished by first reading the data from the hard drive and transferring it to physical memory. Depending on the amount of RAM in your computer, portions of the open files may be paged to disk in the paging file because the entire file cannot fit in the available physical memory. This results in slower overall performance because in order for an application to read the entire file, existing data in the physical memory cache has to be paged back to the hard disk to make room and then other unread portions have to be pulled back from the hard drive into physical memory. This carefully orchestrated memory swap requires a lot of CPU, memory, and hard drive processing time. Whenever memory paging occurs, it slows down the overall performance of your computer.

If you use your computer for anything that requires fast reads of hundreds of files, such as indexing your MP3 collection, you might notice that it takes your computer a while to read these files. This is because the file system has only a certain amount of physical and paging file space allocated to it, which results in increased paging activity. Depending on the amount of physical memory in your computer, you might be able to get away with increasing the memory allocated to the NTFS file system on your computer. This will increase the performance of high disk read operations.

Before you get started, you need to analyze the available physical system pool memory on your hardware. Increasing the NTFS memory allocation on a machine without enough of the right type of free memory will result in a decrease in overall system performance because other system components have to use less memory, which can increase paging.

Follow these steps to determine if you can increase the memory allocation:

1. Click the Start button, type **perfmon** in the Search box, and then press Enter.

2. When the Reliability and Performance Monitor loads, click Performance Monitor under Monitoring Tools.

3. Press Ctrl+I to add performance counters.

4. Navigate to the Memory section and expand it.

5. Locate and select Cache Bytes Peak and press Add.

6. Locate and select System Cache Resident Bytes and press Add.

7. Press OK when both counters are added.

8. Switch to the Report View by pressing Ctrl+G until you see the performance counters listed, as shown in Figure 11-3.

9. Note the values of all three counters on a sheet of paper so that you can reference them even after a reboot.

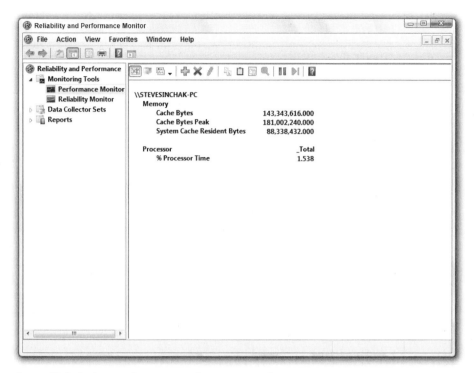

FIGURE 11-3: System pool memory performance counters

Now you need to analyze the counters you just gathered. Cache Bytes Peak shows the maximum amount of physical system pool non-page memory in use since your computer was last rebooted. This number is very important because the memory manager in Windows Vista limits you to 256MB (268,435,456 bytes) of physical system pool non-page memory regardless of the amount of RAM in your computer. If your Cache Bytes Peak value is within 20MB of the 256MB limitation, this is a big red flag to not attempt this hack. In that scenario, you might slow down your computer even more by implementing this hack.

Next, let's take a look at your total System Cache Resident Bytes. This is the current size of the file system cache in physical system pool non-page memory. When you implement this hack, this value can increase by up to 50 percent. Take 50 percent of the System Cache Resident Bytes value and add it to the Cache Bytes Peak value. Make sure that it is below the 256MB limit.

If your results of the two tests above are on the borderline for passing, I would still implement this hack. It is easy to undo this setting and it will not harm any of your hardware or have a permanent effect on the performance of your computer.

Follow these steps to increase the memory available to the file system:

1. Click the Start button, type **Command Prompt** in the Search box, and then press Enter.

2. Command Prompt appears at the top of the list in your Start menu. Right-click the shortcut and select Run as Administrator.

3. After Command Prompt has loaded in the Administrator context, you will be able to access the NTFS configuration utility. At the prompt, type **fsutil behavior set memoryusage 2**.

4. Close Command Prompt and restart your computer for the change to be active.

After your computer has restarted and you load up your usual applications, check to make sure that your Cache Bytes Peak value in Perfmon is still well under 256MB. Also find the difference between your new System Cache Resident Bytes value and the value before the change. Add that to the old Cache Bytes Peak value you wrote down earlier to ensure that the sum is also less than 256MB. If it is greater, you might be stealing memory from other system components, resulting in an overall slowdown in performance.

If you notice any decrease in performance or have bad results from the preceding test, undoing the change is very simple. Just type **fsutil behavior set memoryusage 1** at the prompt instead and reboot.

Speeding Up the User Interface

Windows Vista is all about the new visual experience. Unfortunately, the new visual features that contribute to that experience can put a heavy load on your hardware. Unless you have a newer PC with a recent graphics card and a fast CPU, you may see a slowdown in performance caused by the visual effects and features. This is noticed most when you are navigating between windows and closing them. These effects can sometimes give the impression that your computer is slower than it actually is because the animation is not running as fast as it was designed to run.

In Windows Vista, you can fine-tune the settings of the entire user interface for maximum performance. You don't want to disable all the settings, however; instead, find a good balance between a good looking interface and what you are willing to compromise for speed. The following paragraphs show you how to do this — so let's dig in!

Fine-tuning performance options

As I mentioned earlier, Windows Vista is all about the new experience that the visual effects create for the user. These new visual effects require more computing power from your hardware than ever before, resulting in slower performance on older hardware.

I do not have the latest graphics card or a fast multi-core CPU, although my hardware does meet the minimum requirements for the new Aero interface, so the new visual effects run. Unfortunately, they do not always run very well and even appear to slow down my system at times. Often the animation effects appear rough and when I drag windows around there appears to be a slight lag. The poor performance occurs because the value ATI video card that I have can barely keep up with the work it has to do.

The new visual interface is provided by the Desktop Windows Manager (DWM). This new composition engine uses your 3D accelerated graphics card with DirectX 9 to draw the entire desktop on 3D surfaces. Because my video card is right at the bare minimum requirements, I need to fine-tune the visual effects of the Aero interface so that it runs better on my system.

Adjusting animations

The visual effects of Windows Vista can be adjusted very easily, allowing you to fine-tune the performance of Windows Explorer to work well with your hardware configuration. This can be done using the Windows Performance Options settings. Click the Start button, type **SystemPropertiesPerformance** (no spaces between words) in the Search box, and then press Enter. This starts Performance Options, as shown in Figure 11-4.

FIGURE 11-4: Windows Vista Performance Options

When Performance Options is started, you will notice three preset options and one custom option:

- **Let Windows choose what's best for my computer:** Windows uses your Windows Experience Index to pick the settings it thinks will result in the best balance of appearance and performance for you.

- **Adjust for best appearance:** Turns all settings on.

- **Adjust for best performance:** Turns all settings off.

- **Custom:** Allows you to manually select the individual settings to use.

Go ahead and select the Custom option so that you have total control over which settings to enable and disable. Now that you have the Custom option selected, you can pick the individual settings that work best for your hardware. Take a look at the following list of the visual effect settings:

- **Animate controls and elements inside windows:** This setting currently does not appear to do anything.

- **Animate windows when minimizing and maximizing:** This effect will animate the window when it is minimized to the taskbar, as shown in Figure 11-5. It is a cool looking effect, but it is graphics intensive and can slow down the performance of the GUI. I recommend disabling this effect to gain some extra speed.

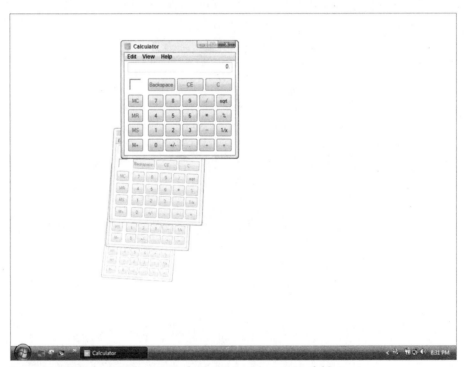

FIGURE 11-5: Windows Vista animated minimizing/maximizing folders

- **Enable desktop composition:** This setting is one way to completely turn off the DWM composition engine that is responsible for the Aero Glass interface. Disabling this will cause your computer to revert to the non-Glass GUI that is similar to the Windows XP visual style engine. Although disabling this feature will give you a big performance increase, it kills the Vista look; therefore, I recommend keeping this setting checked.

- **Enable transparent glass:** One of the most graphics intensive operations of the Aero Glass interface is the transparent glass. This requires various calculations to be run that blur the background behind the glass to complete the transparent effect. Disabling this will give you a performance increase on less powerful graphics cards. Glass still looks good even if transparency is disabled, as shown in Figure 11-6.

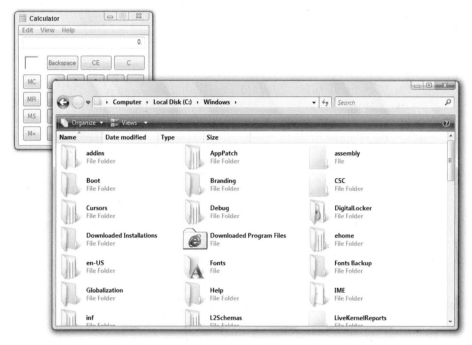

FIGURE 11-6: Non-transparent Aero Glass

- **Fade or slide menus into view:** This effect allows the menus that pop up throughout the system to fade in. You will experience this when you navigate through a menu bar or when you right-click something. This effect does not affect the performance of the system except for when the effect is called on. Some users who have older computers and slower video cards can experience better performance by disabling this effect.

- **Fade or slide ToolTips into view:** This effect will allow the ToolTips in various parts of the system to slowly fade in when either an event occurs or you hold your mouse over the object. This effect doesn't affect performance of the system of most users, but once again, those with older systems should disable this effect for better performance.

- **Fade out menu items after clicking:** This effect will fade the submenus in the Start menu out after you click an item within the menu if you are using the Classic Start menu. Unless you are using the Classic Windows 2000–style interface, this setting will not affect you. This effect, just like the other fade effects, is slower on older systems and should be disabled for best performance.

- **Show preview and filters in folders:** This feature allows Windows Explorer to show previews of files that are in your folders. For example, it can show a thumbnail of a Microsoft Word document, depending on the type of view you have selected. Disabling this item will increase the performance of Windows Explorer.

- **Show shadows under menus:** This effect displays a light shadow when pop-up menus are displayed, giving more of a 3D appearance to the flat interface. Unless you have a really old computer, I don't recommend disabling this setting.

- **Show shadows under mouse pointer:** This effect allows the mouse to have that semi-3D effect. However, it is not applied to the mouse when the mouse is over certain applications, such as Microsoft Word. I have not found this effect to affect performance.

- **Show thumbnails instead of icons:** This feature allows you to view thumbnails of your images instead of the associated file icon. Unless you have problems with a slow hard drive on your computer and a low amount of RAM, or have directories with thousands of pictures in them at once, I feel this feature provides more value and is worth the performance decrease. However, if you don't like thumbnail views of your images, disable this to gain speed while browsing your image files.

- **Show translucent selection rectangle:** When this effect is enabled, you will see a nice-looking blue border with a semi-transparent blue interior when you drag the mouse to select items instead of the old dotted line box as we have all seen in older versions of Windows. Figure 11-7 shows the two different types of selection rectangles. On older machines, I have seen this effect work very slowly and often interfere with the mouse's selection of items because it seems to use up a lot of the CPU. On the average computer, this effect presents no problems at all. If you have a slow machine, then disable this effect; otherwise keep it enabled and enjoy the nicer look.

- **Show window contents while dragging:** If you are using the Aero Glass interface and experience a lag when moving windows around, disabling this option will help because you will see a box outline instead of the entire window image when moving it. If you have to deal with a tiny lag, then keep this effect enabled because it definitely looks nice when it is enabled.

- **Slide open combo boxes:** This effect has no noticeable effect on performance. I do not understand why anyone would want to disable this effect, but if you are the type of person that cannot wait an extra 7 milliseconds to view the contents of the combo box, then knock yourself out disabling this one.

- **Slide taskbar buttons:** This setting allows you to disable the animation of taskbar items when windows are closed and opened. As your taskbar becomes more cluttered, Windows Explorer often likes to group your windows together or resize all those items to make them less wide. When it does this it animates the transitions so it looks pretty. However, I have noticed that this effect is often very rough on systems like mine that just meet the bare minimum system requirements. Disabling this effect will also make your computer appear to be faster because it instantly reorganizes the tasks instead of the slower transitions.

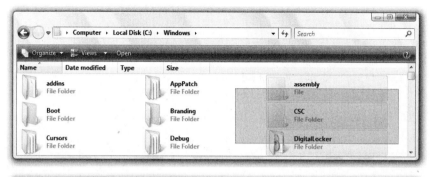

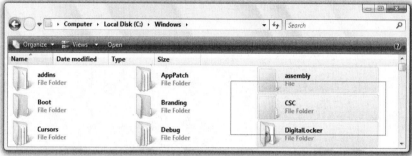

FIGURE 11-7: Selection rectangle comparison. A translucent selection rectangle appears on top.

- **Smooth edges of screen fonts:** This feature seems to depend more on your video card and monitor than your system. Use of any type of font smoothing will require it to do more work. On older machines, I would disable this effect. Also, if you have a cathode ray tube (CRT) type monitor, you will not benefit all that much by having this enabled. The font smoothing effects, especially ClearType, work best on flat panel LCD monitors.

- **Smooth-scroll list boxes:** This has no effect on performance based on my tests. You would have to be crazy to disable this effect because it is just so cool.

- **Use a background image for each folder type:** This has a small effect on performance when browsing through folders. On faster computers you will not notice anything, but on the average and older computers, this is something that you can live without. Furthermore, some of the background images are so light that they do not show up on some monitors such as my old laptop's LCD screen, which did not have good contrast with light colors. My advice is to get rid of them.

- **Use drop shadows for icon labels on the desktop:** Unless you do not like the look of this feature, I do not recommend disabling it. The performance benefit of disabling it is insignificant.

- **Use visual styles on windows and buttons:** Disabling this effect is one way to make your computer look like it is from 10 years ago. If you do not like the Aero Glass look and also do not like the non-glass visual style, disabling this will give you the classic Windows 2000 look. You will see a huge performance increase, but your GUI will also look really old, so the choice is up to you.

Now that you know what all the settings do, just uncheck any of the options that you would like to disable and press OK to save your selections. Your computer will then pause for up to 15 seconds while it adjusts all the settings.

If you ever change your mind and want an effect back, just go back to the Performance Options tool and recheck any options you disabled.

Disabling Aero Glass for faster performance

Now that you know how you can fine-tune the settings of Aero Glass on your computer so that it performs better, you may still want to make Windows Explorer even faster. Disabling the Aero Glass composition engine will allow you to have a much faster user interface experience on slower hardware. However, you will lose most of the cool visual effects, such as the windows transitions and the cool new Flip 3D window switcher, as shown in Figure 11-8.

FIGURE 11-8: Windows Vista's Flip 3D Alt+Tab replacement

Disabling Aero Glass will turn off the Desktop Window Manager and Windows will use a visual style engine similar to what was in Windows XP. The older visual style engine works great on slower hardware that ran XP well. However, the look of the user interface is a little different, as shown in Figure 11-9.

FIGURE 11-9: Windows Vista's non-Glass look

If you are willing to compromise the Glass look for a big increase in performance, follow these steps to disable Aero Glass:

1. Right-click the desktop and select Personalize from the menu.

2. Select Windows Color and Appearance from the top of the list in the Personalization window.

3. On the bottom of the window, click Open classic appearance properties for more color options.

4. When Appearance Settings loads, select Windows Aero Basic from the color scheme list.

5. Press OK and you are finished.

Windows Classic look for maximum performance

If you are a performance freak and need the best possible performance out of Windows Vista at any expense, then you are still in luck. Windows Vista still has the old Windows 2000 classic look built into the operating system. Enabling the old classic look will take you back in time and make your Windows Vista PC feel like Windows 2000 with all of the benefits of

Windows Vista, as shown in Figure 11-10. Reverting back to the classic look will also free RAM and extra work for your CPU, resulting in the best possible user interface experience.

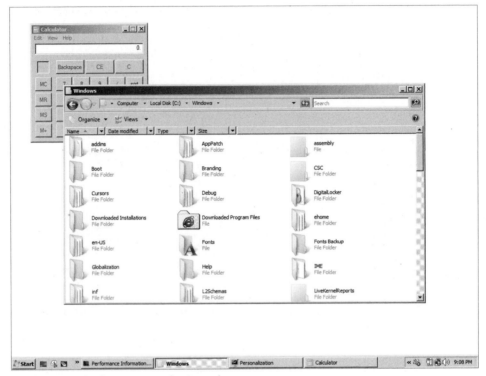

FIGURE 11-10: Windows Vista in classic mode

If you are willing to sacrifice all of Windows Vista's great look for performance, step into the time machine:

1. Right-click the desktop and select Personalize from the menu.

2. Select Windows Color and Appearance from the top of the list in the Personalization window.

3. On the bottom of the window, click Open classic appearance properties for more color options.

4. When Appearance Settings loads, select Windows Classic from the color scheme list.

5. Press OK and you are finished.

Welcome back to 1999. Make sure you are ready for Y2K.

Adjusting Explorer's Search

The ability to search files and folders is available throughout the user interface in Windows Vista. Almost every window has a search box that allows you to find documents, images, applications, and other files almost instantly. Accelerated by the Windows indexing service, Windows Search can quickly search through a file index that is continuously updated by the indexing service running in the background. In order for a search in Windows to be successful, there needs to be a good balance between the amount of time it takes to get results and the overall system performance decrease caused by the background indexing service.

There are some cool tricks that you can use to increase the success of a search while also increasing overall system performance by reducing the amount of work the indexing service has to do. First, let's look at adjusting the scope of where Explorer searches for an item when browsing through folders. Then you will look at adjusting some settings on the indexing service as well as how to use Windows Search without an index. All these hacks will help you increase the performance of Windows Explorer and your overall system performance.

Adjusting the search scope

Typically when you use a search box when browsing through folders looking for files, you are not interested in contacts, e-mails, and application shortcuts that are similar to your search term. Instead, you just want to find a file or document with the name you are searching for. By default Windows Search automatically searches for all types of information matching your search term. By limiting what it is searching through, you can increase the speed of your results. After all, it just makes more sense to find only files when you are searching from a window displaying the contents of a folder.

Adjusting the scope of a search is very easy to do. If you want, you can even have different search scopes for different folders. This allows you to have it both ways. For example, if you are browsing files in the C:\Windows directory and you want to search for a specific file, you can configure Windows Search to look only in the C:\Windows folder. It is also possible to configure the scope of a search placed in a different folder, such as your home folder, to search all information available. Follow these steps to adjust the search scope for any folder:

1. Click the Start menu and select Computer.

2. Navigate to a folder for which you would like to change the search scope. Press the Alt key to bring up the classic menu bar.

3. Click Tools on the menu bar and select Folder Options.

4. When Folder Options loads, click the Search tab.

5. Under Search Behavior, select Search filenames only.

6. If you would like to increase the performance even more at the cost of losing additional functionality, uncheck "Search subfolders while typing in the search box" located under Search Options.

7. After you have made your changes, press OK to save them.

Your updated search scope is now activated.

Adjusting the Windows indexing service

The search scope is just one part of the search feature in Windows. The real brains behind allowing you to quickly search through the various types of files on your computers are in the indexing service. This service runs in the background and monitors only folders and file types it was directed to monitor. Any files located in folders where the indexing service monitors are read and indexed. That indexing data is then stored in a centralized database.

The indexing service allows you to search through the Start menu search box and find all files, documents, and images that match the search term in both the filename and within the document. If the file indexed is a popular file format, most likely there is a reader for it within the indexing service. In theory, you could search for the word "the" and find all documents and e-mails on your computer that contain that word. This is all controlled by the settings for the indexing service.

You can adjust the settings that the indexing service uses to index only the types of files and locations you care about, which will reduce the amount of work the indexing service has to do. This will increase the overall performance of your computer, causing it to have more free resources because they are not wasted indexing files you don't care about. Adjusting these settings is easy once you know where to do it. Just follow these steps to get started:

1. Click the Start button, type **Performance Information** in the Search box, and then press Enter.

2. Select Performance Information and Tools when it appears on the top of the list.

3. After Performance Information and Tools loads, click Adjust Indexing Options on the left menu.

4. When Indexing Options loads, you will see all the locations the indexing service is currently monitoring, as shown in Figure 11-11.

FIGURE 11-11: Indexing Options for Windows Search

5. Click the Global Settings button to bring up the settings for all the users on your computer.

6. Select a location on the list and press Modify. This is where you can fine-tune exactly where the indexing service looks. You can even navigate between locations while on the Modify screen by using the summary list on the bottom of the window.

7. Navigate through the list of drives and folders and uncheck any locations you do not want the indexing service to monitor.

8. Adjust the file types that the indexing service reads by clicking the Advanced button and then the File Types tab.

9. Scroll through the list and uncheck any file types that you do not want the indexing service to keep track of. By default, a ton of files are checked. Reducing the number of files that the indexer has to monitor will greatly improve the performance.

10. Go back to the Index Settings tab in Advanced Options and under troubleshooting, press the Rebuild button to wipe out your existing index and replace it with a new one containing only the file types and locations you want.

11. When you are finished, press OK to close the Advanced Options window and then the Close button to activate your changes.

You are now finished adjusting the Windows Indexing service for maximum performance while preserving the ability for fast searches in Windows Explorer.

Using Windows Search without an index

As I mentioned earlier, the indexing service plays a key role in accelerating searches within Window Vista. Although this service provides a lot of value by allowing you to quickly search thousands of files, it is not a requirement of Windows Search. It is possible to completely disable the indexing service. However, searches with Windows Search will require much more time to complete and can cause your hard drive to do a lot of work while Windows Search iterates through folders and files instead of just accessing a search index.

Disabling the indexing service will save your computer extra memory and CPU time required to run the application in the background. Depending on how often you use the Windows Search feature, you can decide if it is worth sacrificing fast searches for a little extra performance from Windows Explorer. Follow these steps if you decide to disable the indexing service:

1. Click the Start button, type **services.msc** in the Search box, and then press Enter. This loads the Services utility.

2. After Services has loaded, scroll through the list and locate the Windows Search service. This is the indexing service. Right-click this service and select Stop.

3. When the service is stopped, make sure that it does not start again. Right-click the service again and select Properties.

4. Locate the Startup type drop-down box. Change the Startup type from Automatic to Disabled.

5. Press OK to close the window.

You have now successfully disabled the indexing service that is used by Windows Search. Although your searches are now slower, you have freed up processing power that can be used instead by other processes such as Windows Explorer.

Summary

You have now finished optimizing Windows Explorer. The things that you have done in this chapter may seem to make only minor changes to the performance of your computer, but these hacks will have a big impact on the performance of Windows Explorer as well as other applications on your system. Tweaking the file system settings, fine-tuning the visual settings, and adjusting Windows Search are all valuable skills to have when you want your computer to run at top performance.

You are now ready to optimize the core Windows components. In the next chapter, you learn tricks to add more RAM to your computer and fine-tune the paging file, and other hacks that will take your computer's performance to the next level.

Optimizing Windows Core Components

T he core Windows components can be thought of as the steel beam structure of a skyscraper. This basic structure of the building provides support for all the other components. Windows Vista is a massive program that has various layers of components that support each other. This chapter is going to help you tweak the core components of Windows to increase the overall performance of your computer. Instead of a steel beam structure, Windows Vista's core components are short-term memory (RAM, a.k.a. volatile memory), long-term storage (your hard drive, a.k.a. non-volatile memory), and the CPU. All the programs that run on Windows, including Windows itself, eventually break down to these three core components.

To get started, you are going to tweak your system's short-term memory using some techniques and features of Windows Vista to increase the speed of memory operations. Then, you are going to hack another critical component, the paging system, and then speed up your hard drive and adjust how your CPU does work. These tweaks and hacks will help you speed up the overall performance of your computer.

Giving Vista More RAM

All the added features and infrastructure components to support Windows Vista require PCs to have more RAM than ever before. The new security enhancements, visual effects, and maintenance processes can eat up a big chunk of your available memory. Microsoft claims that the minimum amount of RAM required to run Windows Vista is 512MB. However, almost every advanced computer user agrees that you need to double any Microsoft recommendation on RAM for decent performance. The last few chapters covered various ways to cut down on memory usage to speed up your PC. Unfortunately, if your computer doesn't have enough RAM, 512MB or less, the tweaks and hacks in the previous chapters will help, but they will not be able to help enough.

Windows Vista and all your applications require a good amount of available random access memory (RAM) to perform at top speed. You can try very hard to cut down on the need for memory by disabling unused features and applications so you have more memory free for the applications you use daily; however, there really is no substitute for RAM. Before I go any further, let's review why RAM is so important to your computer.

RAM is the fastest type of memory on your computer. No matter what you use your computer for, RAM is always in constant use. Your computer uses RAM as a high-speed temporary storage location to store data and applications that the CPU is currently working with. Every time you launch an application, Windows has to load it from your hard drive into RAM so that the CPU can execute the code. Depending on the available memory, Windows may have to kick some other data currently in memory out. That is called paging, which is covered in greater detail later in this chapter. Paging is a slow process because it saves current memory back to the slow hard disk. It is best to avoid paging as much as possible so that as little time as possible is lost trying to make room so your applications or data can fit in memory. When you consider all the memory that Windows Vista uses on top of your normal applications, you will see why it is so important to have the right amount of high speed memory available.

Adding RAM to your computer

Sometimes your only option to add even more speed to your computer is to give it more of what it likes most, RAM. If you have a low amount of RAM in your computer — say you are right at the bare minimum requirements according to Microsoft to run Windows Vista and you have already tried all the performance enhancements in this book — I recommend upgrading your RAM as a final move. I have never seen any hardware upgrade influence the speed of a computer greater than upgrading the RAM. Upgrading the amount of RAM you have in your computer is an easy and low-cost method to jump-start the speed of your computer. Unsure if you have the skills to do it yourself? No problem — just follow the recommendations that follow for help with buying and installing your new RAM.

Buying RAM for your hardware

Picking out RAM can be very confusing because there are so many different types of it. The following are two main points that will take the complexity out of buying RAM:

- **Type of RAM your hardware requires:** You can usually go to the Web site of your manufacturer, type in your model number, and find the exact type of memory that will work with your hardware. Alternatively, you can visit the manufacturer of your motherboard. I recommend writing down the type of memory your manufacturer states you need and buying the memory from a different company. Use a price comparison Web site to find the best deal on the type or RAM you need. Often the major manufacturers rip you off on the pricing of RAM. When you know what kind you need, you can get it from pretty much anywhere and usually much cheaper.

- **Number of open RAM expansion slots:** In order to add memory to your computer, you need to consider the number of open RAM expansion slots you have on your motherboard. Most computers have either two or four slots and depending on your manufacturer or if you built it yourself, you may be using up all the slots. If your slots are all in use, don't worry — you can still upgrade your RAM. Pieces of RAM usually come in combinations of 256MB, 512MB, or 1GB of memory per stick. Say you have two RAM slots and they are both currently full with two 256MB RAM chips; you can still buy two 512MB chips to replace them, which doubles the amount of RAM you had.

Installing your new RAM

Once you have ordered or picked up your new RAM, it is really easy to install it yourself. Keep in mind that opening the case may void your warranty. Having fun yet? Follow these steps to pop in your new memory:

1. Unplug all the cables on the back of your computer, including the power cable.

2. Use a Phillips screwdriver or push the case release button to remove your case.

3. When you have access to your motherboard, locate the memory expansion slots, as shown in Figure 12-1. Attach your anti-static wristband at this time. Don't have one? No big deal. Just touch any part of the metal case frame with your hand to discharge yourself.

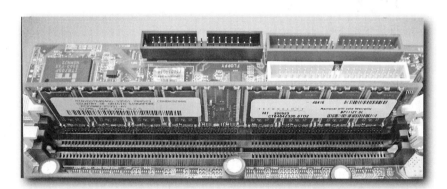

FIGURE 12-1: RAM expansion slots

4. Removing any existing pieces of RAM is very simple. Push the plastic or metal clips away from the sides of the stick of RAM. This will usually cause the RAM to pop out.

5. Putting a new stick of RAM in is just as easy. While the plastic clips are open (pushed away from the sides of the slot), align the chip the correct way so it fits in the slot properly and gently push down. As the stick of RAM goes down, it will cause the plastic clips on the sides to snap in place.

Put your case back on and hook up your cables and you are now finished. If you have any errors when your reboot on your BIOS screen or if your computer does not recognize the new RAM you put in, make sure you got the right kind and that it is seated properly in the slot.

Using a USB storage device to add memory

While upgrading the amount of RAM you have in your computer is a good last resort if you are having performance issues, Windows Vista introduces a cool new way that you can assist the amount of RAM you currently have. As I mentioned earlier, any time your computer has to kick applications and data out of RAM because there is not enough room slows down your computer because it has to store that data on the slow hard drive. In Windows Vista a new feature called Windows ReadyBoost allows you to use faster solid state memory devices, such as a USB memory device, to store this data instead of your slow hard drive. This provides an instant boost to system performance without your even having to open the case.

How does it work? The concept is simple. Solid-state USB 2.0–based storage devices have a faster read and write speed than most hard drives on the market. Windows ReadyBoost, with the assistance of Windows SuperFetch, another caching technology, works with a memory management system to redirect cached data to the high-speed device. At any time you can remove the device if you need to use it for another purpose. To protect the data that is cached on your removable USB device, Windows encrypts it so that if the device is removed, your data is safe.

Setting up Windows Vista to use your USB drive to increase performance is very easy. To get started, you will need a 256MB or larger USB 2.0 drive. Then follow these steps:

1. Plug your USB drive into one of your available USB ports.

2. After your computer recognizes the new device and it shows up in Computer, make sure that you have at least 235MB of free space on the drive. Right-click the drive and select Properties, as shown in Figure 12-2.

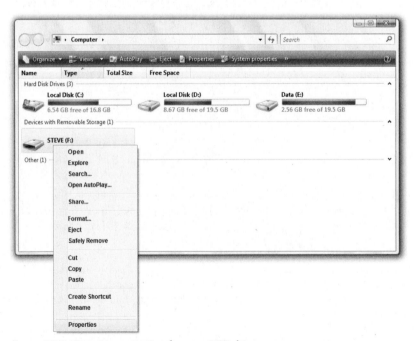

FIGURE 12-2: Opening properties for your USB drive

3. When the Properties window is shown, click the ReadyBoost tab.

4. Select Use this device and adjust the slider to set the amount of space to use for ReadyBoost, as shown in Figure 12-3.

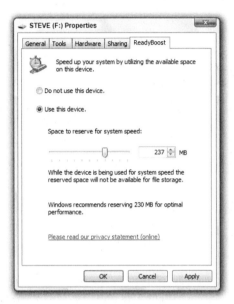

FIGURE 12-3: Using Windows ReadyBoost to increase performance

5. Click OK when you are ready and Windows ReadyBoost is now set up on your computer.

After you set up Windows ReadyBoost on one of your USB devices, it can be removed at any time. You can disable it at any time by selecting Don't use this device on the ReadyBoost tab you worked with earlier. Also, after you set up Windows ReadyBoost on your USB device, it cannot be used for Windows ReadyBoost on another Windows Vista computer without first having Windows ReadyBoost disabled on the computer it was set up with.

Tweaking the Paging File

The Windows paging file, also known as the swap file or virtual memory, is very important to the operation of Windows Vista. As I mentioned earlier, the operating system uses the paging file as a place to store data that was once in physical memory but was kicked out because Windows needed the space for other purposes.

Every ounce of data that the CPU works with has to be in physical memory before any work can be done. When you start an application, Windows loads the program from the hard drive into physical memory so the CPU can execute the code. Because most computers have a limited amount of physical memory (RAM), Windows has a complex paging system that allows applications that are running to be temporarily moved out of physical memory to make way for other applications. This data that was in memory is stored back into a file on the hard drive called the paging file.

Providing a critical memory feature by allowing the operating system to use more random access memory (RAM) than the computer actually has allows users to use more robust programs without upgrading their memory.

The exact method that the system uses to decide what programs will stay in the physical RAM and what programs will go is very complex and next to impossible to alter. However, there are several paging file hacks that will help you optimize your computer's use of the paging file. With the help of hacks to the system Registry, you can prevent certain files from being pushed into the paging as well as completely disabling the paging file to prevent the entire system from using it.

This next section guides you though the steps of optimizing the paging file for your computer.

Disabling the paging file

If you have a large amount of RAM in your box, you have the ability to stop the operating system from pushing any data out into the paging file. This will cause faster memory management and memory access than is physically possible for your RAM. Reading and writing directly to the RAM is always significantly faster than having to use the page file. Reading and writing to the paging file requires multiple steps and that takes time. First the data has to be copied out of physical RAM to the hard drive, and then the new data must be loaded from the hard drive into RAM and then executed. The hard drive is a big bottleneck in this situation.

If you have more than 2GB of RAM in your computer, you can consider disabling the paging file. If you have less than 2GB of RAM, do not even consider disabling the paging file or you will be running into problems.

What can happen if you disable your paging file? If you have enough RAM, nothing. But if you do not have enough RAM, your applications may refuse to load or even crash. For example, if you run Photoshop and are working on a large image, you will run into "out of memory" errors and the application will crash, causing you to lose all your work. This is a pretty extreme example, but it *can* happen to you if you don't have enough RAM.

Basically, stick to the 2GB minimum and you will have no problems. But be aware that if you ever choose to run some memory-intensive applications, such as rendering a two-hour 3D movie, you could run out of memory easily.

So, now that you know the concerns, you are ready to follow these steps to disable the paging file:

1. Click the Start button, right-click Computer, and select Properties.

2. When System has loaded, click Advanced system settings, as shown in Figure 12-4.

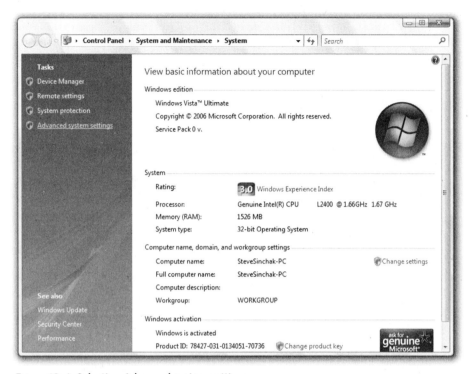

FIGURE 12-4: Selecting Advanced system settings

3. Under the Performance section, click Settings.

4. Click the Advanced tab and then press Change under Virtual memory.

5. This will load the Virtual Memory screen. Uncheck the box that says Automatically manage the paging file size for all drives.

6. For each drive listed in the box that has a paging file configured on it, select the No paging file option and press Set, as shown in Figure 12-5.

7. After you have gone through the list and verified that you no longer have any paging files configured on your drives, click OK to exit.

Your paging file will now be disabled after your reboot. Feel free to delete the pagefile.sys file from your hard drive after your reboot to gain a few hundred megabytes of free space.

If you do not have enough RAM to disable the paging file completely, follow the directions in the next section to adjust the size of the paging file for best performance.

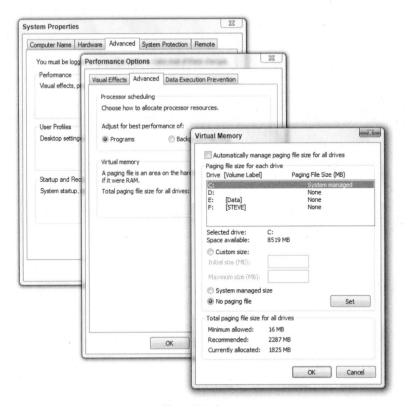

FIGURE 12-5: Using No paging file in Windows Vista

Adjusting the size of the paging file

The size of the page file can be set automatically by the system or it can be set by the user. In some situations, having the page file managed by the system is a good idea, but in others, it is better to manage the paging file yourself.

The biggest argument for setting the paging file size and limit manually is to eliminate growing of the page file when it is set by the system. When the system is managing the size of the paging file, it will monitor the size of the file and will then automatically make it larger when it is needed. This causes two problems. First, it will cause a noticeable delay for all applications running on your computer because the computer has to expand the paging file and this is a hard disk–intensive operation. Second, allowing the system to grow and shrink the paging file causes fragmentation errors.

For the sake of having enough speed, your page file should not have any file fragments. In the next section on defragmenting you will learn exactly how to fix this. But before the defragmentation can be successful, the page file needs to have a constant size. If the page file will be growing frequently, and because the defrag utility has no clue by how much, the defrag utility cannot put the file in a place on the hard disk so that it will never get fragmented, as is the case when you set the page file manually to a constant size.

Setting the paging file to a constant size does have some disadvantages. For example, the lost disk space taken up by the paging file can be as high as 5GB. Additionally, when you set the maximum paging file size manually, you are setting a limit that your computer can never go above. Should you run an extremely memory-intensive application and your limit is too low, your paging file will fill up and you will be out of luck in much the same way as when you completely disable your paging file.

The previous example illustrates why setting the correct paging file size is so important. An easy way to calculate the maximum size of your page file is to take the recommended size of the page file from the Virtual Memory Settings window, as shown in Figure 12-6, and multiply it by 2. If you are having problems finding where your computer states the recommended size, perform the following steps to change the paging file to a constant size because this value is on the same screen as the one on which you will be working.

FIGURE 12-6: Virtual Memory settings showing
the recommended paging file size

Now that you are ready to optimize the paging file to a constant size, follow these steps:

1. Click the Start button, right-click Computer, and select Properties.

2. When System has loaded, click Advanced system settings.

3. Under the Performance section, click Settings.

4. Click the Advanced tab and then press Change under the Virtual memory section.

5. This brings up all the page file settings. Modify the custom values so that the initial and maximum sizes are the same. To do this, you first need to enable the option to set a custom size, so select the Custom size option.

6. Enter the value that you calculated in these two boxes, as shown in Figure 12-7.

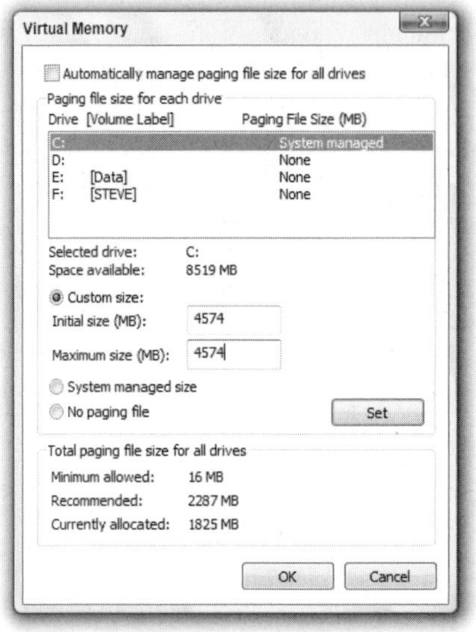

FIGURE **12-7: Setting the paging file to a custom size**

7. Click the Set button and then click OK to exit.

After you restart, you will be using the new constant size paging file. You are now ready to run your defragmenter to defragment the paging file to ensure optimal performance.

 Caution The method that I use to calculate the size of the constant paging file is a very conservative and effective approach. However, if you feel the need for more free disk space, feel free to play around with the calculation, such as multiplying the recommended amount by only 1.75 or maybe even 1.5. Although if you do that, keep in mind that you will be increasing your chances of maxing out your paging file.

Changing the location of the paging file

The paging file can be placed on any storage device in your computer. If you really wanted to, you can even move the paging file to an external hard drive connected over USB. Although this would probably slow down your system because an external hard drive is often slower than a hard drive connected inside your case, it is still possible. However, if you have multiple hard drives in your system, and I am not talking about multiple partitions on the same drive, you may see a performance increase if you move your paging file off the main system drive.

Moving the paging file off your main drive will allow it to be accessed faster in situations in which your primary hard drive is busy. When users add hard drives to their computers, these new hard drives are typically faster than the hard drives that the computers came with because of advances in technology over time. Moving your paging file to the faster hard drive will also help performance.

Changing the location of the paging file is very easy. Just follow these steps and you will have it done in no time:

1. Click the Start button, right-click Computer, and select Properties.

2. When System has loaded, click Advanced system settings.

3. Under the Performance section, click Settings.

4. Click the Advanced tab and then press Change under the Virtual memory section.

5. Now that you have the Virtual Memory settings displayed, select the drive on which your current paging file is located from the list of drives.

6. Before you make any changes, write down what the initial and maximum size text boxes contain. Then, click the No paging file option and press the Set button.

7. Select the hard drive on which you want your new paging file to be placed from the list of drives.

8. When the new hard drive is highlighted, select the Custom Size option and enter in the numbers that you wrote down before. If you are not using the Custom Size mode, click the System Managed Size mode but reconsider what was talked about in the last section because it will help your performance.

9. Click the Set button, click OK, and you are finished.

After a reboot, your system will be using the paging file on the new hard drive. Feel free to delete pagefile.sys from your old hard drive location; it no longer is needed there.

Defragmenting Your Hard Drive

Fragmentation is everything when it comes to maintaining your hard drive. Over time, as your hard drive fills up and you install and uninstall programs and games, the files on your hard drive can become fragmented, as Windows has to find open spots on your hard drive to place the file. Often the file is broken up into thousands of little pieces and scattered all over the hard drive. This cannot cause any significant problems for your computer, but it can cause a noticeable performance slowdown, which can be easily cured by just running a software program known as a *defragmenter*.

Defragmenters do the simple task of moving the bits of the files around on the hard drives so that they are all placed together. This arrangement allows the hard drive to load a file faster since the head, which is the arm that reads the data off the plates inside the drive, does not have to scatter all over the place to read the data.

In Chapter 8, I discussed using several utilities to defragment the boot files. The same utilities can be used to defragment the whole drive as well as the special files. The next section concentrates on two of those special files since defragmenting the whole drive is done at the same time.

Defragmenting the Windows paging file

The Windows paging file can be quite large, as you know from the previous sections. After you have created a constant size paging file, or if you just want to defragment the paging file, you can defragment the file during the next system boot. Windows will not allow any program to move the paging file around on the hard drive when the operating system is in use. The main reason Windows does not allow this is that other programs are running in the background, as are operating system services that will depend on the paging file. Defragmentation can be done only during the boot because very few files are in use at that time.

The built-in Windows defragmenter does not defragment the paging file during a normal defrag. Microsoft has a workaround for this limitation. It tells users to do a normal defrag first, and then after the free space is consolidated, to delete the paging file by disabling it and then recreating it right after a fresh defrag. Doing so will cause the operating system to create one big, continuous file on the hard drive.

There is nothing wrong with Microsoft's approach — it will accomplish the task — but there is an easier way to do this. I recommend that, if you have not already done so, you download the disk defragmenter utility called Diskeeper, by Executive Software (www.executive.com), which was discussed in Chapter 9. All that you have to do to defragment the paging file is to run a boot defrag. By default, the option to defragment the paging file is already set. If you do not remember how to do a boot defrag, go back to Chapter 9 and review the step-by-step instructions in the section "Boot-time system defrag with Diskeeper."

Defragmenting the NTFS master file table

The master file table, or MFT, is very important to the operation of the file system on your computer. Think of it as a phone directory of all the files on your computer. It is a big database of every file on your computer and it is stored on the hard drive. As the number of files and directories on your computer increases, so does the master file table. Over time, the master file table can also become fragmented. Because the master file table is so important to computer operations, it is used any time you want data from the hard drive. Defragmenting it will help your performance.

The built-in defragmenter will not defragment the MFT. Microsoft recommends that you adjust the amount of space that is reserved for the MFT, then back up your drive, then do a full reformat, and then restore your whole drive. This seems like way too much effort to me. Once again, Diskeeper comes to the rescue. Also, by default, when you perform a boot defrag, the option to defragment the master file table is already selected.

Using the Diskeeper method instead of the Microsoft method will save you hours of time that you would otherwise waste backing up and restoring your drive.

Adjusting Your Application Priorities

Ever since the introduction of the multitasking processor, operating systems have been able to handle running multiple programs at once using the new task switching and segmentation features provided by the CPU. These new technologies made it possible for operating systems such as Windows to be created. Even though PCs today are able to multitask, they still really can do only one thing at a time. In order for the operating system to support running dozens of applications at once, it has to slice up all the available processing time and give each application a turn. Although this is starting to change now with the introduction of multi-core processors, each core can still do only one thing at a time.

Operating systems use a variety of techniques to determine which application will get the next available slot to use the CPU. One of the factors that determine this for Windows Vista is the priority level at which the application is running.

Every application that runs on your computer has a priority level attached to its runtime record. By default, the operating system starts each application at normal priority, which is right in the middle of the priority spectrum. Applications can run and be assigned six different priority levels, ranked from highest to lowest: Realtime, High, Above Normal, Normal, Below Normal, and Low. Because the CPU can do only one thing at a time, the different priority levels allow the operating system to decide which application will get the next CPU burst. If an application is running at the High or Above Normal priority level, it will get more CPU time than an application running at the Normal level.

As you can see, the priority you give an application can affect how fast the program runs.

Using Task Manager to adjust priorities

Windows Task Manager is something that everyone experiences when they have problems with a frozen program. However, you learned that Task Manager is a very useful utility in Chapter 8. Another use of Task Manager is to change the priority at which an application is running. This capability can be very useful when you have a lot of programs running on your computer.

Caution

Setting any application to Realtime can be dangerous because doing so allows the application to hog all the CPU time. Trying to exit a program that is running at this high priority is next to impossible if for some reason it crashes or is stuck in a loop. It takes a very long time to just load Task Manager to end the application because the program is hogging all the CPU time.

If you have an application that has a high need for CPU operations such as rendering a video clip or a game, you can adjust the priority of the application by following these steps:

1. To load Task Manager, click the Start button, type **taskmgr** in the Search box, and then press Enter. If you have User Account Control enabled, you will need to run Task Manager under an account that is a member of the Administrators group on your computer. Alternatively, you can type **runas /u:Administrator taskmgr** to start Task Manager in the Administrator permission level but while you are logged on.

2. After Task Manager loads, click the Processes tab.

3. Right-click the name of the process for which you would like to adjust the priority, select Set Priority, and then select the level, as shown in Figure 12-8. Your change is now complete.

Tip

If your computer has multiple processors or multiple cores, or supports hyperthreading, then you will notice an extra option, Set Affinity, when you right-click a process. This option enables you to specify on which CPU the application will run (or which virtual CPU, in the case of hyperthreading users).

FIGURE 12-8: Using Task Manager to adjust application priorities

Using Task Manager to change the priority levels is great. However, there is one downside. When an application on which you have altered the priority level is closed, the priority level it was running at will be lost. The next time that the program is started, the program will be running back at the default level. This downside can be a pain in the butt for some users; however, a cool trick will fix this problem, as discussed in the next section.

Starting applications with a user set priority

A wonderful command built into Windows Vista allows you to start any program and specify its priority. This cool utility is called the Start command. Using the Start command with priority flags followed by the executable enables you to start any program at a priority level of your choosing.

For the sake of demonstrating how to use the command, assume that the Calculator is set at high CPU priority. Follow these steps to set the command:

1. Open Notepad to type the command so that it can be turned into a batch script file. This can be done by starting Notepad from the Accessories item in the Start menu's All Program entry.

2. After Notepad opens, type **start /high calc.exe**. If you want to start the Calculator at a different priority, you can replace /high with **/low, /normal, /realtime/, /abovenormal**, or **/belownormal**.

3. After keying in the priority level, click the File menu bar item in Notepad and select Save As. Change the file Save As Type to All Files and type **launchcalc.bat** in the file-name box. You can call the file anything you want, but make sure that it has the .bat file extension so that Windows knows to execute the commands in the file.

4. Specify a location on your hard drive to save it, such as your desktop, and click the Save button. You are now finished and can exit Notepad.

Now that you have created the batch command file, you are ready to start your new shortcut.

Tip

This tweak will work only if you run each batch file as an administrator or disable User Account Control. This is another tweak that is affected by User Account Control. Learn how to disable this in Chapter 14.

The same technique can be applied to any program on your computer. Instead of typing calc.exe at the end of the command, type the name of the executable of the program that you want to start.

Additionally, this command can be used on nonexecutable files such as documents. For example, you can type **start /high mydocument.doc** to start Microsoft Word in the High priority level with your document opened.

Using WinTasks to profile your priorities

Another great utility, made by Uniblue, is called WinTasks Pro. This utility is like Windows Task Manager, but on steroids. It offers tons of new features that Windows Task Manager does not have, such as the ability to see individual CPU and memory graphs for each application, scripting capabilities that allow the user to set up triggers based on CPU and memory activity for each application, and most important, the ability to have preset profiles for application priority levels. In addition to these features, it has built-in information about quite a few commonly known processes to help users figure out each process that is listed because they are often not easily identified by the process name.

Having a profile for your open application priority levels enables you to automatically change the priority of several applications at the click of a button.

WinTasks 5 Professional can be downloaded from www.liutilities.com/products/trial/. Download a copy now and install it if you would like to follow along with these steps, which guide you through creating a profile of your priorities:

1. To start WinTasks, click the Start button and type **Start WinTasks**. The shortcut will appear at the top of the list. Right-click the shortcut and select Run as administrator.

2. After WinTasks loads, you will see a list of all the different processes running on your computer. You can adjust the priority at which each process is running by right-clicking on the process and then selecting either Increase or Decrease Priority. Go ahead and change the priorities of all the applications that you have running to what you would like them to be.

3. When you are satisfied with all your priority changes and are ready to create a profile of them, click the little key icon on the Presets toolbar, as shown in Figure 12-9. If you do not see the Presets toolbar, select View ⇨ Toolbars ⇨ Presets.

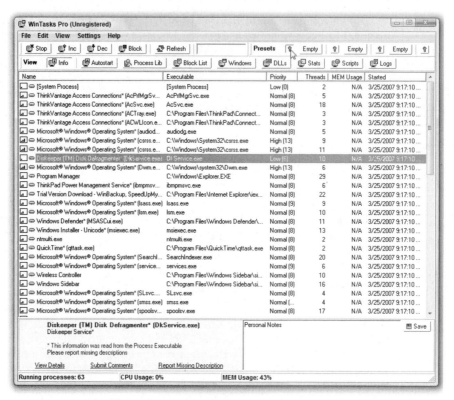

FIGURE 12-9: WinTasks Professional Presets save icon

4. Type a name to save the state of all the priorities as in the Save Preset window and press OK.

5. Next to the key icon that you pressed, you will notice the name showing up in the button to the right of it. Every time you press this button it will reset all the priorities to what you changed them to for this preset.

6. Repeat the previous steps, changing the priority levels for each application to a different value and then clicking on a different key icon to save the new preset again.

Now that you have multiple presets of application priority levels, you can easily switch between them by clicking the buttons.

The capability to create separate presets of priority levels for different applications allows you to optimize certain programs, depending on what you are doing. For example, you can create a profile for your processes when you want to play a game. To do that, you can decrease the priority of many of the system processes and applications running in the background so that a game running at normal or higher priority will have more CPU time.

Lower the priorities of all the other background applications, such as your instant messaging programs. This will allow your game to run faster because these other background applications will have a lower priority.

Summary

You have now finished optimizing the core components of Windows Vista. First you learned how to add more memory to your computer and about the new ReadyBoost feature of Windows Vista that allows you to gain some of the benefits of adding RAM without even opening your case to speed up memory access. Then, you learned how you can adjust your paging file and adjust your application priorities to speed up your hard drive access and how your CPU works.

Next, you looked at way to speed up your network connection. You started with browsing the network and your network card and worked your way outward to speeding up your Internet connection.

Speeding Up Your Web Browser and Network Connection

Y our browser and network subsystem play a major role in the use of your computer. People are spending more and more time using their web browsers and the Internet, making the web browser the most used application on many users' computers. Now that you have optimized almost every major component of the operating system, let's cover the most used application and components it is dependent on, the web browser and the network that connects you to the Internet.

First you will optimize the speed of both Internet Explorer and Firefox by tweaking the number of active downloads. Then I show you some great utilities that will increase the speed of your downloads, followed by tweaks that will speed up your network.

Optimizing Your Web Browser

On my computer the web browser is the most used application second only to my e-mail program and instant messenger. For society in general, the web browser is the most used application on the computer. Considering that you have already optimized, tweaked, and hacked almost every other component of the operating system for speed, it's important to cover the most used application as well. Using the following tweaks, you can make your web browser work faster than ever before. How is this possible? Both Internet Explorer and Firefox have to adhere to web standards that specify how many connections a browser can make to a web server. By default in both Internet Explorer and Firefox, that amount is two at a time. The following tweaks will show you how you can dramatically increase that number to speed up and increase the parallel downloading of files your web browser needs to display a web page.

Speeding up Internet Explorer

Microsoft has made sure that Internet Explorer follows Internet standards by allowing you and your browser to download only two files at a time from any server. If you visit a web page with a lot of images and required files, such as CSS styles and JavaScript, you can easily end up with a scenario where your web browser has to make more than 40 requests to the web server to download all the files and then assemble the web page. Requesting only two of these 40 files at a time is going to be a lot slower than downloading, say, 10 of them at a time.

By tweaking hidden registry values, you can direct Internet Explorer to break Internet standards and download more than just two files at a time. Modifying this setting is simple to do, but be careful; the standards police will be after you. Follow these steps to speed up IE:

1. Click the Start button, type **regedit** in the Search box, and then press Enter.

2. After Registry Editor loads, navigate through HKEY_CURRENT_USER\Software\ Microsoft\Windows\CurrentVersion\Internet Settings.

3. Right-click in an open space and create a new DWORD key, as shown in Figure 13-1.

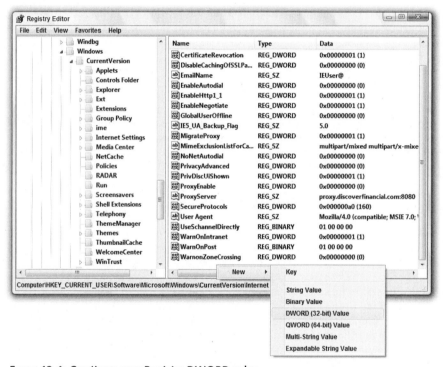

FIGURE 13-1: Creating a new Registry DWORD value

4. Type **MaxConnectionsPerServer** as the name of the new DWORD key.

5. Right-click this key and select Modify.

6. Set the base to Decimal and enter a value greater than 2, as shown in Figure 13-2. I like to use 15 as my value here. Press OK when you are done.

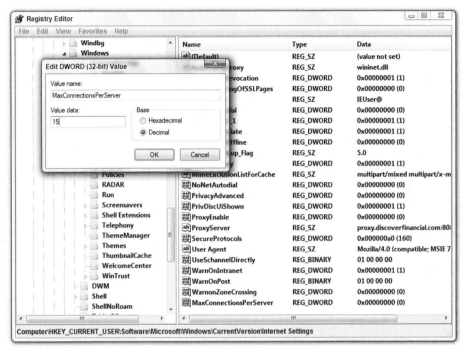

FIGURE 13-2: Setting the value of MaxConnectionsPerServer

7. Create a new DWORD key and type **MaxConnectionsPer1_0Server** as the name.

8. Right-click this key and select Modify.

9. Set the base to Decimal and enter the new value. Use the same value as used in step 6. Click OK when you are finished.

10. Exit Registry Editor and reboot your computer.

After your computer has rebooted, your new Internet Explorer settings are active. If you ever feel like undoing this tweak, just go back into the Registry and delete the MaxConnectionsPerServer and MaxConnectionsPer1_0Server keys that you created and reboot. Congratulations, you are now speeding on the information superhighway.

Speeding up Firefox

Firefox suffers from the same limitation on file downloads imposed on it as Internet Explorer by Internet standards. Thankfully, there is an easy way to modify the number of simultaneous downloads in Firefox as well. Additionally, you can do a few other things to speed up Firefox, such as reducing delays and enabling parallel downloads (which Firefox calls *pipelining*). Instead of editing the registry, you can use a cool hidden feature in Firefox to hack the raw configuration settings built right into the browser. Follow these steps to speed up browsing with Firefox:

1. Open a copy of Firefox if you do not already have it open.

2. Type **about:config** in the address bar and press Enter.

3. Scroll down the list and locate network.http.max-connections-per-server, as shown in Figure 13-3.

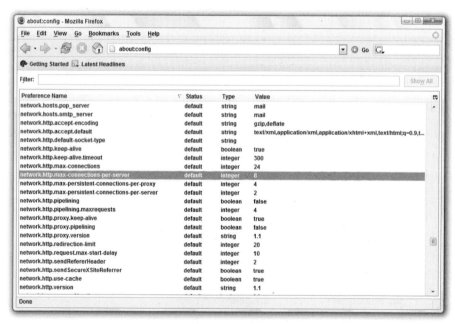

FIGURE 13-3: Modifying the configuration of Firefox

4. Right-click this setting and select Modify. Enter a higher value, such as 15, and press OK.

5. Enable parallel downloads, which is known as pipelining in Firefox. Scroll further down the list and locate network.http.pipelining.

6. Right-click this setting and select Toggle.

7. Scroll down and modify network.http.pipelining.maxrequests. Set this to a value of at least 15 and press OK.

If you use a proxy server to connect to the Internet, you will also want to toggle network .http.proxy.pipelining.

8. Let's reduce the paint delays in Firefox. But be careful with this one; according to the Mozilla Foundation, if you have a slower machine, this tweak can actually slow down Firefox. Right-click anywhere on the configuration screen and select New and then Integer.

9. Enter **nglayout.initialpaint.delay** in the name box and then **0** in the value boxes that pop up.

10. Close and restart Firefox to activate your new optimized settings.

Accelerating your downloads

The most popular web browsers do not currently include advanced download managers that have the ability to actually speed up your downloads. Have you ever noticed that when you download a file from a server, it almost seems that the server you are downloading from is setting a maximum speed on the file you are trying to get? I run into situations like this all the time. I am downloading a file and it seems to be stuck at some slow speed for my broadband connection. While that file is downloading, I start downloading another file from the server and this one also is downloading at near the same speed. No matter how many more additional files I download at the same time, they all seem to be stuck at the same speed, as if there is a maximum speed set for downloads.

Some web servers set a maximum download speed for file downloads, whereas other servers use various technologies to share their bandwidth among the other visitors, and others just seem to be inconsistent. All these situations can be helped with the use of a download accelerator application. Download accelerators work in much the same way as if you were downloading multiple files from the same server at once, only they download multiple chunks of the same file from the server at once. For example, in the scenario outlined previously, using a download accelerator that divides my file I was trying to download into four equal chunks. I was able to download the file almost four times faster than if I were to download it in one big chunk. There is no magic going on here; the download accelerator is just breaking up the file, which results in more actual connections. If a web browser has a set maximum download connection speed, when you have four connections downloading at once versus just one, the combined speed of four is always going to be much faster, which means your download finishes more quickly.

Some of the more advanced download accelerators do more than just split up your files. They search the web for other servers that also have the same file you are downloading and then determine the speed the files can be downloaded from the alternative sources. If the other sources are faster, the accelerator will switch and download the file from the faster server.

Various download accelerators are available. Some are free and others are shareware. Take a look at Table 13-1 for a list of popular download accelerators. For this section, I am going to use the Free Download Manager to speed up downloads.

Table 13-1   Popular Download Accelerators

Application Name	URL	Price
Star Downloader	www.StarDownloader.com	Free or $19.95 for advanced version
GetRight	www.GetRight.com	$29.95 for basic version
Free Download Manager	www.FreeDownloadManager.org	Free
Internet Download Manager	www.internetdownloadmanager.com	$29.95
Download Accelerator Plus	www.SpeedBit.com	Free, Ad supported

Using the Free Download Manager to speed up your downloads

The Free Download Manager is a very comprehensive download accelerator that includes many additional features that will help you manage your connection and find files on top of just downloading them. All you are interested in right now is finding ways to speed up downloads, so I am going to get right to the point. If you have not already done so, visit www.FreeDownloadManager.org now and download the latest version of the Free Download Manager.

After installing the latest version of the Free Download Manager and rebooting your computer, you are almost ready to get started using the download accelerator. First, you need to configure the Free Download Manager to allow you to split files into more than four chunks so that you can maximize the speed of your downloads. Follow these steps:

1. Click the Start button and then type **Free Download Manager** in the Search box. After a few seconds the shortcut will appear at the top of the selection of choices. Click it to start the download accelerator.

2. After the Free Download Manager loads, press and hold the Ctrl key and press the number 3. This will change your traffic usage mode to Heavy mode and will prompt the traffic mode change box, as shown in Figure 13-4. Heavy mode will allow you to download up to 7 files at once and split a single file a maximum of 20 times.

3. Click OK on the confirmation window and you are finished.

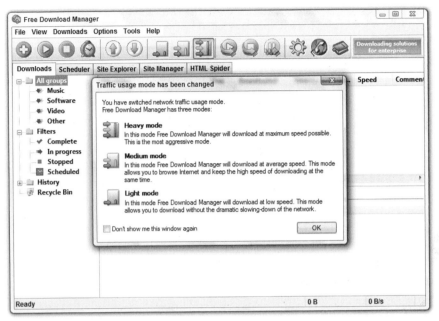

FIGURE 13-4: Changing the traffic usage mode to Heavy mode to allow for more downloads and file splits

You are now ready to begin downloading files with the Free Download Manager. Open a copy of Internet Explorer and browse to a Web site that you frequently download a lot of files from. Free Download Manager integrates with your web browser so that when you click a file to download, the Free Download Manager automatically takes over. Follow these steps to download files with the Free Download Manager:

1. When you click a link to download a file, the Free Download Manager will take over and prompt you, as shown in Figure 13-5. This is where you will select where you want the file to be downloaded to and other advanced settings. Locate the Advanced button on the bottom of the window and click it. This brings up the Advanced properties window.

2. You need to adjust the number of chunks the download accelerator splits the file into. Locate the Sections group on the Connection tab and increase the Maximum number to a higher number, as shown in Figure 13-6. I like to set my maximum number to 10. When you are finished, press OK to return to the Add download window.

3. After you have the Save to folder specified, make sure the Start property is set to Automatically and press OK.

Your file download will now begin. When the Free Download Manager is open and your file is downloading, click the Progress tab to see a graphical view of what parts of the file have already been downloaded.

FIGURE 13-5: Free Download Manager prompting you with the Add download window

FIGURE 13-6: Setting the number of chunks the download accelerator splits the file into

Speeding Up Your Network Connection

The speed of your network connection does not just depend on the speed of your hardware. Windows is an operating system that is designed to work on a variety of different hardware and network setups. Because of the abstract nature of the operating system, it cannot be optimized for user-specific hardware setups.

Depending on the type of network connection you have, you might be able to tweak your connection so that the speed of your Internet connection as well as of your local area network will be faster. By hacking the system Registry and editing the TCP/IP parameters, you can fine-tune the values so that you can take advantage of the more reliable, faster Internet connections such as DSL and cable. Windows Vista has a new advanced network stack that does a much better job than previous versions of Windows of calculating what the best values are for your connection. However, the exact algorithms it uses are kept secret, so you never will know if it truly is using the optimal values for your specific network makeup. Because of that simple fact, I still feel it is best to set these values manually.

The next sections guide you through the steps of increasing both the speed of your local area network and your Internet connection.

Disabling unneeded protocols

Every computer comes with programs installed that you do not need. As with extra programs taking up space, extra protocols are just wasting your network connection and can actually slow it down. How is this possible? By default, a few different protocols are installed on your computer to allow for maximum compatibility with other computers on a network; these protocols each require bandwidth to operate. Most users will not use too many protocols, and their computers will use up a portion of their connection as they respond and transmit information for these protocols.

Additionally, with extra protocols installed on your network adapter connected to the Internet, you increase your risk that you will have security-related problems. One of the most common risks for broadband users is having the Client for Microsoft Networks networking protocol enabled on their connection and no firewall to block the public from their computer. This protocol allows everyone on their network, or local neighborhood if you have a cable connection without a firewall or router, to connect to the users' computers and view any files that they may be sharing. This fact alone should be a good enough reason for you to turn off the extra protocols. But with them disabled, you will save a little bandwidth as well.

Viewing protocols on your network adapters

Viewing the protocols installed and active on your various network adapters is very easy. Just follow these quick steps and you will be viewing them in no time:

1. Click the Start button, right-click Network, and then select Properties.

2. On the side menu, click Manage network connections. This will show a list of all the network devices installed on your computer.

3. Right-click any of the devices and select Properties. This will bring up a list of the protocols installed as well as active on your adapter (see Figure 13-7). The protocols that are installed but are not active are indicated by the absence of a check in the box.

FIGURE 13-7: Network adapter protocol list

Disabling a specific protocol

Now that you have the list of installed and active protocols on your screen, you are ready to disable a protocol. To do so, just click the check box to remove the check. Then click OK and the protocol will no longer be active on the network adapter. Take a look at Table 13-2 for help with the default Windows protocols. Any other protocols you may have listed that are not in Table 13-2 should be researched online before being disabled.

For optimal speed configuration, disable all protocols except for Internet Protocol Version 4. Note, however, that by doing so you will no longer be able to share or access shared files and resources, and certain programs and features that rely on the other protocols may not work.

Table 13-2   Windows Vista's Networking Protocols

Protocol Name	Function
Client for Microsoft Networks	Used to access other shared resources on your local network running the File and Printer Sharing for Microsoft Networks protocol.
QOS Packet Scheduler	Used to provide traffic management on your network for applications that support the protocol.
File and Printer Sharing for Microsoft Networks	Used to share your printer and files on your computer with other computers on your local network.
Internet Protocol Version 6 (TCP/IPv6)	New version of the IPv4 protocol that is not very widespread. Unless you are connected to an IPv6 network (99% of you are not), you can safely disable this protocol.
Internet Protocol Version 4 (TCP/IPv4)	Primary network communication protocol. Do not disable this protocol.
Link Layer Topology Discovery Mapper I/O Driver	Used to discover other computers connected to your local network.
Link Layer Topology Responder	Used to identify your computer to other computers connected to your local network.

Also keep in mind that if you have multiple network adapters in your computer — such as a wireless adapter, a wired network adapter, and a dial-up modem — you will have to repeat the preceding instructions for each device.

Summary

This chapter completes the final chapter in Part II, "Increasing Your System's Performance." I covered speeding up every aspect of Windows Vista, from the moment you press the power button to using your most frequent applications. In this last chapter, I went over how to speed up your web browser and download files faster. Then, I went back to optimize the system components that you need in order to browse the Web, the network.

The next part of *Hacking Windows Vista* covers securing your computer. Windows Vista has a lot of cool new security features that will help you address your security problems. The next few chapters show you how to use those new features as well as many additional security hacks that will help make spyware, adware, and hackers a distant memory.

Securing
Your System

part

Windows Security

Security is one of the most important issues in the Windows computer world. Over the years, as Windows gained popularity and as it grew to become the dominant operating system on the market, it became the prime target for hackers and other individuals who want to find ways to compromise your system. Additionally, we continue to use our computers for more and more activities, which results in a massive amount of highly valuable and confidential information stored inside. Today it is not uncommon to have personal financial information, hundreds of personal documents, and thousands of priceless digital photos all stored in our computers. As the amount of personal data stored on our computers increases, the reward to compromise a system increases as well. This creates an enormous need for a secure operating system that will keep your data safe.

According to Microsoft, Windows Vista is the most secure version of Windows released in history. While there has been a massive effort to completely rework the security model in Windows Vista, and Windows Vista is definitely the most secure version of Windows ever released, it is still not perfect. Security patches are still released to protect users from new attacks, and a lack of education on the new security features results in many users' not using them.

This chapter will help you get the most out of the new security features in Windows Vista and lock down your computer using common industry best practices to protect your computer from getting compromised.

Actively Protecting Your Computer

The days when running an antivirus program on your computer alone was enough to protect it are long over. Now you need to play a more active role in the process of protecting your computer. The types of threats are changing very quickly. Currently, the most effective way to compromise a computer is by taking advantage of the human factor — that is, tricking you into running some code that will install a malicious program on your computer to help someone steal your data and take over your machine. Another effective method to compromise a computer is to exploit a known vulnerability in the operating system to break in. In this situation, a user is not up-to-date on their security patches and they are basically leaving the door unlocked so that anyone can just step right in and install and steal anything they want.

Taking an active role in securing your computer involves keeping up-to-date on the latest security news so that you know about new vulnerabilities and methods hackers are using to compromise your computer. Additionally, you need to know what to look out for to make sure that you do not fall for any undocumented hacks or tricks, as well as to make sure the known vulnerabilities are fixed on your computer.

This section is going to help you with all the aspects of actively protecting your computer. First, I show you some great ways to keep up-to-date on the latest security news. Then, I show you how to make sure that Automatic Updates in Windows Vista is working properly and that your computer has all known vulnerabilities fixed. Finally, I give you some pointers that will help protect you from falling for most undocumented and unknown hacks and tricks to compromise your computer.

Staying up-to-date

One of the largest parts of taking an active role in protecting your computer's security is keeping up-to-date with the latest trends and news on active vulnerabilities. There are various Web sites and newsletters that can help you stay on top of the latest Windows security news. Take a look at the following sites and sign up for some of the newsletters to say on top of the latest security threats:

- **Microsoft's Security at Home Newsletter:** This newsletter is targeted at less technical home users and has a lot of information on good techniques for better "human" security, as I mentioned earlier. The newsletter is free and you can sign up at www.microsoft.com/athome/security/secnews/default.mspx.

- **TechNet's Microsoft Security Newsletter:** This newsletter, which targets advanced computer users, goes into more depth concerning the latest security patches released, in addition to general security news. This newsletter is also free and you can sign up at www.microsoft.com/technet/security/secnews/default.mspx.

- **TrendMicro's Security Info:** This is a security Web site that will help you find out about the latest viruses, malware, and vulnerabilities for Windows Vista and popular applications that run on it. Visit www.trendmicro.com/vinfo/ to get the latest news.

- **McAfee Dispatch:** This newsletter will alert you of the latest virus threats as well as keep you up-to-date with general virus-related news. The newsletter is free and can be subscribed to at http://dispatch.mcafee.com/us/.

- **US-CERT:** This is the federally funded Computer Emergency Readiness Team Web site, which provides information on the latest security news and vulnerabilities for Windows Vista and every other computer software product, including applications that run on Windows. US-CERT is a very comprehensive Web site that has several RSS feeds that you can subscribe to with your favorite RSS reader or with Internet Explorer. Visit www.us-cert.gov to use this massive resource.

Updating Windows Vista

Another key part of actively protecting your computer is to make sure that all the known vulnerabilities have been fixed. Every month, Microsoft releases new security patches for all their products that fix security holes and increase the security of Windows. It is very important to make sure that your computer is set up to automatically download these new security patches and that it is working properly. With the new Windows Update feature in Windows Vista, this is easier than ever before.

Updating Windows Vista is quite simple and is something you need to do every month. Follow these steps to make sure that Automatic Updates in Windows Vista is working properly and that you have the latest security patches installed:

1. Click the Start button and then Control Panel.

2. Under the Security section, click Check for updates.

3. Make sure that your computer has the latest security patches installed. Click Check for updates from the top of the left menu, as shown in Figure 14-1. If any updates are available, make sure you install them right away by clicking Install Updates.

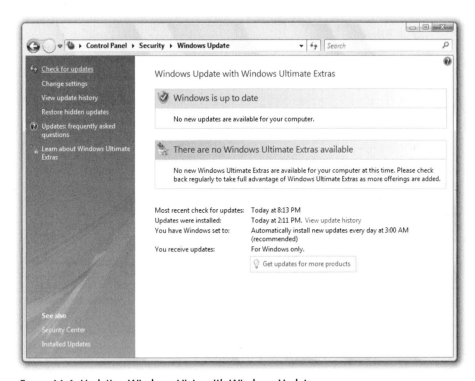

Figure 14-1: Updating Windows Vista with Windows Update

4. Now that your computer is up-to-date, make sure it stays that way by making sure Automatic Updates is set up and running. Click Change Settings to bring up the Automatic Updates details.

5. Make sure that the Install updates automatically box is selected, as shown in Figure 14-2. I also like to adjust the install time from 3:00 AM to a time I know my computer is going to be on. Because my computer is usually on when I am at lunch, I use 12:00 PM for my update time.

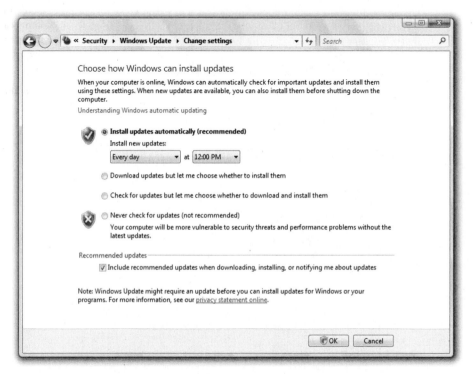

FIGURE 14-2: Configuring Automatic Updates in Windows Vista

6. After everything is set, click OK to save your changes.

Windows is now up-to-date and will remain up-to-date when Microsoft releases new security patches for Windows Vista.

Active security tips

As I mentioned earlier, one of the easiest ways to break into a computer to install malware or steal data is through the human factor. This works by taking advantage of the fact that we do not usually read the fine print for an application that we download or are just click-happy and click Yes on any dialog box that pops up. If you exercise a little caution and follow the upcoming recommendations, you can take the human element completely out of the picture. So, let's get started.

Don't get in the habit of clicking Yes/Continue/Allow

In Windows Vista, User Account Control provides more control over what applications automatically get installed on your computer. The days of visiting a Web site and getting junk automatically installed on your computer are over. In Windows Vista, User Account Control, when configured properly, requires you to authorize almost all changes to your computer, including system configuration changes and installing new programs. To some, these prompts can become overwhelming and result in the habit of just clicking Continue on all of them that pop up. Such behavior completely bypasses the new security features in Windows Vista, allowing almost anything to completely take over your system.

The next time you get a User Account Control pop-up, click the Details arrow, as shown in Figure 14-3, to find out exactly what you are allowing.

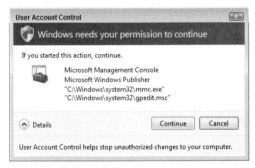

FIGURE 14-3: Viewing details on a User Account Control pop-up

Watch out what Internet Explorer plug-ins you install

Internet Explorer plug-ins are notorious for bundling all sorts of extra junk along with the application, especially those by Web sites that offer some free application. There is usually a reason why the application is free. Most companies are in business to make money and they have to make money some way. They usually get paid for bundling additional software with their software. This can result in a bunch of new applications popping up on your computer when you thought you installed just one.

Most of the more popular Web sites are a little more forthcoming about what extra junk they are going to install on your computer. You can find if they are going to install any other applications by reading the user agreement that everyone just clicks right past and by paying attention to the installation options. There are usually check boxes that enable you to prevent other applications from being installed. If you are visiting a lesser-known Web site or a Web site that may have illegal or adult content, I highly recommend not installing any plug-in unless you do research and can verify it is a legitimate plug-in.

If you didn't start it, be cautious

If you are using your computer and you are hit with a surprise User Account Control pop-up, one that you did not expect, be very cautious about clicking Continue and allowing the request to be granted. For example, let's say you are typing a document and all of a sudden User Account Control wants you to approve a system change. This may be a big indication that your computer is infected with some sort of malware or virus that is trying to change your system settings. I recommend doing a full system virus and malware scan immediately to make sure that your computer is clean.

Secure your network connection

One of the best ways to secure your computer is to place it behind a firewall or a router device that will protect it from malicious Internet traffic. By blocking the public access to your internal network or wide open access to your computer, you can effectively kill the potential for certain types of direct attacks.

In the next chapter, I show in greater detail how you can use firewalls to protect your computer.

Protect your accounts

Your account is safe only as long as no one has or can guess your password. Make sure that you have a password on all your accounts and that it is never written down anyplace. The next section will help you secure your computer accounts and pick complex passwords that will be hard for anyone to guess and hack with brute force techniques.

Controlling Your Computer Accounts

Your computer's physical security, as well as online security, depends on how easy it is to access your accounts. This book is going to show you many ways that you can protect your computer but almost all of them can be defeated by an account on your computer that has a poor password or no password at all. This is why it is critical to ensure that you computer is protected by accounts with strong passwords. Anything less will weaken your entire security defense.

This section will show you how you can manage your user accounts in Windows Vista to make sure they are all well protected.

Managing user accounts

Windows Vista includes various accounts that are set up when you install or buy a Windows Vista computer. These accounts are usually disabled by default, but there are few quick tips that will ensure they can never be used to again. The other accounts on your computer can be protected, too. Follow the steps in the next few sections to secure all your accounts.

Using complex passwords on all your computer accounts

All the accounts on your computer should have a complex password associated with them in case your computer is ever exposed to the Internet. Passwords such as easy-to-remember words and predictable key combinations such as "asdf" just do not cut it. These types of passwords are vulnerable to brute force dictionary attacks where an intruder can use special software to try hundreds of combinations to hack into your account.

A complex password is a password that is at least eight characters long and consists of upper-case and lowercase letters, as well as numbers or other symbols. "Ftm3D8&-" is an example of a complex password. Something like that is impossible to guess and will take quite some time for a brute force technique to crack it.

Using complex passwords on all your accounts might not be easy at first, but after a while they will grow on you and you will have no problem remembering them. To prevent losing access to any encrypted files, it is best to log onto each account on your computer that does not already have a complex password and then change it. If you use the Set Password function in Computer Manager, as you did for setting the passwords for the Guest and Administrator accounts, you risk losing access to any files that were encrypted under the user's account.

Follow these steps to safely change a user's account password:

1. Log onto the user's account you want to change the password for.

2. Press and hold Ctrl+Alt+Delete so that the secure desktop is shown (see Figure 14-4).

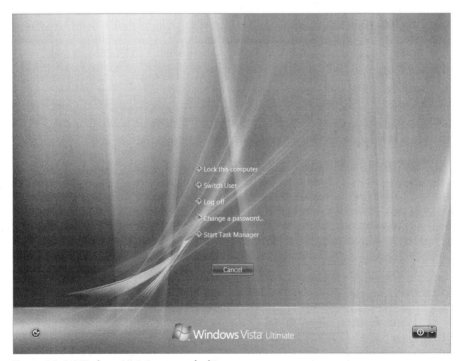

FIGURE 14-4: Windows Vista's secure desktop

3. Click the Change a password button.

4. Type the old password once and then the new password for the user twice, and click the blue arrow button.

The password for the account has now been changed.

Assigning a password and renaming the guest account

One of the default accounts set up in Windows Vista is the Guest account. This account can be useful if your computer is in a public place such as a library and a low rights account is needed. However, for most of us, this account is just another possible security hole because it cannot be deleted. It is disabled by default but it could be enabled again by a virus or malware if your computer ever gets infected. The best way to neutralize this account is to give it a random password and rename it to eliminate the chances that some script will be able to use it.

Follow these steps to protect this account:

1. Click the Start menu, right-click Computer, and then select Manage.

2. After Computer Manager loads, expand Local Users and Groups and select the Users folder. All the local computer accounts will be listed, as shown in Figure 14-5.

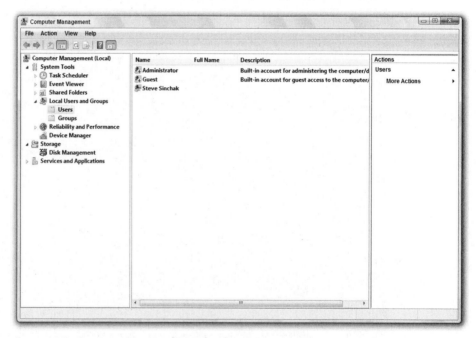

FIGURE 14-5: Computer Manager listing local computer accounts

3. Right-click the Guest account on the list and select Set Password.

4. A warning screen will appear, telling you about what may happen if you proceed. Disregard this message and click Proceed.

5. When the Set Password window appears, type in a completely random password that is a complex password and is also at least 20 characters long in both boxes and click OK. The new password will now be set.

6. Rename the account to confuse any malicious scripts that might be looking for it. Right-click the Guest account again and select Rename.

7. Type a new name for this account that has some random letters and numbers in it. You just want to make it different from Guest.

8. When you are done renaming it, click Enter and you are finished.

Your Guest account is now more secure than ever.

Secure the Administrator account

The Administrator account is the most important account on the computer because it has the highest permissions and can do anything it wants to the configuration and settings of your computer. Securing this valuable account is critical to the overall security of your computer.

This can be accomplished by ensuring the account is disabled, setting a strong password, and renaming it so that it is harder for malicious scripts and viruses to try to use. Doing this is very similar to securing the Guest account as you just did in the last section.

Follow these steps to protect your Administrator account:

1. Click the Start menu, right-click Computer, and select Manage.

2. After Computer Manager loads, expand Local Users and Groups and select the Users folder.

3. Right-click the Administrator account and select Properties.

4. Check the Account is disabled option if it is not already selected, as shown in Figure 14-6. Then, click OK to save the changes.

5. Right-click the Administrator account and select Set Password.

6. A warning screen will appear, telling you about what might happen if you proceed. Disregard this message and click Proceed.

7. When the Set Password window appears, type a completely random complex password that is at least 20 characters long in both boxes and click OK. The new password will now be set.

8. Rename the account to confuse any malicious scripts that might be looking for it. Right-click the Administrator account again and select Rename.

9. Type a new name for the account that has some random letters and numbers in it. I like to use AdminDisabled2341 as a new name.

10. Press Enter and you are finished.

Now both of the built-in Windows Vista accounts are secured.

FIGURE 14-6: Disabling the Administrator account

Clearing the last user logged on

If you use your computer in a corporate environment or are just forced to use the classic Windows 2000 style logon screen, it is very important to clear your username from the user-name box so that potential intruders will not be able to figure out your username before they can even try to break your password. Using the local security policy to your advantage, you can configure a setting that will automatically clear the username of the last person that logged in. This will add another layer of protection on your account by putting it in stealth mode.

Follow these instructions to turn on this setting:

1. Click the Start button, type **secpol.msc** in the Search box, and then press Enter.

2. After the Local Security Policy editor has loaded, expand Local Policy and then select Security Options.

3. Scroll through the list and right-click "Interactive logon: Do not display last username" and select Properties.

4. Select the Enable box, as shown in Figure 14-7, and then click OK.

5. Close the Local Security Policy editor and you are finished.

The next time you reboot, your username will be hidden.

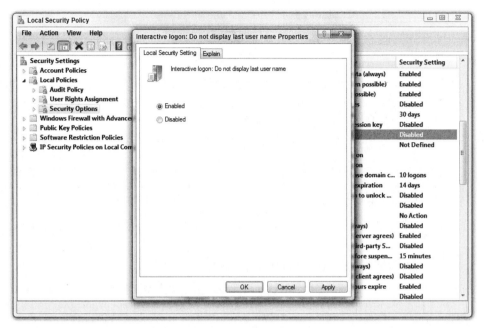

FIGURE 14-7: Hiding your username with the Local Security Policy editor

Setting the Account Lockout Policy

To complement the new complex password that your accounts now have, I recommend configuring the Account Lockout Policy to add even more security to your accounts. The Account Lockout Policy enables you to protect your account from an intruder trying dozens or even thousands of possible password combinations to try to guess you password. When this policy is configured, after the intruder has entered the wrong password a set number of times, the account will then be locked out for a set amount of time. After that time interval has passed, the account is unlocked and the whole process is reset.

This provides valuable additional security for your accounts that will eliminate the effectiveness of certain brute force tools that will try every possible combination to hack into your account. By using the Account Lockout Policy, you can increase the amount of time required to try every possible combination into an unfeasible amount of time required.

Setting the Account Lockout Policy is very similar to configuring your computer to not show the last username that was used to log in. Follow these steps to configure the lockout policy for your computer:

1. Click the Start button, type **secpol.msc** in the Search box, and then press Enter.

2. After the Local Security Policy editor has loaded, expand Account Policies and then select Account Lockout Policy.

3. Right-click Account lockout threshold and select Properties.

4. Increase the number of invalid logon attempts from 0 to a higher value to enable the feature. I like to use 5 as my number of invalid logon attempts before my account is locked out.

5. Click OK to save the setting. A Suggested Value Settings window pops up that will automatically populate the two other settings, Account lockout duration and Reset account lockout counter after. Click OK here as well to use the default values.

6. If the 30-minute duration of the account lockout and before the account lockout counter is reset is too long for you, just right-click each setting, select Properties, and modify the value. I typically use 10 minutes for both of these settings because I think it is a nice balance between added security and inconvenience when I may be using my computer half asleep and type in the wrong password more than five times.

Your Account Lockout policy is now set up and will begin protecting your computer immediately.

Tweaking User Account Control

You are probably very familiar with User Account Control (UAC) by now because almost every time that you make a change directed by this book you get a UAC box popping up asking you to confirm the changes. This is a great new security feature in Windows Vista but is also probably one of the most annoying for new users. It provides standard users an easy way to do things that only administrators have access to by prompting them for an admin account while also confirming with an administrator any changes that are occurring to a system when they are logged on.

User Account Control provides total control over all changes to a system. If you try to install a program, install a plug-in, or access any application that has the capability to change critical system settings, UAC goes into action and makes sure that you really want to do what an application is trying to do on your computer. In terms of the security of your computer, UAC is great because it catches when applications, scripts, and even Web sites try to do things to your computer that cause a critical change. However, if you initiate the change, such as trying to install a program or modify a Windows setting, you also have to deal with the pop-ups because of the way UAC is designed.

User Account Control works by monitoring the Application Programming Interface (API), system components, and application configuration files, to find out if an action needs higher privileges. If an action is found, then it prompts a UAC box for your authorization. The method UAC uses to detect the actions is the reason why you are sometimes bombarded with UAC authorization pop-ups because to the system it is no different if a user initiated the action or if a script generated it. Because of the design of UAC, it is impossible for Microsoft to cut down on certain types of pop-ups. However, they have built in the functionality that allows power users such as you the ability to change the behavior of UAC and even disable it completely. Although I am against completely disabling UAC because of the value that it does add for protecting your computer, it can use a little tweaking and the next section is going to show you just that.

Controlling User Account Control

The new User Account Control in Windows Vista plays a big role in the overall security of the operating system. No longer do you have to worry about software secretly getting installed or scripts running that change critical system data running without your knowledge. Instead, you have to worry about getting bombarded with UAC pop-ups that require you to authorize almost every change this book asks you to do. Thankfully, Microsoft did not implement this feature without adding the ability for power users to tweak it to make their lives easier while still benefiting from some of the protections of UAC.

Configuring UAC is done through modifying the Local Security Policy. You have already done something similar with the Local Security Policy editor when you set the logon screen to clear the last logon and set up the Account Lockout Policy. You can tweak nine different settings for the UAC, as described in Table 14-1.

Table 14-1   User Account Control Settings

Setting Name	Function
User Account Control: Admin Approval Mode for the Built-in Administrator account	This determines whether an Administrator that is logged on and working will get UAC prompts. This account is usually disabled, so this setting is useless.
User Account Control: Behavior of the elevation prompt for administrators in Admin Approval Mode	This determines which type of prompt an Administrator receives. You can choose between just prompting for consent, a prompt asking for the admin password, or disabling the prompting altogether.
User Account Control: Behavior of the elevation prompt for standard users	This determines the type of UAC prompt standard users receive. By default, this is set to prompt for credentials, but it can be set to disable prompting.
User Account Control: Detect application installations and prompt for elevation	This allows you to disable UAC prompts for installing new applications.
User Account Control: Only elevate executables that are signed and validated	This setting is disabled by default, but if you want a super-secure system that can run only applications that are signed with a certificate, you can enable this.
User Account Control: Only elevate UIAccess applications that are installed in secure locations	This allows UAC to elevate only those applications that are in secure locations such as your local hard drive. An unsecured location may be an untrusted network drive.
User Account Control: Run all administrators in Admin Approval Mode	Similar to the Admin Approval Mode for the built-in Administrator account, this setting applies to all accounts that are members of the Administrator security group.

Continued

Table 14-1   *Continued*

Setting Name	Function
User Account Control: Switch to the secure desktop when prompting for elevation	Allows you to specify if you want to switch to a secure desktop, one where other applications and scripts do not have access, to protect the UAC prompts from being manipulated by scripts and applications instead of end users.
User Account Control: Virtualize file and registry write failures to per-user locations	Provides the ability for users running as standard users to be able to still run applications that might previously have required administrative rights. This redirects system registry entries that are protected by admin permissions to local user locations so the application will still run.

Changing the UAC settings is easy to do with the Local Security Policy editor. Just follow these steps to modify the settings:

1. Click the Start button, type **secpol.msc** in the Search box, and then press Enter.

2. After the Local Security Policy editor loads, expand Local Policy and select Security Options.

3. Scroll to the bottom of the list to see all the UAC security policies. Right-click a policy and select Properties to modify it.

4. When you're finished, click OK to save the changes.

As you can see, editing the User Account Control's settings is very simple. If you are fed up with the User Account Control and want to completely disable it, all you need to do is set both the "User Account Control: Behavior of the elevation prompt for administrators in Admin Approval Mode" and "User Account Control: Behavior of the elevation prompt for standard users" policies to no prompt and you will no longer have any annoying prompts. However, you will have just killed one of the best security features in Windows Vista. That is why I believe that it is possible to still use User Account Control while decreasing some of the annoying prompts. The next section will show you how I like to configure my UAC settings for a good balance.

A good compromise between User Account Control and security

While many people want to disable UAC completely, I am against this because of the added security it provides to Windows Vista. Instead, I like to configure my computer in a way that I can get the best of both worlds — being able to install applications and freely configure Windows settings without getting bombarded with UAC prompts, while still getting the security of UAC. How is this possible? Use two accounts!

All too often people like to use their computer logged on with a user that is a member of the Administrators group. They do this accidentally or without even knowing it because when your account is created as part of the end of the Windows Vista setup, it automatically adds it to the local Administrator security group. The end result is a situation in which you have to be treated as a standard user and authorize every single change in order to secure the system. I offer a better solution to secure the system that will greatly reduce the number of prompts you see that is very simple and almost easier to use once you get the hang of it.

This is how it works: You will have two accounts on your machine. One for your day-to-day use that will be a low-rights standard user account with UAC running, and another account that will have full admin rights with UAC disabled so that you can easily install and change system settings with it when needed.

To do this, you need to convert your administrator level account down to a standard user account. Next, create a new administrator account that is for the sole purpose of installing and managing applications and changing system settings. You will then configure UAC to not prompt authorizations on that special admin account so that you can be free of the UAC annoyances when using it.

After creating your two accounts, you will have your standard user level account that you will use 99 percent of the time for your day-to-day work that is protected with UAC, ensuring your computer is secure. Then, when you need to make a bunch of system changes or install a bunch of applications, you can use fast user switching to switch into the system configuration admin account you created to quickly make your changes without having to worry about UAC.

Follow these detailed steps to configure your computer this way to get the best of both worlds:

1. Convert your account to a standard user account. Click the Start button and select Control Panel.

2. Under the User Accounts and Family Safety section, select Add or remove user accounts.

3. Select your account from the list of accounts.

4. Under Make changes to your user account, select Change the account type.

5. Select Standard user instead of Administrator and click Change Account type. You have now finished converting your account to a standard user account.

6. Create a new account that you are going to use only for installing and managing applications and changing system settings. Go back to Control Panel and select Add or remove user accounts again. This time select Create a new account.

7. Type the name of the account; I like to use System Configuration as the name of my account. Then, select Administrator as the type of account and click Create Account. You are now finished creating the separate administrator account. Now, the only part left to do is configure UAC to not show prompts to your new admin configuration account.

8. Go back into the Local Security Policy editor by clicking the Start button, typing **secpol.msc** in the Search box, and pressing Enter.

9. Navigate through Local Policies and Security Options and locate " User Account Control: Run all administrators in Admin Approval Mode." Right-click this policy and select Properties.

10. Select Disable and click OK to save the changes. You are now finished setting up UAC to not run for your system configuration account.

After you are finished with these steps, you can easily switch to the configuration account with higher rights by pressing and holding Ctrl+Alt+Delete. Then click Switch User and select the configuration account. When you are finished doing your work that required higher rights, just press Ctrl+Alt+Delete again and switch back to your low rights session.

Using File Encryption

Do you have important documents on your computer that you don't want anyone else to see? Sure, you can set file permissions on files so that only your account can read them; isn't that enough? Unfortunately, it is not, as there are many ways that file permissions can be manipulated and your account password replaced if someone has physical access to your computer. If your computer is stolen or if someone breaks into your office or home, the only way to truly protect important data is to encrypt it.

Windows Vista includes two different levels of encryption: file level and hard drive level. The file-based encryption is a feature of the NTFS file system, whereas the drive-level method is a feature in Windows Vista called *BitLocker Drive Encryption*. The main difference between the two is that BitLocker Drive Encryption can encrypt your entire drive or partition so that even the file system is protected. Everything on the drive, including the operating system, is encrypted so that no one will even be able to boot up the OS if they do not have access to the device where the encryption key is stored. The security of BitLocker Drive Encryption comes at the price of performance and requires certain hardware, which is why file level encryption is often preferred. So, I am going to cover that first.

Encrypting your files

File level encryption in Windows Vista is very easy to do. However, there are some steps that are best taken before you start encrypting files to make sure that you can always decrypt your files at a later time no matter what events occur. This next section will show you why it is important to set up a Recovery Agent in Windows Vista.

Setting up a Recovery Agent

What happens to your data if some day you forget your password and someone has to set you a new one or if you are forced to reload Windows Vista because of a major Windows or hardware failure? In all of these events you will end up losing access to any files you encrypted earlier because of the way the encryption system is safeguarded. If you encrypt files on your computer, you want to make sure that they are safe and no one but you can read them. Windows needs to make sure that your encrypted files can be decrypted only by the account that wanted them protected.

If someone else has an administrator account on your computer, he has the access to set a new password for your account and then he can log on using your username and password. Typically, anyone logging on to your account has full access to all of your encrypted files; however, in the preceding scenario, to protect your files Windows removes access to them so that even your account can no longer access the files. This feature has both good and bad effects. It is very good because it is smart enough to still protect your data; however, you can also lose access to your own documents. There is, however, a solution to this dilemma: Using local group policy, you can specify a recovery agent that will give you the ability to always decrypt your own files.

This works by instructing the encryption system to add an extra certificate to a file when it is in the process of encrypting. This extra certificate belongs to what is commonly called the *Recovery Agent*. Setting up the Recovery Agent is two-fold. First you must generate the certificate assigned to the Recovery Agent. Then, you need to set up the encryption system to use it. Follow these steps to get your Recovery Agent up and running:

1. Log on to an account on your computer that is a member of the Administrators group.

2. Click the Start button, type **cipher /r:rafile** in the Search box, and then press Enter.

3. When prompted, type a password to protect the Recovery Agent certificate and press Enter. You will have to do this a second time to confirm the password was entered correctly. When the command is finished, it will have generated two files: rafile.cer and rafile.pfx. I will go into more detail on these files later.

4. You are going to use rafile.cer to set up the Recovery Agent on your computer. First, however, you need to move that file to a location that is accessible by all users on your computer. Click the Start button and then click your username on the top-right side to bring up your home folder. This is where the files generated were placed. Right-click rafile.cer and select Cut.

5. In Computer, go to your C drive and create a folder called RA. Paste rafile.cer into that folder. Now you are ready to set up the encrypted file system to use that recovery agent certificate.

6. Click the Start button again, type **secpol.msc** in the Search box, and then press Enter.

7. Expand Public Key Policies, right-click Encrypted File System, and then select Add Data Recovery Agent.

8. Click Next on the wizard welcome screen and then click Browse to specify the location of rafile.cer. It should now be in `c:\ra\` if you followed steps 4 and 5 correctly.

9. After the file is selected, Windows will give you an error saying that it cannot determine if the certificate has been revoked. Ignore this message and click Yes. Your window should now look similar to Figure 14-8.

10. Click Next once more and then click Finish and you are done. The Recovery Agent is now set up.

FIGURE **14-8:** Adding a Recovery Agent to Windows Vista's encrypted file system

It is very important to remove the other file, rafile.pfx, from the computer and burn it to a CD or store it on a USB thumb drive. Then place the CD or USB thumb drive in a safe or safety deposit box to ensure it does not get into the wrong hands. If you ever need to decrypt your encrypted files, you will use rafile.pfx. If anyone gets a hold of that file and can then guess your password that you entered when you created it, all your files can be decrypted. That is why it is so important to remove that file from your computer and put it in a very safe place.

If you ever have a need to decrypt your own files after losing access to them for any reason, copy the rafile.pfx back to any computer that you want to decrypt your files on and double-click it. Then, just go through the wizard to import the certificate and enter your password when prompted. You will now be able to access and decrypt any files needed.

Setting files to be encrypted

Now that you have your Recovery Agent set up and the PFX file removed from the computer and placed in a safe location, you can safely and securely encrypt the files on your computer. To do so, just navigate to a file or a folder that you would like to encrypt on your machine and follow these steps:

1. Right-click a file or folder and select Properties.

2. On the General tab, click the Advanced button.

3. Check the Encrypt contents to secure file box and click OK, as shown in Figure 14-9.

FIGURE **14-9: Encrypting files with the encrypted file system**

4. Click OK to exit Documents Properties and you are finished.

If you ever want to decrypt a file, just uncheck the Encrypt contents to secure file box that you checked previously and click OK.

Using BitLocker Drive Encryption

BitLocker Drive Encryption is a new feature in Windows Vista that allows you to encrypt an entire drive or partition. This drive-layer encryption even encrypts the file system and operating system files so everything is secure. BitLocker Drive Encryption is the most secure Windows security option. This feature is ideal for laptop owners who have sensitive data on their drive as well as desktop users who can't risk their information getting into the wrong hands.

BitLocker Drive Encryption works by encrypting the entire partition, including the file system, with a 256-bit encryption algorithm. Using a Trusted Platform Module (TPM) chip, USB thumb drive, or a typed-in passkey, BitLocker protects your encrypted partition. When you boot up your computer, BitLocker starts to load from a small unencrypted partition, prompting you to insert your USB key or passcode to begin booting Windows Vista. If everything checks out, BitLocker unseals the encrypted partition and starts running the normal boot code. Failure to insert the USB key or correct passcode will result in a failure and an inability to even boot Windows.

Using this new security feature of Windows Vista is not very easy and has strict hardware configuration requirements. Currently, if your hard drive is not partitioned correctly to use this feature, your only option is to reinstall Windows Vista. However, if you want rock-hard security, this may be worth it.

Hardware requirements

For the most secure setup, BitLocker Drive Encryption requires a TPM chip version 1.2 or newer built into your computer. It is possible to set up BitLocker Drive Encryption on a computer without a TPM device or using a USB drive, but your only source of protection is a passcode and the physical USB drive.

Configuring your hard drive

BitLocker Drive Encryption works by first booting into an unencrypted partition to run the unlocking code and then boots the encrypted partition. This requires a very specific partition configuration to work properly. First, you need to have a small partition that is at least 1.5 gigabytes and is set to active that will be used for the initial boot information. Then you need a second partition that is designated for the operating system.

When I install Vista, I usually just create one partition that has the boot information on it as well as the operating system. Because BitLocker Drive Encryption requires a separate partition for the boot information, my only option is to reconfigure my partitions and reinstall Windows Vista.

Because you will need to re-install Windows Vista, you can use the diskpart utility that is part of the WinPE install environment that is on the Windows Vista installation DVD. In order to complete the next steps, you will need a bootable copy of the Windows Vista installation DVD. When you have one, follow these steps:

1. Insert the Windows Vista installation DVD into your computer and restart.

2. While the computer is starting up, press the correct key for your system to boot from the DVD. The exact key for your system is usually shown on the first screen when you turn on your computer. If you do not see any options, consult the user guide that came with your computer or contact your manufacturer.

3. When the setup loads, select your language, time and currency format, and the keyboard layout, and click Next.

4. On the next screen, click Repair your Computer.

5. System Recovery Options will show up; click Next on this screen as well.

6. On the recovery tool window, select Command Prompt.

7. In Command Prompt, type **diskpart** and press Enter to launch a more advanced partition editor.

8. Type **select disk 0** and press Enter to select your primary hard drive.

9. Type **clear** and press Enter to erase the current partition table.

10. Type **create partition primary size=1500** and press Enter to make the first partition that is 1.5GB.

11. Give this drive a letter. Type **assign letter=b** and press Enter.

12. You are almost done with this partition, but you still need to set it as active. Type **active** and press Enter.

13. Now you need to create the partition for the operating system. Type **create partition primary** and press Enter to create a new partition with the rest of the free space on the drive.

14. The last thing to do with diskpart is to assign the new partition a drive letter. Type **assign letter=c** and press Enter.

15. Now that you are finished with diskpart, you can exit it by typing **exit** and pressing Enter.

16. The last step is to format the two new partitions you just created. First, type **format b: /y /q /fs:NTFS** and press Enter to format the boot partition. Then type **format c: /y /q /fs:NTFS** and press Enter to format the operating system partition.

You are now finished configuring the hard drive to work with BitLocker Drive Encryption. Just close Command Prompt and then close the recovery options window and you will be back to the main Windows Vista installation screen. Click Install Now and install Vista to the new operating system you created. You should be able to easily find it when you select where to install to because it is the larger one of the two.

After properly configuring the hard drives and reinstalling Windows Vista, you are ready to get started using BitLocker Drive Encryption. The next section guides you through that.

Using BitLocker Drive Encryption

Using BitLocker Drive Encryption is easy when you have your hard drive configured properly and have reinstalled Windows Vista. Just follow these steps to get BitLocker up and running for you:

1. Click the Start menu and select Control Panel.

2. When Control Panel loads, click the Security heading.

3. Click BitLocker Drive Encryption.

4. If your computer is configured properly, you should see a Turn it on link, as shown in Figure 14-10, next to your operating system drive. Click that link now.

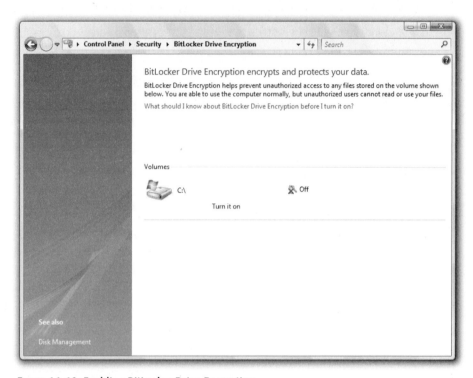

FIGURE 14-10: Enabling BitLocker Drive Encryption

5. Select the type of device you will be using to protect your computer and follow the onscreen steps for your method of protection.

After you complete all the steps the wizard guides you through, your computer will begin encrypting the hard drive automatically. Congratulations, your computer is now even more secure. Keep in mind that you will need to insert your USB drive every time you want to boot your computer if you choose the non-TPM option. Failure to insert it will result in your computer not booting. Make sure that you keep your emergency recovery passcode stored in a safe place, as well as your USB drive, in the event you choose to use that option.

Using BitLocker Drive Encryption with a USB Storage Device

If your computer does not have a compatible TPM chip, you can still use BitLocker Drive Encryption with a USB storage device. However, Microsoft has recently decided to hide this option from users. A local group policy change must be made to turn this option back on.

1. Click the Start button, type **gpedit.msc** in the search box, and press Enter.

2. When the Group Policy editor has loaded, navigate through Computer Configuration, Administrative Templates, Windows Components, and BitLocker Drive Encryption. Right-click Control Panel Setup: Enable advanced startup options and select Properties.

3. Select the Enabled option and click OK.

You can now use a USB storage device with BitLocker Drive encryption again.

Summary

This chapter was all about making what Microsoft is calling "the most secure operating system ever released" even more secure. First, I talked about ways to actively protect your computer by keeping up on the latest news and trends and making sure that your computer is up-to-date on the latest security patches. Then, I showed you how to configure User Account Control in a way that balanced both usability and security by creating a separate configuration administration account while running as a standard user the majority of the time. Finally, I covered the two different types of encryption available in Windows Vista: file level and drive level with BitLocker Drive Encryption.

The next chapter builds on the secure foundation this chapter created by securing your computer from attackers getting in from over the Internet. I will show you how you can configure hidden firewall settings to turn on the two-way firewall that is normally turned off. Then I will go over the latest tools to fight spyware and viruses.

Internet Security

The Internet is the primary source of conveyance for almost all of the attacks on your computer. Someone may be trying to break in to steal information or a worm from another infected computer may be trying to use the latest exploit to infect your box as well. So how do you protect your Internet connection? That is the topic of this entire chapter. I am going to show you how you can test your computer and see how vulnerable it actually is. Then you'll find out how you can use the firewalls to build a "brick wall" around you computer. Additionally, you'll discover how you can protect yourself from other Internet threats such as spyware and what to do to clean up an infection.

Analyzing Your Security

The first step in securing your Internet connection is detecting where you are vulnerable. Your specific network setup (for example, if your computer is behind a hardware firewall or router) will affect how exposed your computer is. For example, if you have a high-speed broadband connection and share it with more than one computer in your home using a router, your computers are already better protected than a computer that is just directly connected to the Internet. By default, most routers act like a firewall blocking all external Internet traffic from coming into your home network. However, if your laptop is infected and you plug it into your home network, all of the machines become vulnerable because the threat is now inside your firewall. I go into more detail of how firewalls work in the next section but first, let's test your connection to see how exposed your computers are to attacks from both the Internet and from other machines on your internal network.

Testing Internet security

Ports are the gateways inside your computer. When a computer program wants to communicate with a remote computer, it makes a connection to the remote computer through a port that it will use to talk with the computer. Each computer has thousands of ports — 65,535 to be exact. You can think of the different ports of a computer as a bunch of different mailboxes. When a program wants to send data to a remote computer, it sends it to a specific port (mailbox) number. Then, provided that a program is on the remote computer that is set up to receive data at a particular port (mailbox), the remote computer can then work with the data it was sent.

Theoretically, nothing is wrong with this scenario. In the real world, however, applications don't always work this way. Applications are not perfect, nor are they always efficient. Sometimes, they are sent data that they are not programmed to receive, which can cause errors and unexpected behavior that may execute the code a remote attacker is sending it. The result is that a remote attacker can gain access or infect your computer using the flaw in the application. The technical name for data sent to a program that results in bypassing security is an *exploit*.

Now that you know the basics of how attacks work, you will use various utilities to check for open ports that allow other users to connect. In theory, if you have no ports open, then it is next to impossible to break into your computer. To detect the open ports on your computer that are open to the entire Internet, it is best to use a web-based port scanner. If your computer is on an internal network and is behind a firewall or router, a software-based port scanner will show you what ports are open internally.

First, let's check your external port exposure, which everyone on the Internet can see. To do this, you will use a web-based port scanner. Various Web sites offer such scanners and are also free of charge. I personally like to use GRC.com to do my testing. Follow these steps to test your external connection:

1. Open a copy of either Internet Explorer or Firefox and navigate to `www.grc.com/x/ne.dll?bh0bkyd2`.

2. When the page loads, click the Proceed button.

3. Click All Service Ports to begin the scan.

4. When viewing the results, make sure that everything is in the green or blue. You do not want any ports to be open, which is indicated with red.

Depending on the results of your test, if you have any ports that are open, you can find out how to close those in the Firewall section. But first, if you are connected to an internal network, it is a good idea to test your internal vulnerability. As I mentioned earlier, it is best to use a software port scanner for testing your internal vulnerability. For this test, I am going to show you how to use Axence NetTools, a comprehensive network tools suite with a fast port scanner. To get started, visit `www.axencesoftware.com/index.php?action=FreeNT` and download the latest copy of NetTools. Then follow these steps to scan your computer's local ports:

1. After you have downloaded and installed Axence NetTools, click the Start button, type **nettools** in the Search box, and then press Enter.

2. After NetTools starts, click the Scan Host option on the far right of the icon bar.

3. In the address box, type **localhost**. If you want to scan a different computer, you can type the IP address of any computer in this box.

4. Set the port range for it to scan. In NetTools you have five options: Services, Ports (Well known), Ports (Well known-extended), Ports (Range), and Ports (Trojans). For this section you are going to use Ports (Range) to scan all possible ports. The other selections scan only the more popular ports where known applications are running. If you want a

quicker scan, I recommend using Ports (Well known-extended). Because you want to do a complete scan here, select Ports (Range). The two ports boxes will be enabled. Enter **65535** in the end port box so that it goes through all possible port numbers.

5. Press Scan next to the address box and watch the results appear, as shown in Figure 15-1.

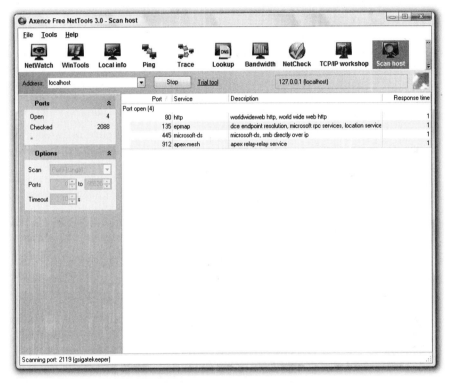

FIGURE 15-1: Using NetTools to find open ports on your PC

It can take over an hour to scan all 65353 ports on your computer, depending on your hardware. Once it is finished, you will have a list of all ports that are open in your computer. You will find out how to close these ports in the next section, "Using a Firewall."

Security Center

The new Security Center in Windows Vista is another easy way to find out if all of your "essential" protection software is installed and running. It is important to have your firewall running, virus software, spyware protection and other security features set up and running at all times to defend your computer against whatever tried to attack it. The Security Center provides a quick overview that you can check to make sure you are fully protected.

Using the System Center is very simple. Just click the Start button, type **Security Center** in the Search box, and then press Enter. When it loads, any alerts will be expanded for you to see. If everything is in the green, you are set. If not, pay attention to the recommendations so that your computer is as secure as possible.

Using a Firewall

In the last section, you found out how potentially vulnerable your computer is to viruses and attackers from the Internet and your internal network. You also know that one way to help fight those attackers is to block access to your computer on all of the ports, which can be gateways into your computer. How exactly do you block all the ports? Use a firewall. A firewall is a special application that acts like a brick wall that is protecting all of the ports on your computer.

When a remote computer attempts to access a computer that is protected by a firewall, it is not able to connect and the data that was sent is ignored and discarded. Depending on the way the firewall is configured, when data is sent to a blocked port on your computer, the firewall will either respond to where the data was sent from with a message that the port is closed or it will do nothing, giving your computer a stealth presence. Most firewall applications are set up by default to run in a stealth mode, which provides the maximum amount of protection. Any remote computer trying to connect or send data to your computer with a firewall installed and running in stealth mode will think that your computer has gone offline because it is not getting a response.

So far, I have talked only about firewalls that block incoming attacks from the Internet. Firewalls can also block traffic originating from your computer going out to the Internet. Why would you want to do that? What if someone installed a key logger on your computer that sends all your information to a remote computer for him to use? Or how about a media player that sends a history of everything that you played to a server for their tracking purposes? With a two-way firewall, you can block outgoing traffic that you haven't authorized.

Firewalls can be a very powerful security device. In Windows Vista, a firewall configured properly can completely eliminate one way an attacker may try to gain access to your computer. The next section shows you how you can use the new and improved firewall in Windows Vista to block incoming attacks and prevent unwanted applications from sending information out.

Using the Windows Vista firewall

The firewall included in Windows Vista is much more advanced than previous Windows firewalls. Microsoft actually calls it, "Windows Firewall with Advanced Security." It has three different location profiles that allow you to customize your firewall rules based on where your computer is. If it is in a public place, you are going to want to have very strict firewall rules compared to if you are in a corporate domain at work or at a private network at home. On top of the location profiles, the firewall has a very complex rule structure that allows you maximum flexibility to create openings in your firewall to permit application or service-related network traffic. Most important, Windows Firewall now has support to block outgoing traffic as well.

The upgrades to Windows Firewall really make it a very powerful security solution that was once provided only by advanced third-party firewall software. The integration of Windows Firewall into the Network Center and other parts of Windows makes it even more powerful.

Unfortunately, Microsoft chose to hide the raw power of the new firewall from most users. You can access the advanced firewall configuration tool only if you know what it is called. Microsoft even disabled outbound filtering because Microsoft thought it would be too much of an annoyance for inexperienced users. The next two sections guide you through the basics of using the advanced firewall configuration tool and enabling the outbound firewall.

Configuring Windows Firewall

You are not going to find an easy link to the advanced firewall configuration tool anywhere in the user interface. The only way to access it is to call it directly. That is exactly what you are going to do. Click the Start button, type **wf.msc** in the Search box, and then press Enter. When Windows Firewall with Advanced Security window loads, you will see the complexity and the power of the new firewall. Maybe it was a good idea Microsoft decided to hide this from inexperienced users after all.

On the main screen you will see a list of the profiles, as shown in Figure 15-2. This is where you can see an overview if the firewall is on and if the inbound and outbound rules are active. The next step is to view the specific rules. You can do that by simply selecting Inbound Rules or Outbound Rules from the list on the left. Go ahead and click Inbound Rules now.

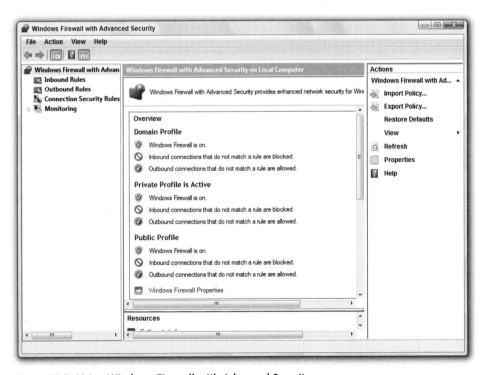

FIGURE 15-2: Using Windows Firewall with Advanced Security

In a few seconds you will see all of the rules currently set up on your computer. If they are enabled, they will have the green icon. If not, the icon will be gray. You can also see what firewall profiles the rule is used in, as shown in Figure 15-3 in the Profile tab. If you ever need to enable or disable a rule, just right-click it and select Enable or Disable. You can also edit an individual rule's properties by right-clicking on the rule and selecting Properties. Working with the Outbound Rules is exactly the same as working with Inbound Rules; Outbound Rules just control a different direction of traffic.

FIGURE 15-3: Inbound firewall rules and the profiles they are used in

For the sake of demonstrating how to add a new rule, let's say that you just installed some type of server on your computer that users will connect to on port 800. Follow these steps to open up a hole so that your users can connect:

1. If the Windows Firewall with Advanced Security window is not already open, click the Start button, type **wf.msc** in the Search box, and then press Enter.

2. After the firewall configuration tool loads, click Inbound Rules.

3. Under Actions in the right pane, click New Rule.

4. The new Inbound Rule Wizard loads and asks you for the type of rule you would like to create. For this scenario, you are going to select Port. Click Next when you have selected Port.

5. You are asked to specify what type of port to open. Unless you have an application that specifically requires a UDP port, nearly 100 percent of the time you will be selecting TCP. For this scenario, select TCP. Also on this screen, type **800** in the specific port box because you want to open up only port 800. Click Next when you are done.

6. The next screen asks you to define the action of the rule. You can choose to Allow the connection, Allow the connection if secure (on a network with IPSEC), or Block depending on what you want to do. Select Allow the connection and click Next.

7. You will need to select what profiles this rule will be part of. By default, all of the profiles are checked; uncheck any profiles you do not want your rule to be part of and click Next.

8. The last step is to name your new rule. Type a name and a description if you want and click Finish.

Your new rule will now appear on the Inbound Rule list. It will automatically be enabled when you click Finish.

Enabling the outbound firewall

In Windows Vista, Microsoft decided it was best to disable the outbound connection filtering because it can cause headaches for many inexperienced computer users. This may have been the right choice but not filtering your outbound traffic can increase the possibility that an application can steal important personal information and send it to a remote computer. If this application is malicious, it can be used to steal personal information such as passwords and bank account numbers. Turning on the outbound firewall filtering and enabling only the rules that grant your normal applications access to the Internet will greatly increase the security of your computer.

Enabling the outbound firewall rules on your computer is easy to do once you know where Microsoft hid the setting. Follow these steps to turn the outbound firewall back on:

1. If the Windows Firewall with Advanced Security window is not already open, click the Start button, type **wf.msc** in the Search box, and then press Enter.

2. When the firewall configuration tool is loaded, click Windows Firewall Properties right in the middle of the opening screen.

3. When the settings window loads, you will see a tab for each of the different firewall profiles. Select the tab for the profile on which you would like to enable outbound filtering.

4. Under the State section, locate the Outbound connections drop-down box and change it to Block.

5. Click OK when you are finished to activate the outbound firewall on the profile you specified.

Windows automatically detects any applications that try to access the Internet or other network resources that are now blocked with the outbound firewall turned on and will prompt you to automatically authorize the application to send information out to the Internet.

Web Browser Security

Now that you have eliminated one method attackers user to enter your computer by blocking your ports with a firewall, it is time to secure the other entry point, the web browser. An attacker can also get into your computer by using an exploit in a web browser by tricking you into installing a web component that has malicious code inside. Internet Explorer has many security settings built in that will help you keep safe. However, there are often tradeoffs including ease of use and convenience. For example, you can disable the installation of all web components for maximum security, but when you really need to install one, it can take longer and require more work than normal.

Internet Explorer 7

Internet Explore in Windows Vista has undergone massive changes and has many new security features, such as Protected Mode. What does that mean? In the past, Internet Explorer was prone to various different attacks, leaving it one of the weakest parts of the entire Windows operating system. Microsoft tried to stop automatic downloading and installation, and Web site exploits, in its release of Service Pack 2 for Windows XP, but we all know that worked only a little. Flaws are still being discovered in Internet Explorer and attackers are trying to find new ways to trick users into installing their malicious code. How do you fix this problem? Simple — you isolate Internet Explorer into a secure environment so that in the future, if exploits are found, they will not work because IE cannot access resources other than its own. That new protection is found only in the Windows Vista version of Internet Explorer 7 and is called *Protected Mode*.

Protected Mode, the phishing filter that protects you against fake Web sites, combined with other security options in Internet Explorer 7, will help you secure your web browser and the other major point of entry for spyware, malware, and attackers. The next section shows you how to get the most out of these new features.

Fine-tuning security settings

You can adjust the security settings in Internet Explorer within Internet Options. Follow these steps to adjust the security settings in IE7:

1. Open Internet Explorer 7.

2. Click Tools and select Internet Options.

3. After Internet Options loads, click the Security tab. The Security tab enables you to manage the individual settings for what is allowed in each of the browser zone settings — for example, if ActiveX controls are allowed to be automatically downloaded and installed in the Internet zone. You can adjust these zones by selecting the zone and then clicking the Custom Level button, as shown in Figure 15-4.

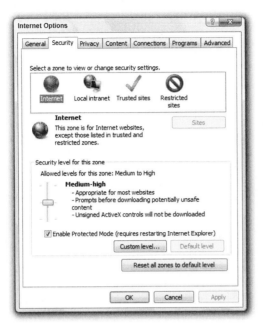

FIGURE 15-4: Adjusting Internet Explorer 7 security zones

4. After the security settings for the zone selected load, you can scroll through the list of settings and check or uncheck any of the settings to enable or disable them, respectively. For optimal security, I recommend disabling a lot of these features beyond what is normally disabled. Take a look at Table 15-1 for the settings I recommend that you change for best security practices. When you are finished modifying all the settings, click OK to return to Internet Options.

5. After you are back on the Security tab of Internet Options, make sure that the Enable Protected Mode box is checked for each of the zones. This is one feature that I believe should be enabled for all zones.

6. You are now ready to move on to the Advanced tab to adjust more security settings. Click the Advanced tab and scroll down the list to the Security section, as shown in Figure 15-5.

7. In the Security section, I recommend selecting Do not save encrypted pages to disk and Empty Temporary Internet Files folder when browser is closed. These two settings will help protect your privacy as well as keep your important online data from Web sites, such as your bank's, safe.

8. When you are finished, click OK to save your changes.

You are now finished configuring Internet Explorer to run more securely and protect you even better when you are online.

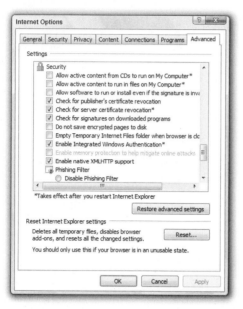

FIGURE 15-5: Adjusting advanced security settings in Internet Explorer 7

Table 15-1   Internet Explorer Security Zone Settings

Settings Name	Function
Loose XAML	I like to select Disable for this option because few sites use it and disabling it means one less feature to worry about getting exploited.
XAML browser applications	I disable this setting as well because it also is not used much.
XPS documents	Disable this option for tighter security. If you don't use this document format, you should have no problems disabling it.
Run components not signed with Authenticode	For tighter security, select Disable.
Font download	Consider yourself very lucky if you ever run across a Web site that uses this feature. Disable it to be safe.
Enable .NET framework setup	Disable this setting. I do not understand why this option is even listed here.
Include local directory path when uploading files to a server	I like to disable this option for privacy and because it should never be needed.
Launching programs and files in an IFRAME	Disable this feature. Really, this should never be done.
Logon	I usually set this option to Prompt for user name and password for maximum security.

Defending Against Spyware and Malware

Spyware has become the largest annoyance on Windows for the last few years. Often hidden in free screensavers and games, these programs can spy on your computer activities and report home various information about your computer habits. Adware is another menace that is closely related to spyware. Just like spyware, it can be secretly installed on your computer and will monitor what you do. Then, when the time is right, some adware apps will display relevant advertisements. Did you ever visit eBay.com and then notice an advertisement for Ubid.com, one of eBay's competitors, pop up on your screen? If so, then you are infected with a bad case of adware.

Your computer can get infected in a number of ways. The most common is visiting a Web site and downloading a free game, emoticons for an instant messenger, or a browser utility such as a search toolbar. Often these utilities are spyware themselves and are also bundled with other spyware and adware. Unfortunately, users never seem to read the terms of service agreements that are presented when they install these free apps on their computer and pass right over the notices that this software will display ads and will monitor your browsing habits.

In Windows Vista it is getting much more difficult for outsiders to install software on your computer that you don't want because of User Account Control. If something is installed, it is because you authorized it when you clicked Allow in the UAC authorization box. What do you do if you made a mistake? This next section shows you how to use the new anti-spyware and anti-malware application called Windows Defender to protect your computer and clean it of any spyware threats.

Using Windows Defender

Because spyware has been an increasing problem for so many Windows users, Microsoft has included free spyware protection in Windows Vista called Windows Defender. Windows Defender works by scanning the files and Registry on your computer for signatures of known adware and spyware applications. The signature definitions that it uses are updated very often and also assisted by Microsoft SpyNet to find out about new, unknown spyware that is not yet in widespread use. When Windows Defender finds a file that looks suspicious but does not know exactly what it is, it sends that information back to the Microsoft SpyNet computers for tracking.

Windows Defender does more than just detect and monitor spyware files. It also monitors applications that get installed in your startup and processes currently running in memory. Using the Software Explorer feature located under Tools, you can harness the power of Windows Defender to fight malicious software that has infected those areas as well. To get started, let's go over the basic uses of Windows Defender.

Scanning your computer

Windows Defender is very effective at scanning your computer for spyware. By default, Windows Defender is configured to scan your computer once a day in the early hours in the morning. If you ever notice something strange happening to your computer and suspect spyware, you can perform the following steps to do a full system scan with Windows Defender:

1. Click the Start button, type **Windows Defender** in the Search box, and then press Enter.

2. After Windows Defender loads, click the down arrow next to the Scan button and select Full Scan, as shown in Figure 15-6.

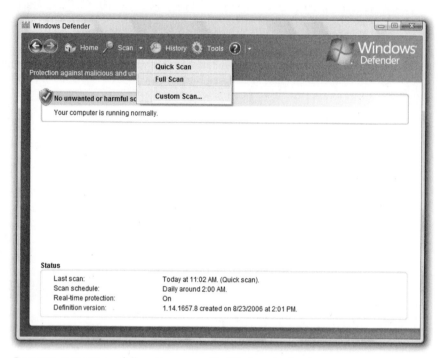

FIGURE 15-6: Starting a full system scan with Windows Defender

3. When the scan is finished, the results are shown. If any spyware is found, click Review Items detected by scanning to find out exactly what was found.

4. On the Scan Results screen, all the malicious software detected by Windows Defender is shown, along with details on what each application is. Click the Remove All button, as shown in Figure 15-7.

Using other anti-spyware software

Sometimes Windows Defender just doesn't detect all the spyware on your computer. You can try to manually kill it using the Software Explorer feature and disable the startup programs, but there is an easier way. Before going for the manual approach, give these two proven spyware utilities a try:

- **Lavasoft's Ad-Aware Personal:** www.lavasoftusa.com
- **Spybot-S&D:** www.safer-networking.org

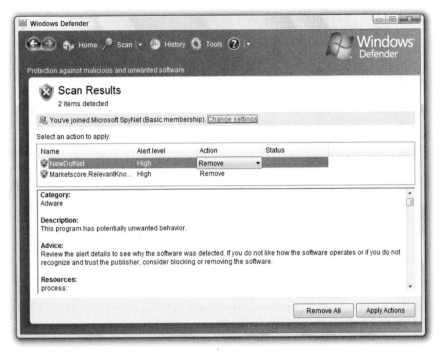

FIGURE 15-7: Removing spyware with Windows Defender

Using Antivirus Software

Antivirus software is the classic PC utility that has always been thought of as absolutely neces-sary if you own a computer. The fact is, in Windows Vista, the need for antivirus software when User Account Control is turned on is significantly lower than in Windows XP because UAC prevents most events from happening that you have not authorized. For example, if you open an e-mail that contains a virus and the virus attempts to reformat a drive, a UAC prompt will pop up asking you to confirm the reformat request. UAC stops the virus dead in its tracks in this situation.

Unfortunately, many people choose to disable UAC in Windows Vista, and UAC will not pro-tect you from all types of attacks. After all, sometimes users click Authorize on every UAC prompt they see, which makes UAC useless. For this reason, I feel it is still a good idea to run some type of basic antivirus program on most computers — especially if you have UAC dis-abled or if the computer is used by beginning computer users.

Note   For more information on UAC, refer to Chapter 14.

Using avast! antivirus software

There are many free antivirus utilities that work well with Windows Vista. My favorite is avast! 4 Home Edition, which can be downloaded for free if it is for home use. This saves a lot of money that you may be spending on mainstream antivirus products and their yearly signature update fees. With avast! 4 Home Edition, all the signature updates are free. All you have to do is register on avast!'s Web site to get a free registration key within 60 days of installing the software.

Similar to other popular virus scanners, avast! has various on-access scanners that automatically scan files when they are opened on your computer. This makes it less necessary to do a full system scan to find files because you can be sure that a file is scanned before it is executed. Additionally, avast! includes support for all the popular mail applications, so you can be confident that your messages will be safe as well.

Using avast! is slightly different from other antivirus programs. Follow these steps to get it up and running on your computer and to perform a full system scan:

1. Visit www.avast.com/eng/avast_4_home.html and download a free copy of avast! 4 Home Edition.

2. Once you have it installed, reboot.

3. Click the Start button, type **avast** in the Search box, and then press Enter.

4. Enter your registration key if you already have it; otherwise press the Demo button. avast! will now perform a scan of running applications in memory.

5. When the in-memory scan is finished, you are ready to set up a full system scan. To do this, you first need to select what will be scanned. This can be done by clicking the drive button located on the top of the right column of buttons, as shown in Figure 15-8.

6. Click the Play button on the left of the screen and the scan will begin.

After the scan has completed, you will be presented with the results and the option to take action on any discovered viruses. With the active protection features of avast!, you do not need to run a full disk scan very often. If a file becomes infected and you attempt to open it, the on-access scan will catch it.

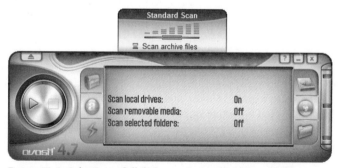

FIGURE 15-8: Selecting a full disk scan in avast! 4 Home Edition

Summary

This chapter has shown you how you can protect your computer from attacks that arrive via the Internet by using exploits and open ports on your computer and by using your web browser. I show you how you can use Windows Firewall to protect your computer and also defend against attacks by increasing the security of Internet Explorer. You wrapped up the Internet security chapter by protecting your computer from spyware and viruses. The next chapter is all about protecting your privacy in Windows. Windows Vista tracks more information about what you do than any other version of Windows. Sure, that information can be useful, but it also can be embarrassing. Find out how to clean it all in the next chapter.

Protecting Your Privacy

Windows Vista keeps track of all activities that you do on your computer. It records the Web sites that you visit, the addresses that you type in, the applications that you launch, and even the files that you open. Why does it do this? The majority of the information is used to tailor your computer experience and power features such as the frequently run programs or recently opened documents lists. These features can be very useful and save you time. Other activities, such as typing in addresses for Web sites, are also logged. As you type part of the address, possible suggestions based on your history will appear. However, these convenient features also make it very easy for anyone to see what you browse on the Web.

Because of the vast amounts of information that Windows Vista records, your privacy is in danger when other people share your computer. This chapter will show you how you can clean all the recorded data from your PC. Additionally, I will show you how you can protect your privacy further by taking advantage of some cool features of Windows Vista.

Internet Explorer Privacy

Internet Explorer is one of the most difficult parts of Windows to clean because it stores data all over your drive, which makes clearing the data more difficult than just deleting one folder. Every time you want to clean all your Internet Explorer history, you need to clear recent addresses, remove history files, erase temporary Web files, and remove cookies. The first part of this section shows you how to clean all the required parts to remove your Internet Explorer history and protect your privacy.

The second part of this section shows you how you can protect your privacy further by configuring other Internet Explorer features.

Removing address bar suggestions

Windows Vista, like other versions of Windows, includes a feature called AutoComplete that is always activated for the address box. This can be a convenient feature because it can help you when typing in an address by presenting you with various suggestions you already used. The suggestions are based on your address box history. Although this feature offers a great convenience, it also will risk your privacy. When I start typing **www.Twea** in my address bar, it automatically suggests www.tweakvista.com because I have visited that site. Anyone who uses my computer and starts typing addresses in manually can see sites that I have visited. If they just type in **www.s** or **www.t**, they will be presented with a small list of all the sites that I have visited that have URLs that start with *s* or *t*.

How do you stop the suggestions? You have to go after the source. Unfortunately, this effort can be a little tricky. The file that stores this information is called the URL cache and is named index.dat. This file resides in your Cookies directory within the root user folder. To remove the information that Windows records, you just have to delete the file. However, deleting this file is not as easy as deleting normal files. The URL cache file is always in use when the operating system is running. And because it is impossible to delete files that are in use, the only way to delete this file is to delete the file in Safe mode or when the system is loading. One solution to this dilemma is to boot into Safe mode with Command Prompt and delete the file. That works because when you boot into Safe mode with Command Prompt, the file is no longer in use.

Follow these steps to delete the index.dat file by booting into Safe mode:

1. Reboot your computer and press F8 repeatedly right after the BIOS power-on test finishes to get the Safe mode boot menu.

2. When the Advanced boot menu loads, select Safe Mode with Command Prompt and press Enter. Windows will now load into a repair environment called Safe mode that has only the core Windows components running.

3. When the logon screen appears, log on with your username and password.

4. When Command Prompt loads after you sign in, you are ready to get started deleting the file in DOS. You are going to want to navigate through C:\Users*Your Username*\AppData\Roaming\Microsoft\Windows\Cookies. In Command Prompt, you will start out in the C:\Users*Your Username*\ folder. Type **cd AppData\Roaming\Microsoft\Windows\Cookies** and press Enter to navigate the rest of the way.

5. When you are at the right folder, you are ready to delete the file. Type **del index.dat**, as shown in Figure 16-1, and press Enter.

You are now finished and can reboot your computer. The index.dat file has been deleted and cleared out.

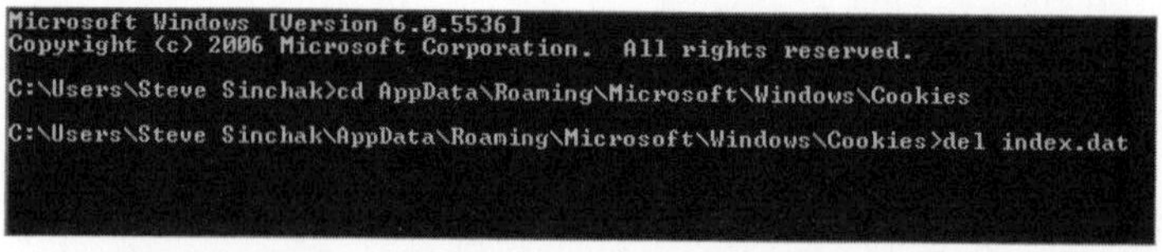

FIGURE 16-1: Deleting the index.dat file in Safe mode with Command Prompt

After you reboot the computer, the file will have been erased. Do not be surprised if you see a new index.dat file generated after you reboot. A new empty file will be generated again to replace the existing file.

Clearing temporary Internet files, history, and cookies

Every time that you visit a Web site, the files for the Web page (such as the HTML and the images) are downloaded and stored in a temporary directory known as *Temporary Internet Files*. Over time, this directory can become full of images and HTML from various Web sites that you have visited. This directory can end up taking up a lot of space on your hard drive. Additionally, a user can browse your Temporary Internet Files directory and find out exactly what sites you have been visiting just as if they were looking at your browser history. If you are concerned about your privacy, or just concerned about disk space, then clearing the temporary Internet files is a must.

The web browsing history is another area that users often like to clear. Internet Explorer, by default, is configured to record all the Web sites that you visit for a 30-day period. If you are concerned about your privacy, your browsing history should be cleaned frequently and history settings configured best for your privacy. Doing so will ensure that any user of your computer will not be able to easily see exactly what you have been doing.

Cookies are also created on your computer when you visit Web sites. Contrary to popular belief, cookies are really not that bad. Most Web sites use them to save user data to a browser. An example of this is site preferences or automatic logon when you visit a Web site. A Web site you visit can detect if the Web site has given you a cookie already that has your user ID stored in it. If it finds one, then it knows exactly who you are and logs you on automatically. Advertisers also use cookies to store personal data. Instead of showing you the same advertisement 50 times, they use cookies to keep track of how many times an advertisement is displayed on your screen.

A common myth about cookies is that they allow Web sites to track what other sites you visit. That is just not true. The only cost of having cookies on your computer is a privacy concern for local users. Any user that has physical access to you computer can browse to the directory that the cookies are stored in and view what Web sites you visit because the cookies are named after the Web site that instructed your browser to put them on your computer.

Clearing the temporary Internet files, history, and cookies is a very simple task. Just follow these steps to clear these files:

1. Open Internet Explorer 7.

2. Click Tools and select Delete Browsing History, as shown in Figure 16-2.

3. When the Delete Browser History Window loads, click Delete All on the bottom of the window to clear all temporary files, history, and cookies from your computer.

4. On the confirmation screen, select Also delete files and settings stored by add-ons, and click Yes. All your browser data will now be cleaned.

Now users will no longer be able to see what Web sites you visit from the cookies and temporary Internet files that are stored on your computer. Additionally, you will have freed up some disk space by deleting these files.

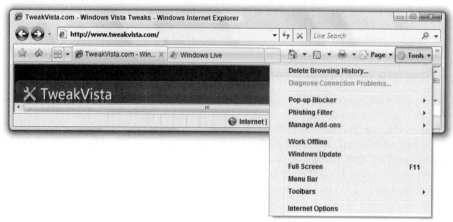

FIGURE 16-2: Clearing browser data in Internet Explorer 7

Adjusting your cookie security policy

As mentioned, cookies are not as bad as some people in the computing world would like you to believe. Instead, the only real risk they present is a loss of some privacy, as I mentioned previously. If you allow your browser to be instructed to create cookies on your computer, over time your PC would have quite a collection of them. Anyone who used your computer would then know what sites you visited, if they knew where the cookie files were located.

The latest version of Internet Explorer includes many new enhancements. One of the enhancements includes a new way of accepting cookies. Now you have the capability to specify if you would like your browser to block all cookies or just certain types of cookies. To be able to use this new feature, you need to understand the two different types of cookies:

- **First-party cookies:** Placed on your computer by the current site that you are visiting.
- **Third-party cookies:** Placed on your computer by remote sites, such as advertisement servers.

If you do not want your computer to accept third-party cookies that are often used for online marketing or if you just want to adjust your cookie acceptance settings, follow these steps:

1. Open Internet Explorer.
2. Click Tools and select Internet Options.
3. When Internet Options loads, click the Privacy tab.
4. You will see the up-and-down slider that allows you to select different levels of cookie security. I recommend that you bypass this and just click the Advanced button instead.
5. After you have clicked the Advanced button and see the Advanced Privacy Settings window, select the box that says Override Automatic Cookie Handling.

6. Your settings for first- and third-party cookies will now be available for adjustment, as shown in Figure 16-3. I recommend that you always accept first-party cookies. You can decide if you want to block all third-party cookies or be prompted to accept them. If you select the Prompt option, a dialog box notifies you that a cookies request has been received.

FIGURE 16-3: Adjusting the cookie privacy settings

7. When you are finished with your settings, click OK to save your changes and return to Internet Options.

8. Click OK once more to close Internet Options.

Now that you have set the cookie privacy setting manually, you can eliminate cookies from being stored on your hard drive in the first place. Doing so will allow you to protect your privacy and still be able to use Web sites that need cookies.

Saying no to encrypted Web pages

If you manage your finances or shop online, then you probably have had experience with using secure Web connections, otherwise known as *SSL*. These secure connections encrypt the data that is transferred from a Web server to your computer. When the data gets to your computer, your browser has a special key that decrypts the information and displays it on your computer. During this process, when the file is decrypted, it is saved in the Temporary Internet Files directory so that the browser can display it.

This default appears to be harmless because the Web page is saved on your computer only. If no one has remote access to your computer, the data would be safe, right? Not necessarily, because your data is now vulnerable to anyone who has physical local access to your computer. If that person is clever and lucky enough, he or she can sort through your Temporary Internet Files directory and just might find some confidential information such as your online banking information. All this information is saved by default on your hard drive for anyone to look at who knows how to get to it. They do not even need to know your password or even log onto your account on the bank's Web site because a snapshot of the Web page is stored locally on your computer.

What can you do to protect your computer from this vulnerability besides setting up better computer security such as complex passwords? There is a cool feature of Internet Explorer that you just have to turn on that will eliminate the problem completely. Simply called Do Not Save Encrypted Pages to Disk, this feature, when enabled, solves your problems. To enable it, follow these steps:

1. Open Internet Explorer.

2. Click Tools and select Internet Options.

3. Click the Advanced tab.

4. Scroll down though the list toward the bottom of the window until you see the Security section.

5. Locate Do Not Save Encrypted Pages to Disk, and check the box to the left of it.

6. Click OK to save and activate your changes.

Now you will no longer have to worry about pages that were encrypted being saved to your drive for anyone who has access to your computer to see.

Disabling AutoComplete

You already know about AutoComplete from the address bar. You have taken care of that privacy problem by clearing the file that stored the information, as shown in the section "Removing address bar suggestions." AutoComplete also tries to give a helping hand when you are filling in text boxes on Web pages. In this situation, AutoComplete works exactly the same as it does with the address bar. As you begin to fill in the text box, several suggestions will appear based on information that you have already typed in.

To get an idea of how this works in action, visit a search site such as Google (www.google.com) and start to type in words for which you want to search. When you do so, words similar to the ones you have typed in the box on other visits to the site will appear. This capability allows anyone that uses your computer to be able to see what other users of the computer have searched for on the site, even if the browser history was cleared.

Clearly, having this feature enabled would be a big concern if you were concerned about your privacy. Disabling the AutoComplete feature is not very difficult and will completely take care of this privacy concern. Follow these steps to put an end to AutoComplete:

1. Open Internet Explorer.

2. Click Tools and select Internet Options.

3. Click the Content tab and then Settings button under the AutoComplete section.

4. After the AutoComplete Settings window loads, clear all the boxes, as shown in Figure 16-4.

FIGURE 16-4: Adjusting the AutoComplete settings

5. When you are finished, just click OK to save your changes.

6. Click OK once more to close Internet Options and activate your changes.

AutoComplete is now a thing of the past. You no longer have to worry that people who use your computer will be shown all the things that you type into your address and text boxes.

Clearing temporary Internet files automatically

Earlier I showed you how to clear your temporary Internet files so that they will not be a privacy concern. Over time, your Temporary Internet Files folder will fill up again and will once again become a privacy concern. One easy way to fix this is to use a cool hidden feature of Internet Explorer that automatically deletes these files every time you close Internet Explorer. This way, you will not have to worry about clearing all the files every time that you use Internet Explorer. Follow these steps to activate this cool feature:

1. Open Internet Explorer.

2. Click the Tools menu bar item and then select Internet Options.

3. Click the Advanced tab and scroll down to the bottom of the screen.

4. Locate and select Empty Temporary Internet Files Folder when browser is closed, as shown in Figure 16-5.

5. Click OK to close Internet Options and activate your changes.

Enabling the automatic empty feature is a great way to easily maintain a clean PC. Keep in mind that this will delete only your temporary Internet files, not your cookies. You will still have to delete the cookies the way that I mentioned previously in this chapter.

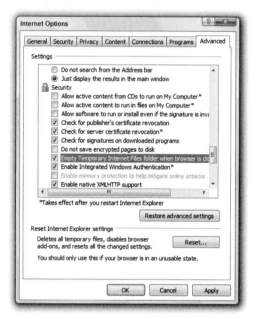

FIGURE 16-5: Setting up IE to automatically clear the temporary Internet files

Windows Interface Privacy

When you have Internet Explorer under control, you can move on to cleaning the rest of the Windows interface. Just like Internet Explorer, Windows Explorer keeps track of the applications that you run and files that you open. It does this so that it can tailor your computer to your personal use with features such as the frequently run programs list on the Start panel. Features like this are designed to speed up the use of your computer. However, the side effect of the convenience is a loss of privacy. The next few sections will show you how to recover your privacy, albeit at the expense of convenience.

Clearing Frequently Run Programs and the Open files list

One of the great new features of Windows Vista can also be a pain when you are concerned about your privacy. The capability to select the programs that you use frequently directly from the Start panel instead of having to navigate through the entire Start menu can save you some time. However, over time, this list can become cluttered with programs that you do not want to be there. Additionally, anyone who uses your computer can easily see what programs you use.

Windows Vista also does something similar with the files that you open. Every time that you open a Word document, a digital image, or any other file, an entry is created in the Recent files list. Although this feature exists, I never find myself using it and it just seems to add another privacy concern.

In Windows Vista, it is very easy to clear and/or disable these features. Just follow these steps:

1. Right-click the Start button and select Properties.

2. Clear the two check boxes under the Privacy section on the Start Menu tab, as shown in Figure 16-6.

FIGURE 16-6: Clearing the program list on the Start panel

3. Click OK to save and activate your changes.

Depending on what check boxes you chose to clear, you may have to go back in and check them again if you would like to use the frequently run feature again.

Removing temporary files from your hard drive

Over time, your hard drive can become cluttered with temporary files left behind from applications and the operating system. These files not only take up space, but they can be tracks of activity on your computer. Removing the temporary files is a great way to clean up any garbage information that is left behind, increase your privacy, and free up some disk space.

Windows has advanced greatly over the course of it existence. In the early versions of Windows, there was just one temp folder that all temp files were located in. With Windows Vista, temp folders are all over the place. To remove the files, you could go to all the different folders and manually erase the files, but there is a better way.

To clear my temporary files from my hard drive, I like to use Disk Cleanup. Disk Cleanup is a utility that comes with Windows Vista that makes it easy to remove your temporary files. It works by automatically checking the known temporary file locations for you and removing the files. With Disk Cleanup, you do not have to worry about where to navigate on your hard drive to delete the files. Instead, just execute the program.

To get started using Disk Cleanup, follow these steps:

1. Click the Start button, type **Disk Cleanup** in the Search box, and then press Enter.

2. You will be prompted to choose which files you want to clean — "My files only" or "Files from all users on this computer." I recommend selecting Files from all users on this computer.

3. If your computer has multiple hard drives, you will be prompted to select which drive you want to clean. Select the drive you want to clean and press OK.

4. After the utility has analyzed your computer, it gives you a report of various types of files that it can clean, as shown in Figure 16-7. Scroll through the list and make sure that only Temporary Internet Files and Temporary files are checked.

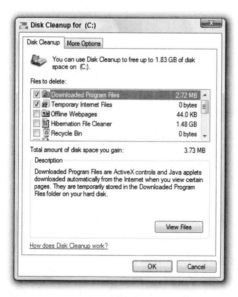

FIGURE 16-7: Using Disk Cleanup to remove temporary files

5. Click OK to run the cleanup.

6. Click Delete Files on the confirmation screen. The utility will now run and exit automatically when it is finished cleaning your hard drive.

Disk Cleanup is the perfect way to easily clean up your temporary files. Now that you know how to use it, I recommend that you run it at least once a month to keep your temporary files under control.

Removing saved passwords

When you visit a Web site that requires authentication or attempt to connect to remote computers, you are given the option to save your password so that the next time that you visit the page or attempt to access a remote resource you do not have to reenter your password. This feature can be a huge convenience, especially if you access a particular Web site or resource frequently. The downside to this convenience is the potential for horrible security and privacy problems that it creates. Essentially, you are taking the password off all the sites and resources for which you saved a password. Anyone who has physical access to your computer can get in using your username and password, even if they do not know your password.

Removing your saved passwords from your computer is a very good idea because doing so will protect your accounts. Removing the password is a little tricky in Window Vista because there is not an easy way to access a list of all the accounts that have passwords stored for them within Control Panel or any other user interface element. Fortunately, there is a great hack that will do just that.

Hidden away in the keymgr.dll system file is an interface for viewing stored usernames and passwords. To use this cool interface, follow these steps:

1. Click the Start button, type **rundll32.exe keymgr.dll,KRShowKeyMgr** in the Search box, and then press Enter.

2. The Stored User Names and Passwords window will load, showing you a list of all the accounts that are saved on your computer, as shown in Figure 16-8. To remove a saved password, select the account on the list and click the Remove button.

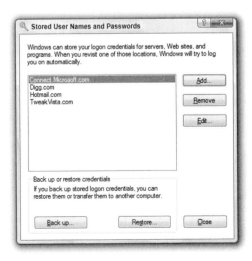

FIGURE 16-8: The Stored User Names and Passwords administration screen

3. Click OK on the Confirm screen and the account is removed from the list, erasing your stored password.

4. Repeat the previous steps for any other accounts that you want to remove.

5. When you are finished, just click Close.

You can also use the Stored User Names and Passwords window to add more usernames and passwords to your computer. If you have a Web site or resource for which privacy isn't a concern, such as some news Web site, just click the Add button when the Stored User Names and Passwords window is loaded.

Setting file and folder permissions

Windows Vista runs on the NTFS file system, which allows users to set file and folder permissions. These permission settings enable you to specify the users that can view a particular file or a whole folder on your computer. In fact, file permissions in Windows Vista are so detailed that you can even specify if a person has the ability only to read your files while preventing them from saving any changes. For the sake of privacy, file permissions are very helpful because they allow you to prevent other users from even being able to gain access to your private folders.

Setting the permissions on files and folders is easy to do. Just follow these steps:

1. Right-click any file or folder for which you want to modify permissions and select Properties.

2. Click the Security tab and press the Edit button.

3. Make sure that your username is added to the list and that you give yourself Full Control. You can do this with the Add button.

4. Remove all users from the group or username list that you do not want having access to this file. It is a good idea to remove the Everyone group because this does include everyone that can access your computer, including guests. Make sure that you do not accidentally remove your username from the list. Also watch out for the SYSTEM account. This is one account that the operating system uses to access files but can be safely removed unless you experience any problems with its removal.

Tip   If you are having difficulties removing users from the username list, this could be because the user is inherited from a parent folder. Permissions are passed down to all subfolders and files. If you want a user to have access to a folder but not its subfolders, then you have to click the Advanced button on the Security tab of the properties window. After the Advanced Security Settings window loads, clear the option that says Inherit from parent the permission entries that apply to child objects. A Security notification box will pop up. Click the Remove button to remove all the inherited permissions so that you can have full control of the folder.

5. Now that you have the list of users and groups taken care of, set the specific permissions that the user has on the file or folder. Select the name of the user that you want to modify, and then check the corresponding boxes in the Permissions for list for the activities that you want them to be able to do, as shown in Figure 16-9.

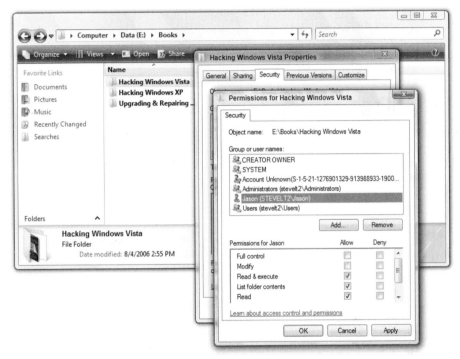

FIGURE 16-9: Adjusting the permissions for Jason. Jason now has permission only to read files in the folder.

6. When you have finished setting the permissions for all the users, click OK to exit the permissions screen.

When you have set the permissions for all sensitive directories, you will have greatly increased your security and privacy. Also keep in mind that file permissions are inherited. Every folder within a folder inherits the permissions of the parent folder unless they are specifically removed. Therefore, if you set the file permissions for a folder, all the subfolders and files will be automatically set with the same permissions. File and folder permissions can be very useful. If you have a program on your computer that you do not want anyone else running, simply set the permissions on that folder so that only you can read and execute it.

Summary

Throughout this chapter, you found out how to increase your privacy with Internet Explorer. Because Internet Explorer records so many pieces of your browsing experience, that information can leave you open to huge threats to your privacy. To fight that, you need to remove histories of sites browsed and addresses entered, as shown in the chapter. Then, you learned how to delete cookies as well as how to set up Internet Explorer to clean up after itself.

The second part of the chapter addressed the privacy concerns of the Windows interface. Just like Internet Explorer, Windows records many of your computer activities. Clearing those records has become an essential part of protecting your privacy. First, you found out how to clean up Windows. Then, you learned about ways to protect your privacy further with the help of permissions. If you follow all the tips that I have outlined in this chapter, you will have a secure system.

You have now finished reading the last chapter of *Hacking Windows Vista*. I showed you how you can customize everything that can be customized in Windows Vista in Part I. Now you know how to make your computer look and feel completely different. In Part II, you were shown how to speed up all the different components that make up Windows Vista. From the boot to the speed of your applications, the chapter provided tips to optimize the performance of your computer. Part III shifted into the topic of securing your computer. You learned how to protect your computer from attackers; defend against spyware, adware, and viruses; and protect your privacy. Now that you have read this last chapter, you are finished with the most complete guide written to fully optimize and improve your Windows Vista experience.

Index

How to take it to the Extreme.

If you enjoyed this book, there are many others like it for you. From *Podcasting* to *Hacking Firefox*, ExtremeTech books can fulfill your urge to hack, tweak and modify, providing the tech tips and tricks readers need to get the most out of their hi-tech lives.